CRAIG CHILDS on the bald eagle

"Eagles have been known to dive five thousand ₁ₑₑₜ wₐₕₒᵤₜ a single change in course and, at the end of that dive, hook into a salmon below the surface of the water. What a human can see at twenty feet, an eagle can see at one hundred and eighty feet. Some smaller raptors, if they please, can read the print of this book from two hundred feet in the air."

On the pronghorn antelope

"The pronghorn was once hunted across Wyoming by the North American cheetah, which explains why the pronghorn came to run more like a cheetah than a deer. The two species nearly match speeds. Twelve thousand years ago the cheetah vanished from this side of the planet and the pronghorn survived. Embedded in the pronghorn's ability to run so outlandishly fast are the cheetahs in their memory."

On the porcupine

"I've always considered the mating of porcupines to be a messy scenario fraught with danger and pain. It is, instead, delicate. Porcupines can easily take all day in their sexual matters, unlike most animals who complete long-awaited copulation in seconds. There is a nuzzling and a courtship process as they stand on hind legs to rub noses."

On the coyote

"The tip of its tail is black because, I have heard, it was the coyote who stole fire and brought it to humans, and he stole it by thrusting his own tail into the first fire, turning the end black. It was the coyote who brought us fire's light and warmth, the beginning of civilization, which we then divvied into all the bits and pieces, the cars and paper clips and budget department stores and backpacks, that make up our lives."

"Curled up in a quiet corner of the college library, I was intending to read a few pages of *The Animal Dialogues*. The next thing I knew, the day was gone, the book was done, and I sat there grinning with the sweet, sad grin of someone who had just finished a delicious, exotic, omnivore's meal. . . . Childs describes encounters with animals as diverse as mountain lions and great blue herons, grizzly bears and swallows, some of which I have encountered myself, others of which I am just as happy to meet on the page. And — take a deep breath — we surely do meet them."

— Chet Raymo, *Los Angeles Times*

"In addition to sharing Childs's wonder, delight — and occasional adrenaline rush — over these encounters, readers learn fascinating facts about a variety of critters. . . . There's also a fascinating discussion of human versus animal fluency in the sense of smell, and of a time when woolly camels roamed in North America. And did you know that porcupines have antibiotic quills because they stab themselves so often? . . . Absorbing accounts of windows into the natural world. . . . Highly recommended."

— Hilary Williamson, BookLoons.com

"There is a terrible beauty here, one that's occasionally violent but always in balance. . . . Childs manages some magical writing in tracing the path of a hawk hunting a rabbit through marks it has left in the snow. . . . His re-creation of the struggle is as vivid as a video of the hunt. . . . Childs has written a powerful book that glimpses past the anesthetized parts of human socialization. . . . If philosophy is an inquiry into how one should live, then in *The Animal Dialogues* Childs has created a natural philosophy for modern man."

— Pete Warzel, *Rocky Mountain News*

"A packed subway train crawls toward Manhattan from Brooklyn. I'm pushed on all sides, smashed against the door reading Craig Childs's *The Animal Dialogues*. Tears well in my eyes as I read about a perfect blue shark dying on a desolate beach. For those of us pressed into spaces devoid of anything resembling the natural world, these stories invoke all that we are missing: the space, the sky, the awe at witnessing animals in their element; the wonder, the pure heart-stopping fear. While these essays may not bring tears to most readers' eyes, they do dwell in the emotional realm. Combining science, history, and lyricism, Childs articulates sublime and untenable moments, those 'stop and pay attention because this will never happen again' moments with a cast of likely and unlikely characters.... As wild spaces become increasingly distant and animals increasingly threatened in their natural environment, Childs's continuing narrative of his 'uncommon encounters' is all the more trenchant. Calmly intruding into this world with Childs, witnessing the singular moment 'so vivid that it detaches from time,' each species' individuality shines, as do their similarities, humans included."
— Sara Rose, Associated Press

"In these tales, Craig Childs rediscovers himself as animal, vulnerable and keenly aware, and reminds us that we are creatures as ordinary and extraordinary as any other.... Childs's synthetic style, where taste is color is light is smell, infuses the essays with bright immediacy and palpable wonder. It is tempting to classify this well-researched, beautifully written collection as natural history. But *The Animal Dialogues* is less about the lore and habits of bear and raven (though these details are present in spades) than it is about what is possible when you confront the wonder and mystery of a living world with wide-open eyes."   — Sarah Gilman, *High Country News*

"A beautiful book.... Mr. Childs is a born storyteller. You may not be especially interested in the domestic arrangements of bighorn sheep or the spawning habits of smelt, but after a few sentences, you find yourself drawn irresistibly in. In part, this is due to his unusual eloquence. Mr. Childs has a distinct gift for the clinching description.... Mr. Childs belongs to a venerable tradition of nature writing extending back to William Bartram, Henry David Thoreau, and John Muir. He shares their keenness of eye and sharpness of ear, along with their obsessive desire to come as close as humanly possible to the elusive lives of wild things; like them, he believes that 'the forest is, without a doubt, eternity.' But he brings other, more personable qualities as well. Some of his exploits are quite goofy. Who else with a dread of rattlesnakes would trek barefoot through a snake-infested desert in pitch darkness, or rescue a trapped and snarling raccoon with his ungloved hands from a waterhole, and not only survive but speak with perfect frankness of both his clumsiness and his fear?" — Eric Ormsby, *New York Sun*

"Childs has had more opportunities than most to be humbled by nature. A mountaineer, wilderness guide, and passionate observer, he's overwintered in a Colorado tepee, crossed the Sonoran Desert on foot, and trekked the outermost beaches of the Queen Charlotte Islands. And in that time, he has frequently renewed the wonder that first struck him at the age of twelve when he followed a black bear into the ponderosa forest of northern Arizona. Neither carnage nor mystical mind-melding ensued: the bear ran off; the boy walked home. But the experience marked him for life.... The power of *The Animal Dialogues* lies in the cumulative impact of its vignettes, which, taken together, offer a portal into a universe that's infinitely larger than human experience alone."

—Alexander Varty, Straight.com

"Eloquent.... Childs's captivating essays, rich in sensuous imagery, are hauntingly beautiful and replete with evocative observations of animal life."   —*Publishers Weekly* (starred review)

"I have long been a huge fan of Craig Childs's nature writing, and I was delighted to discover his newest offering, *The Animal Dialogues*. This is a book to read slowly and savor, accompanying Childs one chapter at a time as he travels through the rain forest of Washington's Olympic Peninsula to the Arizona desert, from the mountains of Colorado to the rapids of the Colorado River, from Alaska to New Mexico, and sharing his experiences—vicariously, of course—with the animals he meets along the way."   —Nancy Pearl, NPR.org

"Childs's new book, written in easily digestible chapters, lets us eavesdrop on his conversations with the animal kingdom."   —Joshua Payne, *Plenty*

"The author has a talent for bringing his encounters home and fashioning them into chromatic, immediate accounts. Some of the experiences chronicled here are quite simply breath-catching and heart-gladdening: following an intermittent stream of ruby-red dragonflies to a water source in a dry land; watching fifty violet-green swallows 'working a cat's cradle into the air'; placing a mouse upon a branch to become a canapé for a northern spotted owl. Occasionally—and profoundly, as the pursuer becomes the pursued—Childs is reminded that his place on the food chain is not necessarily at the apex. Surprise, a mountain lion!... Childs's great accomplishment is to excite our thrill in an animal's beauty and strangeness, then arouse our protective instincts by pointing out its vulnerability. Each of these pieces is a personal invitation to get outdoors and celebrate all things furred, feathered, and scaled."   —*Kirkus Reviews*

THE ANIMAL DIALOGUES

THE ANIMAL DIALOGUES

Uncommon
Encounters in the Wild

Craig Childs

BACK BAY BOOKS
Little, Brown and Company
New York   Boston   London

Back Bay Books / Little, Brown and Company
Hachette Book Group
237 Park Avenue, New York, NY 10017
Visit our Web site at www.HachetteBookGroup.com

Originally published in hardcover by Little, Brown and Company, December 2007
First Back Bay paperback edition, March 2009

Back Bay Books is an imprint of Little, Brown and Company. The Back Bay Books name and logo are trademarks of Hachette Book Group, Inc.

Many of the essays in this book first appeared in Craig Childs's *Crossing Paths*.

Illustrations on pages 7, 9, 68, 91, 107, 127, 150, 215, 236, 240, 252, 290, 299, 314, 317, and 319 copyright © 2007 by Neil Flewellen
All other illustrations copyright © 1997 by Sivi Ruder

Library of Congress Cataloging-in-Publication Data

Childs, Craig Leland.
The animal dialogues : uncommon encounters in the wild / Craig Childs. — 1st ed.
p. cm.
ISBN 978-0-316-06632-7 (HC) / 978-0-316-06647-1 (PB)
1. Animals — North America — Anecdotes. I. Title.
QL151.C45 2007
590 — dc22   2007026010

10 9 8 7 6 5 4 3 2 1

RRD-IN

Printed in the United States of America

For
Jasper and Juden

CONTENTS

AUTHOR'S NOTE

Some of the stories in the following pages originally appeared in a book I wrote in 1997 called *Crossing Paths*. Other stories have been written since then. They need not be read in any particular sequence or all in one sitting. They are not in chronological order. I have hoped, in fact, that you, the reader, might come upon this book by accident, finding it on a desk, left open to a passage on mountain lions, or flipping its pages until you are caught in the stares of fifteen sorcerous ravens. This is how each story came to me: unexpectedly, halting my breath before I could draw it in. If you are one of those people who insist on reading books from left to right, I recommend a sip of clear water before starting each new chapter. Even better, I suggest that before you read the next story, you open your door and walk into the woods where only birds and spying raccoons might see you, or into a desert of lizards and jackrabbits, if that is what is at hand. Paw up the dirt and taste it on your lips. Drink out of a stream or from the lucid depths of a bedrock water hole. Return to your house, where this book waits on a table. Pull up a chair and see what other wild creature comes to speak with you.

GREAT BLUE HERON

I was very young when I woke before dawn and grabbed the small knapsack beside the bed. In it I placed a spiral notepad, a sharpened pencil, a paper bag containing breakfast, and a heavy thrift-store tape recorder with grossly oversized buttons. I walked outside, through the neighborhood, and at the edge of a field full of red-winged blackbirds, I took out the tape recorder. Their officious prattle lifted like shouts from the stock market floor. I pushed *record* and listened.

In time I moved on, recording birds in different trees, in other lots. I ate cold toast with careful bites. Writing things down: the time, the place, what the bird looked like. My penmanship was terrible, shaky, typical for elementary school. I wanted so badly to be able to write like an adult. Occasionally I would just make loops with the pencil so that it looked like cursive. I worked at the entries, putting the last letter or two of a word on the next line if it wouldn't fit. It was important, as important as anything, and I acted as if I knew what I was doing, as if I knew something about birds. Which I did not. I understood only that they flew and that they did it well. I would hold the pencil in my teeth and hum thoughtfully as I had seen the adults do.

With my tape recorder, I walked these fields fanning below the east side of the Rocky Mountains in Colorado. So rarely was I awake at this time of the day that it felt like my birthday or Thanksgiving. I had not known that the sunrise was so lavish and that you could actually feel the color when it reached your face. I had a fantasy of running away to the woods, becoming a nomad and a hermit, but soon enough the sixty minutes of tape ran out. I returned home. There I ate breakfast a second time.

Not for decades would I hear of John James Audubon or Aldo Leopold or Ann Zwinger. In these decades I would grope into the land. I would be blatantly watched by grizzly bears and humming-birds. I would blow dust from tracks and crawl on my stomach through forests to see the animal. My truck would be buried axle-deep in the sandpits of New Mexican back roads. I would become a river guide in the North American deserts and take young students from cities into the wilderness, teaching them how to smell for coyotes and how to let tarantulas walk over their hands. I would rope into canyons looking for all the fear and quiescence and exquisite forms that roil in the wilderness.

Now I go out walking. Sometimes for a hundred miles, circling mountain ranges or following canyons for weeks and months. More often it is a quarter mile in an afternoon, shuffling around the trees, looking for a soft place to sit. Out of habit, my eyes train on shapes and movements, and if I see any animal, it is invariably unexpected. I have no idea how proficient trackers do it—choosing their animal, then finding it. I choose a coyote and I get a very rainy day. I choose an elk and get a deer mouse. Then a mountain lion comes from behind while I am crouched, looking at its tracks.

To see the animal, you must first remain very still. You may have to huddle in the dark of a street culvert for three nights before the raccoon comes. You may have to sit naked on the tundra before the grizzly finds you. Or you will simply have to be there, driving the highway the moment that a caravan of unhurried red-backed salamanders passes from one side to the other. That is when you must leave your car and get on hands and knees in the roadway. Just be careful not to touch the salamanders, because the acid from your fingerprints will burn into their backs. When you encounter an animal, it may be as startling and quick as the buzz of a rattlesnake. Or you may have time to note the shift of wind and the daily motions of light.

Times that I have seen the animals have been like knife cuts in fabric. Through these stabs I could see a second world. There were stories of evolution and hunger and death. Cross sections of genetic histories and predator-prey relationships, of lives as cryptic as blood paths in snow. I have talked with those at the Division of Wildlife who know. I have rummaged through clutters of skulls and skeletons in a musty museum basement and read the reports of field biologists. But it is outside where the grip of the story lies.

———

It was at a guide house near the Colorado River in Arizona that I saw the great blue heron. We were cleaning gear at the end of a river-running trip. Open ice chests and tired people. Equipment was being moved with dry, cracked hands that bleed as they often do midway through the season. The man behind me told me to look up, and I pulled my head out of an ice chest. Sweeping into view twenty feet above was a great blue heron. It had the monstrous wingspan of a flying dinosaur, its snakelike neck stretched ahead, its long legs trailing behind. As it reached the telephone pole directly over our heads, its wings changed. Feathers spread with the fullness of a parachute. They stalled the air, these domed wings suddenly occupying more space than both of our bodies combined. With limber figure-skating grace, it landed on the flat of the pole top. The wings remained out for a moment, the heron teetering for balance. Then they closed.

"Jesus, look at that bird," said the person behind me. And, Jesus, I looked at it. Head to toe, it was nearly five feet tall, a subtle steel blue that tricks the eyes. It surveyed the landscape of mobile homes and river equipment below. From our vantage point we could see straight up its body. Its head was colorful, with contrasting grays and blues and the yellow of its saber beak. Balanced on the long neck, the head moved independently of the body. Head motions were a language in themselves, with the weight of the back of its skull balancing the lightness of its beak.

People came and shunted gear, maneuvering around us. We did not move. The two of us were cradled by this bird, taken in as if it were a magician. You see these herons on the river daily, sweeping out from the riverbank, swerving among the dazzling white egrets. You see them wait until the last moment before they fly and screech, as if doubting you have the effrontery to come this near. But never a view like this. Not straight up, not right into its eyes. You want to ask questions now, now that the heron is so close. But you can't. You can't get a word out. You just stare for as long as you can because suddenly it will be over, you will get your name back and life will begin again. The two of us down here are members of a species famous for road building, artwork, and claims of superiority. People of reason, we ask many questions and give voluminous answers, but for now we were dead silent. The heron had us. It is a stalker, one so patient and still that time turns to ice as it waits and watches for fish in the shallow water. It held to the telephone pole perch, its slender, armored toes overhanging every edge. It straightened its feathers, leaned back and preened through them, aligning the steel-wire breast feathers that swept out at their tips like whispers. Its eyes tilted down, an adaptation useful for when your food swims at your feet.

You cannot look at this bird and decide who is superior and who is not. The encyclopedic vocabulary of a raven is no more admirable than a red-spotted toad's ability to drink through its skin. The human penchant for deciphering the world has no greater merit than the unusually large eyeball of a pronghorn.

People kept moving. Stoves and dry boxes were carried in and out, arranged and rearranged. Knots were tied—double half hitches, trucker's hitches, bowlines, clove hitches—securing equipment to the top of the van, tying off tarps and random lengths of rope. The heron's neck retracted into a slight S shape. Its center of gravity shifted down. You see them do this before they fly, and they always pause as if to make certain that this is the moment. Its wings opened and flashed against the sky. With one stroke it was off. With two and three it glided. Air foiled beneath it, turning to an invisible clay of a very certain shape. The bird raked us with a stone-ground voice as it turned west toward the Colorado River, back to the desert and the water, away from the guide house and mobile homes where once there had been desert and water for as long as heron generations could remember. The heron was then gone.

The man with me said only "Mmm." What else was there to say?

You see these things, even if you are not looking. You come out and the animals will find you, even if you never know they are there. Whether you are observant, curious, unaware, reluctant, or apathetic, they will find you. As they move around you, they will make tracks of different sizes, different gaits, different numbers and shapes of toes and claws, leaving signatures as they turn their weight into the ground to watch you. Their scents will have the sweetness of wool or the dark molasses smell of good soil. Always there will be a brilliance of form and function in such discreet and flagrant abundance that the universe must be nothing but a bottomless grab bag of ingenuity.

This book is a collection of my own encounters, staring at animals for as long as they would stay. The experiences are translated, now made of words, like trying to build the sky out of sticks. Verbs and nouns do not always change to the weather as they should. They may not dry out and crack on hot days. Even my eyes have betrayed me as I have watched a tiger shark, losing its shape and its direction, and my ears have been misled as I have listened for a mountain lion in a canyon.

I have written this book to share nuances that I have witnessed, to cultivate a familiarity with animals in their most original of contexts. At times I have been blasphemously arrogant and then learned from them to be quiet. In the mere studying of short-tailed weasel tracks in snow, I have been instructed in temperament and precision. There is, of course, an instant drama to an encounter, but remember that beyond the single moment is the long and ornate process of living.

The life of an animal lies outside of conjecture. It is far beyond the scientific papers and the campfire stories. It is as true as breath. It is as important as the words of children.

Ardea herodias

Animalia

ANIMAL

A nimals are watching. Right now they are in the woods, many of them looking back over their shoulders or peering down at us from bridges of tree branches as we march below, snapping dry wood with our boot soles and squashing soft, fleshy mushrooms.

My companion stops.

"Did you hear that?"

I stop too, listening to a chittering forest of birds.

"What?" I ask.

"Something moved over there," he says. "An animal."

We both drill our eyes through the trees.

I am sixteen years old and, like my friend, I am lost in the mountains of western Wyoming. Not interminably lost, we just do not know exactly where we are—besides being on an untrailed flank of the Teton Mountains, over our heads in jackstraw timber. We had taken off from a road at a random point that morning and barged our way into a steep forest where no signs point the way. We wanted to see what it was like in here. Day packs are slung on our backs, containing water and some food. We have no maps, no compasses. No whistles, flares, or shelters. We have knives in our pockets and the clothes we are wearing—all that is needed for a day of going nowhere.

I peer with my friend through a thousand broken shadows, seeing no movement save for twigs springing back as small bark-colored birds flit from one tree to the next. All the way along, we have been hearing animals snitching and scratching, elk lumbering about with heavy sounds, pine squirrels chattering, scolding from overhead. But all we have seen are these few birds. Everything else is lost to us behind tree trunks nearly touching one another. I squint to see better.

"How big an animal?" I ask.

"Big," he says. "I didn't see it, but it sounded like something big."

"I don't see it."

"I don't either."

Only so long can we stare at nothing, so we start moving again, ducking under branches, touching the ground with our hands, and leaving the big animal—whatever it was—behind. Drunken, wild forest, it is far denser than we anticipated, battering our shins as we step through trapdoors of dead wood. Our hands slash in front of us, clearing branches and beards of dry, stringy lichen. Spiderwebs snap like trip wires across our lips, our foreheads, our arms. We've been side-hilling for hours, taking so many brief, natural paths that we don't really know how to get back.

Ahead we find a big dollop of scat on the ground and we stand around it, sweat dripping from our eyebrows, wiped on the backs of our hands. The scat looks like a big can of hash dumped on the ground. It is full of berry hulls and black digested meat.

"Bear," my friend says.

"Yeah," I agree. "A big bear."

"Grizzly, you think?"

"What's grizzly scat look like?"

"I don't know."

My friend turns a grin toward me. "What if it is a griz?" he says excitedly.

Should we be excited? I wonder. Better than being nervous, I suppose. I don't want to see the bear. I just like the tingle in my spine telling me there is one nearby.

"Let's keep going," he says.

"Yeah," I agree.

Stupid kids, why not?

All we have to follow are animal trails, faint inclinations left by elk or deer or bear that passed through. Even squat clearings left by waddling porcupines come in handy. They are all short-lived, ending as suddenly as they began, putting us back in thick trees where birds send warnings ahead of us, criers calling through green crowns. I crawl under a toppled tree, and my nose grazes the ground. I smell leaf rot and animals. It is the odor of spices in an earthy, slightly unpalatable dish: bonemeal, bobcat urine, wood fungus, worm dung. This is the other side of the coin from the rest of my life, from doors and walls and movie screens. This is the place that does not belong to humans. Animals have scuffed the ground, shat upon it, cleared twigs out of the way, folded down grass in their sleeping. They are talking, leaving messages written in scents on leaves and tree bark, whistling to one another, hearing voices in the distance.

As we move, a deer bounds away, stabbing its hooves into the ground with punctuated sounds. Only the tips of its fawn-colored ears are visible over ferns and serviceberry bushes. We look for the deer, but it is gone that fast, vanished back into the folds. After that, a gray jay sails in and lands on a branch to see who we are, its soft, inquisitive eyes following us. I feel as if we are dragging tin cans into the wilderness, startling animals from their many private gardens.

A little farther comes a sound like the weight of an elk crashing through dead branches. My friend and I freeze, both listening and wondering if the weight of an elk might also sound like the weight of a mountain lion. I step up on top of a rotten stump, and see nothing.

"What is it?" my companion asks.

Not taking my eyes off the forest, I say, "I don't know. A big animal. Sounds like an elk."

By this age I was accustomed to going out with no adult supervision. My mother had tried Little League on me, and a goofy local version of Boy Scouts, but in the end she just had to shoo me out the door and send me hiking. Both my parents took their own, separate interest in wild places—my father building great fires and showing me the taste of whiskey on cold Arizona mornings, and my mother lightly tramping the mountains of Colorado and Wyoming, picnicking atop slender timberline ridges. With such parents I learned not to fear wild animals, only to know they are there.

The forest deepens. We come into a stand of old-growth trees where Douglas fir and short-needled spruce muscle their way toward the light. No longer is there ground to walk on, only decades of huge trees downed from windstorms and disease. We balance across trunks as big around as cars, fifteen feet off the ground, and follow each other down into warrens of shattered debris.

We do not know that a large predator is watching us from only a few feet away. We do not know we are blithely stepping into its territory. We know nothing until it leaps.

A rush of motion and sound explodes from between fallen trunks directly beneath our feet. Blood jacks straight into our muscles. We take wings. We fly. Not once do we look down, not even glimpsing the color of this creature. It is large, something with strong lungs. I can hear its claws grinding dead wood. The animal fills the forest with a territorial uproar unlike anything I have ever heard. I am gone.

Before my conscious mind even recognizes the true presence of danger, before a second passes, I am turned around and a good twenty feet away, trying to outrun my companion with all my might.

The animal's voice breaks the air at my back. My mouth goes instantly dry, my whole body cold and fast from adrenaline. I sail over dead trees. Feet barely touch anything solid. I spot a snowmelt swamp cupped nearby into the slope and I think of diving into it to escape this beast, but all I can see is myself bogged to the knees with some unknown creature feasting on my torso. For all I know this is an undiscovered animal, a huge, clawed primate, a meat-eating Sasquatch. I'm not ready to die.

We run through our own cacophony of snapping branches, our hands flinging tree limbs out of our way like we're deflecting daggers in midair. Down the steep slope only our boot tips touch ground. I become an acrobat, no gap between hand and eye, no coordination needed because I am right now a single muscle sliding like pure light between the trees.

They say not to run. Stand your ground or curl up in a fetal ball. Protect your head and your vital organs. Bear, mountain lion, wolverine: whatever the case, do not turn and run. Do not reveal your back and initiate a chase. By the time such warnings enter my mind, I am making a full-speed exit, hoping my companion will fall prey first and give me some extra seconds.

The forest comes to an end and we break into an open, day-lit meadow exactly where we had started hours earlier. A couple of miles in the distance is a road and the car we left there. We had beelined our way back, sprinting down the mountain as if we knew exactly where we were going. We stumble to a halt, panting, leaning over with hands planted on our thighs. We turn and look back. There is no beast. Whatever it was, it has not pursued us. After a minute of watching, my heart pumping but winding down, I say, "Mountain lion. You think?"

"Yeah." My friend exhales. "Mountain lion."

"Or a bear?" I ask.

"What does a bear sound like?"

As I look into the trees, I wonder how many animals are now

settling from our loud, desperate visit. How many eyes had watched us pass, how many heads turned to see us careening through the woods? We overturned their applecarts, stampeded through their bedrooms and dining rooms, threw open their doors. We start laughing. We laugh at ourselves. We laugh at our good fortune—both the fortune of encountering what must have been a large predatory animal and the fortune of it not running us down and devouring us. We chide each other, letting our guard drop a little. But we do not take our eyes off the dark wall of trees. There is an animal inside with the smell of us fresh in its nostrils. I realize that it had not been attacking us. We would have been easy to catch. Instead, the sound of its voice was strictly territorial, designed to root down into our spines and trigger a flight response. We did as we were told. We answered the animal clearly, playing our part in the conversation with everything we had.

When my companion finally turns and walks into the meadow toward the road, I linger. I am not ready to render myself back into a human being, not ready to return to a car and an asphalt highway. I want to stay just a moment longer. I peer into the forest, where every bit of darkness and light has a face, a set of eyes looking out at me. Nothing emerges. I feel the tug at my back, my friend walking away, and I turn to catch up and become human again.

Animalia

Carnivora

BEAR

I

When I first saw the bear, I was twelve years old. The bear was a couple of years old, relatively equal to me in age as far as bears go. It was a black bear, mottled and scroungy as it came out of winter into spring, carrying a changing wardrobe on its back. It was in the ponderosa forest, beside the rusty propane tank and the clothesline. This was the far edge of my grandparents' home in the White Mountains of Arizona. I lived here at times and grew familiar with its forests, with the high, roaming mountains thick with pines and bears.

The bear was startled and went rigid upon our meeting. Its neck craned. Nose went into the air. I turned and ran the other way, into the house. I grabbed a camera and ran back out. There was a stream of noise, people asking me what on earth I thought I was doing.

Their words scattered behind me like agitated dust as I jumped off the porch in an open sprint.

The bear was farther into the ponderosas now, far past the propane tank. When it saw me beating toward it through the trees, it too began running. Later in my life I would learn not to be so thoughtlessly bold. Now, though, I was charging into the territory of the bear, pushing my way through because it did not matter who an animal was and who I was. There were none of these things. I was a stone, the wind, a child. Of course you remember this, when nothing else mattered. Nothing. Anything. Anywhere. But here. Now. This.

The bear took me past the ponderosas and beyond the gnarled oak trees along the meadow. It took me through the aspen forest honeycombed with black, scrutinizing eyes. I opened a trough out of the delicate purple irises, ferns, and tall grasses. The camera was in one hand and my finger was on the shutter button. When the bear stopped I would bring it to my eyes and take pictures. But it did not stop.

Every few seconds it looked back and grunted disapprovingly, annoyed that I was following. It turned ahead and ran with bursts of speed. The fur on its flanks rolled like a baggy coat. We dove through the aspen forest, into places I had never seen. We passed under the barbed wire fence where a bent, shot, and rusty yellow sign hung at the Apache National Forest boundary. A tag of tawny hair was snagged on a barb. Bear fur. The fallen aspens were gray and pickup-sticked across one another, decked with dog mushrooms. I watched my feet, huffing and trying not to trip over the forest debris. I kept the bear at the edge of vision, paying attention only to what was a few bounds ahead.

There is an account in Alberta of a yearling black bear frightened off by a coyote. The weight ratio was probably one hundred fifty pounds to thirty-five pounds. Still, the bear walking the shore of a lake skittishly fled into the forest upon seeing the coyote. The coyote merely sniffed a patch of grass and kept walking. The bear popped from the forest well beyond the coyote and, looking carefully over its shoulder, continued along the lakeshore. The researchers who saw this concluded that the bear had recently broken from its family. Finding no historic evidence for a yearling black bear to fear a coyote, they assumed it was stricken with "some level of temporal insecurity."

I stopped in the forest with a jerk. Almost ran flat into the bear. It was a short distance away, turned to face me. It was still. I did not see its lungs rapidly expanding and contracting like mine. It contemplated me with curious impatience, lifting its nose to smell me. The camera swung by its strap, near my waist.

A sound came from my mouth. Not a word, just a sound. Now I was with the bear in the aspen forest past the barbed wire fence with the yellow sign and far beyond the rusted propane tank at home. We were children, the bear and I, with unjaded stares for each other. We were just old enough to run far off on our own. Children of different sizes, of course, and it did not occur to me until many years later that a bear of this size, being so aggressively dogged by someone of my small stature, could have easily removed my face with a paw swipe. Since 1900 there have been about fifty human fatalities from black bear attacks in North America, most of them in remote regions where bears have not been habituated to humans. (The opposite is true of fatal grizzly attacks, which tend to occur in places more frequented by people.) But this was not what I was thinking then. I believed that that bear and I were exchanging bits and pieces of each other through smell and color. We were studying each other, assaying our various characteristics. We were standing in an aspen forest, face-to-face, watching. Nothing had ever been as silent as this. No afternoon nap, no light snowfall.

The bear twisted with a grunt, its shabby coat waving as it landed on forepaws. It ran into the forest, and I did not move. You encounter an animal like this, and it is so vivid it detaches from time. The cogs and wheels of convention instantly unravel. So vivid was this encounter that I later wondered if it actually happened. But I was there, standing in the recess between aspens, as quiet as I had ever been. It happened. The bear was here.

When the bear was gone from sight and the cracking of branches was no longer audible, everything caved into the hole left behind. Time began again. I thought about following the bear, but I had come far enough. The camera ceased swinging from my arm and hung like the pendulum of a broken clock.

I I

There were thunderstorms in Alaska somewhere. They were the shapes of fists rising into the atmosphere. There were no good maps at our disposal to tell us what was out there besides clouds. I sat in the canoe in a quiet space between rapids and watched them elevate, columns of cumulonimbuses ascending at different rates and spreading into anvils as they hit cold, high-level winds. My feet were propped against the gear, my paddle dragging in dark, tannic water from the stern. I had come to the headwaters of the Fortymile River with a friend named Todd Robertson. This was the Dennison Fork, one of many forks of the Fortymile providing a grip on these nameless mountains. We had been twenty straight days in the wilderness before coming to this river.

Todd had hunted out the Fortymile from a photocopy of a hand-drawn map. He traced the only road, a winding dirt thoroughfare, back to the headwaters of the Fortymile, and convinced me that we could get there. We hitchhiked with a canoe from Eagle, catching a ride in a camper shell filled with mosquitoes and fresh caribou antlers still strung with rotting, fetid velvet. The truck swerved into the interior of the state through a blizzard of stabbing jolts and hairpin switchbacks. At the end of the day we were rolled out of the back, violently nauseated. We shuffled our canoe to the river. As we shoved in, getting our paddles in place, a moose crossed the river. We passed eye to eye and swept downstream, out of sight.

We were running the river blind, though we had heard rumors of big white water between here and the Fortymile's confluence with the Yukon River. It was a crazy stretch of water, and the canoe became awash in heavy rapids, beating through rock gardens and broadsiding waves that towered out to smack our faces. We scouted some of the rapids. We would then chart our course, a careful pathway usually involving a slip into an eddy to bail water before we were thrust into the next waves. Maps and plans lose integrity within the grind of a rapid. It all became yelling and digging with the paddles and hoping to God we wouldn't vanish into a hole. Todd and I had guided rivers together, had run deep into rapids in Colorado, so here at least we were able to work tightly. But there had never been rivers down there that ran through this kind of wilderness. Never so much unaltered land. The canoe tilted into the froth, so that from the stern I was lifted on the gradient to see everything; then we were in, Todd's arms and paddle lost in the white. The work was exhausting, living foot by foot, fast enough to barely push the boat out of holes.

In the deepest whorls of wilderness, where the valley moves from the state of Alaska into Canada's Yukon Territory, we found prints less than a day old of wolves and grizzlies. We slept on islands, contemplating what would happen if our canoe wrapped and broke against a rock. A person cannot walk away from this river to find help without becoming a legend. We had no wish to become legends, either as people who made it or as people who did not. We brought duct tape for repairs and enough food for weeks. When the rapids played into long, silent pools, we no longer thought of boat repairs. We drifted. For miles we did not speak. Then it came again, the noise of swift water scooping into rocks ahead.

The days left us tired, and we chose different sides of this cobbled island to sit and rest. Camp was in the center, between us, and the canoe was dragged high to shore, embellished with new creases and scrapes. The island was a scuff in the river. The canyon was steepled with black spruce. I watched the water, dark and rolling over boulders, flowing with the sheen of black silk. At a rock, it tattered into white shapes like a sketch by M. C. Escher. My eyes roamed lazily around the shore. Above the water, as if the Escher drawing had moved naturally to a different image, was a grizzly bear.

The bear was watching me. It presented the entire side of its body to the river, a mass of blond fur, outlined only at the blunt face and blocky head and the round hump between shoulder blades. The bear's shore and mine were separated by twenty feet of water. There was no solace in this distance. I had seen a bear swim a mile of swift, cold water here, much swifter and colder than this. The bear walked downstream, fixing on me now and then. It entered a collection of blueberry bushes and scanned our island.

I called Todd over, and he walked across the island. Now there were three of us: the bear, Todd, and me. The bear continued plodding past. Across the river from our camp, the grizzly took a seat. It found a cluster of birch trees, and it rolled onto its rear like a very large person sitting to tell a story.

We studied the bear closely, without speaking, and the bear peered about, looking at perhaps us, perhaps our gear, or just perusing the world. We did not have guns. It was a conscious choice not to bring that kind of weaponry, even after some folks, experienced with the region, suggested otherwise. We feared we might shoot each other (there have been several cases of someone being shot by a partner who was trying to shoot a bear during an attack). Or we might shoot a grizzly in the foot and subsequently have our bodies ripped up and scattered over the landscape. It is better not to shoot at a grizzly unless you are certain of killing it. Their braincases are long and narrow, more so than those of most animals, and getting a bullet into that target is not a simple task with quivering aim.

Weeks earlier we had camped along an Alaskan river called the Salmon, ten miles upstream of the town of Hyder. While eating our meal beside the canoe, we had witnessed a horde of well-armed men and women piling out of a nearby forest. With dirt on their faces and ripped clothing, they looked like a small military team on maneuvers. It was a biological survey crew studying fish in the creeks.

One of them had carefully eyed our camp, a high-powered rifle hanging from her shoulder. "There are grizzlies all over the place," she warned. "Better watch yourselves." Hard words to sleep on.

Still, we had not brought a gun to the Fortymile. It would be presumptuous of us to believe the presence of a bear in a birch grove meant we would need a weapon. Grizzly bear attacks are so rare that, should one occur, you would have to shrug at the irony, curl into a ball, and hope to survive.

There were no trees for us to climb on our small island, in case the bear should cross over. Although trees make for fair escapes from grizzlies, rarely is there enough time during an attack to get your hands on the first branch. Incidentally, two people in North America have been killed by falling from trees they were using for escape. In both cases, the bear gave the body furtive sniffs and left without troubling it further.

We discussed leaving the island, getting gear to the boat quickly and pushing down the river. Again, the thought made us both feel presumptuous. There were more grizzlies here than on the Salmon, and we were as likely to come upon another at the next site. We were in a land well populated by bears, and it was best simply to live rather than to chase ourselves in circles with fear.

Our patience thinned before the bear's. It had no engagements to call it away. Slowly, we left the shore and walked to camp. We looked up often to see the bear. It reached to scratch its foot, turning its forearms, which rotate from joints like a human's or a gorilla's. *Ursus arctos,* once *Ursus arctos horribilis,* is a bear made famous by its unpredictable face-to-face conflicts with humans. Its common name, grizzly, has no relationship to its legendary ferocity but simply refers to its shimmering, mottled, grizzled coat. This animal's hairs were gold-tipped, so below its luminescent dusting, the bear looked dark, as if there were a ghost in there.

Most animals show themselves sparingly. The grizzly bear is six to eight hundred pounds of smugness. It has no need to hide. If it were a person, it would laugh loudly in quiet restaurants, boastfully wear the wrong clothes for special occasions, and probably play hockey. It would also pursue secret solitude, disappearing for weeks on end while people were expecting it at upcoming meetings. At the moment, it was bold and aloof, making sure we knew we were being watched, but keeping its distance. As a function of time and patience, our uneasiness faded. We kept looking and the bear kept sitting.

We constructed our separate tents on different parts of the island. The bear monitored our activity. It watched us enter our tents. It listened to us tighten zippers and dig into our bags. My last thoughts into sleep were to keep alert, to not lose contact with the world. My next thoughts could be greeting a grizzly at the door.

I woke at about three. This far north the sun was still up, although very low, riding through the mountains as if looking for something it lost on the ground. Black spruces dressed the mountains with shadows. I opened the tent and looked outside. Water sounds, rocks rounding themselves in constant motion. I remembered the grizzly, and it startled me that I had forgotten. I glanced at the birch grove where it was last seen. There was no grizzly.

I could sleep now on the fact that a grizzly was in the forest. At any moment we could cross paths. The world became far more elaborate once I knew that this bear and many more surrounded me, and I sat there for some time, looking into the dim land around the Fortymile.

III

We had come by foot, navigating the marshy humps of the tundra. Air from the Arctic Ocean was frigid, pressing moisture against the north edge of the mountains. It was weather for ravens. I listened to their deep wing beats as they passed and could hear their muffled, gravelly calls. We were on a far corner of the Arctic National Wildlife Refuge where caribou antlers were thrust into the ground, overgrown with tundra, like sacred artifacts. I flared my nostrils, taking in fresh air. It stung my nasal passages. Hunks of clouds adhered to the coolness of the mountains like cotton candy to a child's fingers.

Autumn had finally come to the Arctic. The air was different, stinging in the morning. The heaviest part of a storm had rolled through the previous night and it tasted of a new season. Its dampness was no longer subtle. Its clouds smothered the mountains. The rain was half snow. Scrubby tundra plants on the north slope of Alaska's Brooks Range, down to the tough, bare grasses, turned ocher and faintly red.

I shifted in my sleeping bag, rubbing my feet together in their damp wool socks. Feet were sore from the tundra, ankles swollen from cramming between tussocks. I pried a hand through the opening to feel the air in the tent. It smelled like a wet dog in there. When I pushed my head through, I saw Todd's tangled hair poking from his own bag. There was no sound of rain. A faint light was on the nylon, the first sun for some time. I reached overhead and pulled down the tent zipper, releasing a spray of water.

I wormed my body from the bag and came to my knees, then up, standing outside at the front of the tent. My feet were still inside, on the hood of my bag. Our packs were lumps beneath a tarp upon which pools of rainwater gathered. There were very few plants more than three inches high on the tundra, and certainly no trees, so the mountains seemed to be optical illusions of size and distance. There was nothing to serve as reference, and the grayness added another dimension to physics. Or took one away. The mountains could be miles high, or just beyond my nose. I stretched my arms and turned to see the world.

Distance immediately came to focus on a grizzly ten yards away.

It was the only thing there, like a roving boulder. We made eye contact, and the bear caught itself midstep toward the tent. One paw suspended above the ground. Eyes locked. An erratic breeze blew through and it riffled the bear's fur just as my hair fluttered. The fur was colored in hot honey, like spent autumn grasses and late afternoon sun. It took ripples out of the breeze. The bear's black nostrils widened. Great lungs filled. I could see the texture of its nose, how it was wet and soft.

The rising agencies of fear one would expect were not there. There was no time for them. No time to cross myself or to believe or disbelieve what I was seeing. It was a grizzly bear. I was sure of this because there was nothing else, no boulder, no tree, no bush. Even the ravens were gone. I knew I should not be staring the bear straight in the eye, that the safest conversation with a bear is held while looking to the side. But it appeared so suddenly, the only thing to look at, that I couldn't break the stare. I rattled a foot against Todd's head and muttered his name.

"What?"

"There's a grizzly out here," I said.

He thought about this. "How close?" he asked.

"Very close."

Todd said no more. There was no movement from inside the tent.

The eyes of most predators are situated at the front of the head for three-dimensional vision. A rabbit or a deer has eyes to the side, reading a broad range of events in nebulous detail. But like a wolf or a weasel or a human, a bear has its eyes placed forward, gathering depth of field, telling it exactly where you stand. You use this kind of vision when you are chasing something, so you know the right moment to pounce.

I was a small animal next to this bear. I didn't have a lot of fat, I certainly didn't have muscles that hid the shape of every bone, and I did not have a rug of fur to top the whole thing off. I felt as if I were built of toothpicks. I was small and I was waiting for an answer from the big bear. The bear inspected me. Behavior is as complicated for bears, especially grizzlies, as it is for humans. Each time I have seen a grizzly, the attitude and outcome have been different. No rules apply. A native in a remote Yukon River village once told me to bluff a black bear when in danger, advice that mirrors the bulk of official documentation stating that a person attacked by a black bear should never lie down or go into a submissive, protective position, but rather should shout and even throw rocks or sticks. When I asked the man about grizzlies, he shrugged and said that nothing works twice. Curiously, in a study of one hundred fifteen human injuries from combined black, polar, and grizzly bear attacks, only two victims were natives.

The distinguishing hump between a grizzly's shoulders is a tangle of muscle draped from the spine to the powerful forearms. These muscles are primarily directed toward digging, and I have watched a grizzly unearth arctic ground squirrels with little effort, tossing cubic yards of dirt into the air. It can also use those limbs to grab an animal and crush it.

Occasionally they will devour black bears. A twenty-three-year-old female black bear, easily three hundred pounds, was part of an Alaskan denning study in the Tanana River flats. In October a tracking plane flew over and spotted a grizzly digging at the black bear's den. When the researchers swept low, the grizzly lunged at the plane. At the time, the black bear was still sending a signal from within its den via a radio collar. The study was left for the winter, and researchers returned by helicopter the following April. They found only a chewed radio collar, small bone fragments, and a large amount of hair from the black bear. She was apparently able to defend the main entrance of her den, which was reinforced with tree roots, but the grizzly dug its own entrance elsewhere.

At our tent, I watched the bear's eyes, waiting for a sign. The nostrils flared, taking in the air. It contemplated that air, judging scents. A breeze came between us several times. I sensed a peculiar familiarity, like looking at my parents and seeing my own traits. There were shocking similarities. I have never seen a bear skinned open, but I've heard some say that beneath the fur, the bear is human. I know some hunters, methodical people who dress animals in the field with precise, wordless turns of a knife. When they stripped the fur loose from a bear, exposing a pale, pink corpse, they covered their mouths in fear. Never killed a bear again, any of them.

I have heard the story about a bear and a woman who made love. It was an old legend, one from the Northwest. I have often imagined them together in a den, a sensual vision of comfort and warmth that I cannot shake. The woman had children, cubs, and became herself a bear because it was a simple evolutionary step, because it was already there, inside her. I have no doubt that if a person turned truly wild, if that person's skin sprouted thick, soft hair and curved claws sprung from fingers, if senses honed themselves to where the nose, run through the air, could read all things, that person would be indistinguishable from the bear.

The woman belonged to two worlds after she made love to the bear. Her human brothers came and killed her bear husband in his den. They tracked him. They cornered him with dogs. They pierced his heart and skinned him clean. She has gone now, the bear woman. She's taken her cubs into the mountains. I think of her sorrow and how she must have wished that the differences could be sewn together. I could see, at the face of this grizzly, why this story persists.

The bear abruptly reared back. Fear struck at my stomach. The air broke with the move. The bear landed away from the tent and went into a full run to get away from me, as if I had fired a rifle over its head. Its fur streaked back with the speed. Its body took to the terrain as if there were no obstacles, as if there were no such thing as friction.

It had to be my scent.

The bear raced across the tundra, and as it moved it gave perspective to the place. The mountains became a distance. Water-falls became volume and size. Land became geography. The bear's shanks flapped as it galloped. It ran until it was small and moved up the incline of the nearest mountain. It ran until details were missing, bolting up the mountainside with intense, impervious power, not slowed at all by the terrain.

All I could smell were damp clouds and water slipping through the tundra. I could not find what startled the bear. I could not smell the humanness, the incomprehensible scent that sends a full-grown grizzly running like a scared cat. I breathed deeper when the bear was a dot of gold light a mile away, not brown at all, when Todd finally came out of the tent. I tried to read what I was breathing. Nylon from the tent, the dank, wet-dog interior of worn people sleeping off the cold, the opening sky, and steam with sunlight fingering the ground.

The bear had smelled something in the breeze, perhaps a memory of humans. Something genetic maybe, or a warning spoken through the air about who I was, that I was one of the woman's brothers.

IV

I've got legs. I can walk. I go into the desert with a pack and only a sheet to sleep under. Around me, Utah summer bakes dry feeder canyons of the San Juan. Uncut sunlight burns through my hat brim, and through my salty shirt fabric, and then through my skin until I feel like nothing but a walking skeleton. My legs carry me. My eyes ache from light, but I am happy, as happy as this lone body can be, a Magellan drifting across my own barren sea.

In the spiraling heat of morning, I look down, and there, printed in red sand before me, is a perfect track left by a black bear. Head hung, breathing with my mouth open, I puzzle over the mark of a broad pad, five oval toes, and five long nicks of claws. An animal wearing a heavy black robe of fur has walked here, unexpected traveler from far away.

Hello, stranger, I think. It is too hot to speak out loud.

Dark prince of the mountains, the black bear belongs to a country of pine thickets and beaver ponds. It is not one to be living among lizards and vacant stone canyons. Nearest I can figure, it wandered down from the Abajo Mountains forty miles to the north—an isolated uplift of alpine forests where a bear ought to be.

What are you doing down here? I ask it.

Perhaps the bear just came down for a look. No doubt it had spent most of its life in a throne of aspen trees and dark spruces, from where it stared down at a pale, blistering desert surrounding it on all sides. Curiosity must have gotten to it. The bear had come to see what this gaunt landscape was all about.

Studying its solitary track, I remember a childhood song, something about a bear going over the mountain to see what it could see. *Is this why you came? Welcome to hell, my friend. Make yourself at home.*

I walk deeper into the desert and start seeing this lonely bear's tracks all around, nosing into dry canyons, pawing across cracked plates of mud where water had once been. It is three or four days ahead of me and walking in the same direction—south. It feels as if we are traveling together, separated by only a few turns of the sky, seeing these same scorched boulders. Feels as though we know each other, two animals out for a long walk to see what we can see. It is probably a male, considering that male black bears tend to range about 20 percent farther than females. Juvenile males in particular enjoy broad, unbounded ranges, sometimes covering hundreds of miles a month.

Eventually I see where this bear is going. Its tracks head down into canyons that finally lead to the San Juan River, a warm, shallow stretch of quick, muddy water. I think, *So this is why you came. For water.* It's been a dry summer, maybe hard luck up in the mountains, springs petering out, streams going dry. The bear must have followed its nose downhill until it finally found a river. Three days behind it, I walk straight into the water, strip off my pack and toss it on shore. I empty my pockets; throw my knife, journal, pen, and binoculars onto dry ground; and dive in. I am still wearing boots and clothing. It doesn't matter. It feels so good, even if the water is bath temperature. I lie down in the river, its shallow bed rubbing against my shoulder blades, cobblestones slick with silt. For hours I lie there, only my face above the surface, shaded by the hat I am still wearing.

Looking up at a bare, blue sky, I remember that other animals have been sighted in odd places lately. Jaguars have been moving from Mexico into Arizona and are establishing a healthy population here in the United States. Wolves, without aid of activists or biologists, have traveled from Wyoming down into Colorado, seen in the southern Rockies for the first time in many decades, one hit and killed by a car while crossing an interstate. Great numbers of animals are in motion these days. Tropical and neotropical species —elegant trogons and eared quetzals, javelinas, coatis, and numerous butterflies and moths— have been documented moving out of the South into new northern ranges in the United States. Armadillos and opossums are suddenly all over the map, skittering out of longtime habitats to find new places.

A friend of mine, a scholar and naturalist named Walt Anderson, has been keeping his eye on these movements and recently said he spotted American robins in the Northwest Territories of Canada, where they have perhaps never been seen. He is aware of animals moving all over the planet. Anderson told me that environment, disease, economics, politics, and population levels all play into these recent migrations. It is difficult to say what is the sole driving factor, if any. There is always a push and pull going on, and put all together, a historically unprecedented number of animals seems to be setting across the world in the past few decades.

Climate zones are shifting north across the globe at a rate of a few feet every several hours, and species are steadily following, sending out scouts to find fallbacks and future niches. A Noah's ark sort of migration seems to be in effect, one by one, two by two, hundreds by hundreds, searching for new homes. Those who have been itching to travel are now set free, cast across the planet.

Whether this one bear is part of a larger movement is hard to say. For me the animal seems simply to be a companion, another desert vagrant. At the same time, we might both belong to this rumbling planetary migration, obeying a twitch in our DNA that persistently whispers in our heads, telling us to go. We've got legs. *Why not?*

When the sun drops in the west and the heat of the day loses its edge, I finally emerge from the water. I step out, and the river drains from my clothing. After an hour I am bone-dry, walking south. Soon the first stars appear, and I find a place to sleep. Out on bare rock, draped in a sheet, I dream of water under a huge sky.

In the dark before sunrise I wake and move again, no particular task on my mind but turning the pages of the world, seeing what comes next. I walk away from the river, farther into the desert. The bear must be behind me now. It has no good reason to go beyond the river corridor, where it can nap under big domes of cottonwood trees and lap up mouthfuls of water. I wonder what the other bears will think when this one returns to the mountains. Like a storyteller, it will carry a new smell home with it. Will they be awestruck, or will they care at all that one of their kind walked to the desert and back?

About ten miles from water I am in need of shade, a place to rest. The sun is too high. I begin scanning the cliffs until I find an alcove that I can reach. I climb up to it so I can sleep out the rest of the day behind a shield of brush. When I get there I find water. A dark seep emits from the rock wall. Just barely enough to drink. I lean in and kiss this faint spring, drinking its thin skin of water. It takes time, but I am patient. I don't have anywhere else to be right now. Soon the inside of my mouth is wet again.

For five minutes I drink, and I let my eyes wander, gazing around this shallow cave. On the ground a few feet away is a heap of bear scat. I pull away from the wall, surprised.

What are you doing here? You're not supposed to be here.

I'm incredulous. I thought I was the only one wandering in this manner, out for a walkabout in arid country.

You're supposed to be at the river, I think. *Unless you didn't come for water, and you really are just traveling.*

I crawl over and have a look at the scat. It is made of devoured beetle armor and ants crushed by bear molars. There are wings of flying insects, grasshoppers and cicadas. The pile is stained brick red by squawbush berries, mostly seed and very little berry, not an ideal diet for an animal weighing a couple hundred pounds. I pick up a twig and poke at the scat, punching through a dry crust formed around it. Inside, the scat is as soft as pecan pie. The bear is still three days ahead of me, still moving.

I step out of the alcove into naked sunlight and scramble to the head of the cliff, where I can see all around. To the south are great walls of sandstone and hard, saffron-colored basins. No water. No shade. Just desert.

I am not going any farther than this. My resources are nearly exhausted. But the bear has gone on. As I peer across this desolate expanse, I think this is not simply a bear looking for water, and not one on vacation from the Abajos. This bear is never coming back. I am captivated and envious, imagining this dark prince ambling onward, appearing in places a bear should never be seen: a vagabond showing his face between huge red columns of Monument Valley, crossing the barrens of the Petrified Forest and the wind-struck Painted Desert. It will hit the Lukachukai Mountains near the New Mexico–Arizona border if it turns left. Maybe it will veer right and scale up into the forests of Black Mesa on the Navajo Reservation. Or it is going straight south, bound for woods along the Mogollon Rim, for the Sierra Madre far beyond that, perhaps aspiring toward the tip of South America, where it can finally stop and peer across a wildly blown sea toward Antarctica.

I look across the distance before me and think, *Good luck to you, traveler. May your legs carry you all the way.*

I return to the shade of the alcove and I sleep where the bear slept. When the sun goes down I rise again. I kiss the wet rock. I turn north and then I walk back.

Ursus americanus

Ursus arctos

COYOTE

I

Ragged and tired. We reached the Aermotor USA windmill after two weeks of crossing the Sonoran Desert. Water cranks out of the desert here like ice from the center of the sun. At the windmill was the first of our two food caches, hidden 112 degrees and a few hundred yards southeast of the well, under a paloverde tree. Our next cache was another week away. Backpacks were dropped as if we were shedding skin, a snakelike move that made sense now. We sat and waited for evening, then got about the small tasks of preparing a meal.

Behind us a single coyote barked a few times. The voice searched the area and found no other coyotes. We looked up, then returned to work. Again the bark came, closer. When it came a third time, we both stood and scanned the crosshatched shadows of paloverdes and creosote bushes. My traveling companion, Irvin Fernandez, grabbed his binoculars and loped in one direction, hunched to the height of the creosote. I saw motion through the spaces, parts of a coyote on the move up a nearby wash. Irvin was fixed on it from another vantage, signaling that he could see it.

The coyote obeys something internal that requires it to sing even when solitary. The singing brings them together. It creates a detailed map of coyotes across a landscape. About a third of all coyotes will be in packs, another third traveling in pairs, and the remaining third going solo.

The coyote barked again, and I was surprised there was no answer. I slipped my flute — long, wooden, and Japanese — from my pack and started playing to see what would happen. Irvin ducked, holding the binoculars to his eyes. I could not see the animal. Thinking it had moved on, I stopped playing. Without losing sight of the coyote, Irvin signaled with a hand to keep going. I played, and as I did he gestured more, winding his hand in the air, saying *Play, play*. I played high and furious. I felt the queer sensation of my brain grasping for air. My embouchure muscles began to ache. Irvin climbed the windmill tower and fused with the fading western sky. Calm evening air kept the blades inert. I walked toward him, covering the sound of my footsteps with flute notes. I was lost in the music as sight became hazy. Finally I stopped and inhaled deeply, my vision dazzling with an oxygen-starved brain.

"It sat down," he whispered to me. "It's just sitting out there, listening."

Slowly I climbed the metal tower, and when I reached Irvin, I turned and held up my binoculars. The coyote was sitting in the open. Truly in the open. The nearest plant was a chuparosa in full, red bloom, twenty feet away. The coyote, perhaps accustomed to strange motions and noises from the windmill, ignored us. Its ears were perked, and after it turned its head in all directions, it ducked nose to tail and closed its eyes. When it did this, it turned to stone.

If I stumbled across it, I would see nothing. The bushy tail made one rock, set against a hind leg that made another, set against the body, which was the third and largest rock. This posture took the coyote's surface area and wadded it into a ball, holding warmth and creating an instant home.

They are omnivores, the coyotes. Watermelons, beetles, deer, kangaroo rats, and flowers, all on the menu. The best way to survive for a long time on this planet, and thus become a highly success-ful species, is not to specialize. Like the shark and the cockroach, who have leisurely waltzed from one global extinction to the next, the coyote is a generalist. Specialists, eating only one type of prey or depending on specific tools to survive, are usually flash-in-the-pan species. They are impressive but generally short-lived. As with most omnivore generalists who must create a matrix of tactics for attaining foods, a peculiar open-ended intelligence has arisen in the coyote. Social orders have formed. Knowing looks have come to their eyes.

The government agency claiming such heroics as regional exter-mination of wolves and grizzlies was known at the end of the 1800s as the Bureau of Biological Survey, sporting the slogan "Bring Them In, Regardless of How." In a marvel of name juggling, it has since become Animal Damage Control and is now Wildlife Services. The agency eradicates any animal Congress and its assorted lobbyists find to be "noxious," from foxes to crows to jackrabbits. The one animal that has gotten under the program's skin, the way a trickster will steal mel-ons from your garden and hurl rinds at you, is the coyote. The more coyotes one kills, they discovered, the more live coyotes one must con-tend with. It is a spit-in-your-face species because of the very point that the coyote is an industrious and unparalleled generalist.

Each western state throws several hundred thousand dollars annu-ally into the coyote-killing pot. A typical year will see the federally man-dated death of ninety-eight thousand coyotes in the United States. In return, coyote populations have risen off the charts. Coyote numbers, by nature of female biology, are designed for rebound. Coyotes are the first species to occupy a devastated area in the way evening primroses grow in the turned sand of roadways. Female coyotes living in areas under light predator control have three to four uterine swellings in a year, each leading to litters of three to four pups. Where the killing of coyotes is more popular, females have around nine uterine swellings. Start shooting coyotes, and they start having more pups.

The response of coyotes to predator control is not just in litter size but in the numbers of females giving birth. When the population is stable, half of the female coyotes in an area will ovulate. When the pack is drastically pared down, all available females will ovulate, including the yearlings, who would normally not ovulate for another year. In a closely related pack where the lead female is usually the only one to bring a litter, the second and third females will mate and dig dens. Field biologists have estimated that if three-quarters of the world's coyote population were destroyed at once, within a year or two their numbers would return unfazed.

They fill spaces like water or darkness. When I have taken students down the lower Colorado, I have checked between their silent dome tents at dawn and found crossword puzzles of coyote prints from the night before. I have woken from my sleeping bag and glanced up to see the darkness of a coyote against the stars, five feet away, stopped in the middle of a group of guides sleeping on the ground. Two hundred years ago they lived only in the Great Basin region, and now they span most of North America, from Costa Rica to Alaska and from the West Coast to the East. It was not until 1938 that a trap in Mississippi caught its first coyote, marking the animal's eastward expansion. Now they are natives to that part of the continent, already genetically altered for their new habitats, with eastern coyotes weighing thirty-five pounds more than their western counterparts. Every now and then a coyote appears in Central Park in Manhattan. They have kept going and are now on Newfoundland, crossing a hundred miles of open water. Some suggest that they hitched on ice floes of the Northeast coast, and I imagine all the ice floes that missed land, coyotes going out to sea, never heard from again.

They have even surpassed geographic extension and have moved into genetic frontiers. DNA analysis has shown that 50 percent of sampled gray wolves from northern Minnesota, southern Ontario, and Quebec now carry coyote DNA. They have been hybridized by the coyote. Wolf genes have yet to be found in the coyotes. They are tough animals, gnarled and ingenious, getting into everything.

Their expansion since the industrial revolution has proved more successful than even human expansion. We built civilization, and they are doing a better job of using it than we are. The naturalist Loren Eiseley once observed that "man's greatest creation...was not really his at all," and he was talking about New York City being used as a flight path for pigeons. I am talking about coyotes on the North American continent. They have populated cities, fitting particularly well into the motherboard grid of Los Angeles. Again, something to be said for being a generalist.

If anything, it is we who are innocent, and not the animals. Naïveté comes with believing that the world is built of words and numerals. Coyotes, which have no use for pronunciations of supe-riority, are intent on survival, reproduction, and life. There is no naïveté in knowing how to survive this well. Coyotes move within a landscape of attentiveness. I have seen their eyes in the creosote bushes and among mesquite trees. They have watched me. And all the times that I saw no eyes, that I kept walking and never knew, there were still coyotes. When I have seen them trot away, when I have stepped from the floorboard of my truck, leaned on the door, and watched them as they watched me over their shoulders, I have been aware for that moment of how much more there is. Of how I have seen only an instant of a broad and rich life.

At the windmill, the coyote on the ground hadn't moved for a half hour. It still did not seem like a coyote at all. If I looked away for a time, then looked back, I had trouble finding it again. It was part of an extended family whose voices I heard often along this open stretch of desert between one mountain range and the next. It was also a solitary creature, sleeping lightly, and maybe it was not my flute that prompted it to stop. Maybe it was just time for a rest, and like all things, when it is time, it should happen.

Occasionally it glanced up to a shift in the wind or the sound of a quail covey. My hands grew sore, gripped to the steel of the windmill. The stone turned back to a coyote. It rose from the ground and stood facing west. It barked. Its tone suggested that it was feeling the terrain with its voice. The coyote allowed enough time for each sound to drift away before introducing the next. Each bark prompted a tug on the tail that turned it under the coyote's belly. The tip of its tail is black because, I have heard, it was the coyote who stole fire and brought it to humans, and he stole it by thrusting his own tail into the first fire, turning the end black. It was the coyote who brought us fire's light and warmth, the beginning of civilization, which we then divvied into all the bits and pieces, the cars and paper clips and budget department stores and backpacks, that make up our lives. Coyote, the trickster. You gave us the stuff for civilization, and now look at us, dangling off a windmill when you can still slip nose to tail and be instantly under cover.

The barks continued into the world, not finding anything. The coyote faced west, expecting an answer and not yielding to silence. The barking was like foreplay, softening air that was then taken up by solitary howling, the coyote's head lifted to send the song upward, tail tucked far under.

The song echoed. The coyote waited. There is a loneliness about a coyote not answered. The spaces are much more open, devoid of the social pleasures of the pack animals. At other times there would be the feeling of the coyotes' having eaten rabbits or mice, unfolding themselves on warm rocks in the day, several of them with lazy eyes, a family.

Now we were all very far away. Alone. Now the land was so huge. It went on as far as a coyote's voice will carry, and there was nothing to impede the sound. The only home the coyote had was that bushy tail, and if I had it, I would curl beneath it and remain very still.

The coyote did not grow anxious. It did not scratch disappointment into the dirt. It howled again. One bark returned from the west, so far away it could have been only a strand of hair slipping over my left ear. Coyote ears stood erect, registering the sound, telling me it was real. Two barks. Then howling. The distant howling kicked a group even farther west into howling. The entire desert, in a few seconds, was a cacophony of coyotes shouting back and forth. The desert changed instantly. It turned from stones to coyotes. Whining went high, with shouts and yelps hurled from all directions. They were everywhere, although from the top of the windmill I could not see them at all.

The first coyote wasted no time in trotting west into the sound. As soon as it was beyond the arroyo, we lost it. Irvin and I climbed down and walked wordlessly to camp. There we returned to our small tasks. Soon we ate hot posole with rice. Isolated coyote packs released songs into the night sky. Their frenetic tones took the desert and pushed it even farther than the loneliness could take it, connecting far points with strings of sound. The two of us with our warm pots of food were no more than objects dangling in a web, witnesses to the lives of coyotes.

II

I wake to the yip-yap howl of coyotes. Under heavy blankets, under a roof corniced with five feet of snow, I open my eyes and listen to rowdy voices in the frozen, hollow wilderness outside. I listen closely, trying to tell where they are, imagining coyotes at the edge of a forest a mile away, calling from windswept clearings. The sun must be coming.

It is still dark, and after the coyotes fade I lie unmoving, listening to my then girlfriend breathe beside me. Our loft is right up against the ceiling, our cabin a mere ten feet by ten feet, a two-hour ski from the nearest plowed road in the San Juan Mountains of Colorado. We are alone but for the coyotes and what few other creatures are still awake and alive in February. I muster all the willpower I can and crawl out from under the blankets, my body flashing into a sheath of frozen air as I climb down a wooden ladder. I grab clothes off a shelf and layer them on, wool socks and long johns followed by pants, button-down shirt, wool sweater, heavy coat. Every layer is alarmingly cold and it takes a while for me to feel my own heat slowly recycling back into my body. While I wait I rattle a wooden match from a box, strike it, and bring a burst of sulfur light to the inside of the cabin. I touch the match to the wick of an oil lamp and seat a glass globe over a single narrow flame, softly revealing a room around me, a space for cooking, reading, talking, and waiting out the deep womb of winter. Cans of food sit on shelves. Books are stacked on one another. A dog-eared copy of *Vogue* magazine is left out, which we both read in the long evenings to remind ourselves that human civilization, with its svelte women and dour young men, is still out there, somewhere far away.

Morning is about fire. I start a pan of water heating on a propane stove, its ring of blue flame hauntingly beautiful. Then I crouch and open the woodstove's small black door, and I take a stick and stir a bed of coals inside. Embers wake, their bright eyes looking up at me. Kindling and rumpled newspaper bring flame, which I blow with long, focused exhalations, warming my lips, my nose, my cheeks. I add sturdy wood that my girlfriend and I cut with a two-person saw the previous summer, every piece of wood prized. I close the door to the sound of crackling and snapping, ingenuity ascending the black flue.

I thrust my feet into a pair of old Sorel boots, then strap the boots into a set of webbed snowshoes. It is the only way out of the cabin. Every morning is a mantra of motions, and at times I feel as if the coyotes and I are constructing the day, keeping the sun moving, preventing winter from settling in for good. Without us, no one else would understand what happened, why the world suddenly came to an end. I open the front door, the only door, onto the thin, icy light of dawn. The sky is clear. The thermometer outside reads twenty below zero. It does not mean much to me, a deep well of numbers that could spin ever downward without my feeling any colder than this. I crunch across the snow on a trail. Everything is smooth and soft with snow but for the bony white trunks of aspen trees surrounding the cabin, and spindles of mountains in the south jetting up to thirteen and fourteen thousand feet.

A crescent moon rests in the east, part of the clock I live in, one of the slowly spinning gears. I peer at it through bare, antlered aspens as I urinate, letting out a steaming arc.

After hot tea and breakfast, we each go our own way. On cross-country skis, my girlfriend heads east into the first strokes of sunlight showing through the aspen grove where we live. I take my skis and head west. There is nothing we are looking for. We go out like riders sent to the horizons, eyes open for whatever trinkets or charms winter has set out.

Everywhere I go I leave a swath of myself, my labor set deeply into elegant folds of snow, my skis buried in my own trough, poles plunging beside me. The snow is a truth-sayer. A bird cannot land without making delicate script where its wings touch down, where its hard toes hop along. Anybody alive out here sets a trail, and so I have become a tracker coming out for my daily read, like opening the newspaper in the morning, seeing what has happened in the world. I pause at lumbering sinks where elk have come through belly-deep, and a bloodstained skirmish where an ermine breakfasted on a flicker that flew too close.

Skiing in and out of meadows on my morning rounds, I stop where a coyote, curled into a ball, slept for about half an hour at the edge of a spruce thicket. A weak shell of ice remains from its body heat. I look up from the coyote's bed and watch its tracks continue along the thicket's edge, the animal woken and getting about its business. *What business would that be?* I wonder.

I follow the coyote's tracks, its C-shaped gallop skirting trees and meadow. Here it burrowed for a rodent and came up with nothing. Here it walked across a barren white plain. Here it stopped in the middle of the plain and stood for several minutes, gazing north.

I halt on my skis on the plain, tuck my poles under one arm, and bend down. I pull off a mitten and place my finger inside one of the prints, wondering why the coyote paused here. I feel a faint crust in its lobes. It had stayed long enough to sink a little, no more than two hours ahead of me. *Why did it stop?* I hold my eyes exactly where it held its, looking at the same summit-filled horizon, the sun blazing over a featureless spread of snow. Maybe it heard something or saw an animal far away. A shrill and sudden wind skates against my back, kicking up flecks of ice. I pull a wool scarf over my mouth, stuff my free, reddened hand into a mitten, and keep going. My skis set long twin tracks across the plain, poles sweeping at my sides, gliding me farther into the day.

This one coyote shows me its business step-by-step, leading me ten miles through the mountains on loops and backtracks and straight trots across clearings. There are other tracks, of course, many different animals. On another day I would go from one to the next, a squirrel handing me off to a deer, deer sending me to a raven, raven leading to a hare. But today I am interested in this coyote alone, coming to know it better by every mile, seeing how it prefers drifting to the right, that it has a very slight limp. I feel its satiation where it drank from a window in the snow, a mumbling creek revealed below. I am getting nearer to the animal, closing on its freshening tracks, ducking under downed trees, plowing through powdery underbrush. Here the coyote had come up from a deep drift like a porpoise. It was hunting blue grouse, which sleep near the ground. In all its romping I cannot tell if it got meat or not, if grouse exploded from their small snow caves one after the next, going up around the coyote like fireworks. I can see its look of bewilderment, even amusement, as it watches grouse launch skyward.

After a few more miles I am half an hour behind the coyote in the long light of afternoon. I have not yet seen the animal, but I wonder if it has seen me. I search for any sign of recognition in its tracks, a pause, the push of a backward glance followed by a quickened pace. But it does not know I am here, and I feel a little embarrassed, like a voyeur. The coyote's moves are so candid, so unspoiled, I think maybe I should not be following this closely. But I have come a long way. It would be rewarding to spot the coyote, if for just a second, to spy it over a rise and watch it go, completely unaware that I had been riffling through its life for hours. I keep on its trail up the slope of a mountainside swept smooth and hard by wind. The light is getting low, and I will not find my way home until well after dark. I have a headlamp with me, and it will be easy to retrace my day, but I will leave my girlfriend wondering what became of me longer than is polite. I pick up my pace, following the coyote as quickly as I can.

Fifteen minutes behind the coyote, I come into a basin cupped against the mountain, a place where a snowmelt lake of topaz will sit in the summer. More coyote tracks appear. Five more, eight, twelve. Coyote packs are more loosely arranged than those of wolves. They are more like get-togethers with friends, neighbors, and relatives than they are alpha-male bureaucracies. I like that about coyotes, their casual sovereignty. Skiing into this pack, I find it difficult to keep sight of my own coyote where it frisked and sniffed among the others, excitedly bounding to see them. I squint behind sunglasses, trying to decipher overlapping coyote tracks, wiping frozen snot off my nose with the back of my mitten.

Five minutes behind my coyote, I check for its scent in the air, the smell of an entire pack, but the wind is blowing and the hairs in my nose bristle with frost. I pull the scarf so that my nose and mouth are covered, and all I smell is my own damp, warm breath.

There is a drop of blood in the snow before me. I stop and stare at it as if it were a ruby set in ice. It lies between the tracks of my coyote, dropped there. I think it must be an injury, a cut paw, but it is not smeared inside the coyote's step. It is a single drop. The coyote, I realize, is female. It is in estrus. Ahead is another blood mark, and another after that. Blood had landed between her tracks as she trotted along with her family and companions, perhaps spurred to let out a bit of herself, sending a message, telling everyone she was now ready, that the clock of her winter was ticking toward spring.

I kneel at this crimson drop and see how fresh it is, only now soaking into the snow, turning from red to pink. She and the rest of her pack are just over the rise, right in front of me, less than a minute away. I want to take off my mitten and pick up the blood, roll it between my fingers, but I do not dare. It is far too personal, not a message meant for me.

I have come far enough, I think. If I ski ahead, appearing in the midst of the pack, they will flee, their winter cover blown. They believe they are alone here. They believe the world is theirs. They are right to think so. I rise and turn back, never having seen my coyote. I start long miles to the cabin and its windows glowing with firelight, leaving the rest of the world to coyotes who are now running across the mountain together, howling and yipping behind me, calling for the frozen night to come.

Canis latrans

MOUNTAIN LION

I

S tanding atop one side of the Arizona landmark called Black Mesa, I was surrounded by jags of volcanic mountains. Saguaro cactus mixed with the illuminated white spines of cholla cactus. I have spent a good part of my life here, in this particular set of mountains.

A route off of Black Mesa is not always obvious or simple. To one side of me was a skirt of basaltic boulders, and to the other, an escarpment of small, steep ravines. I hiked to the latter with a saguaro-rib walking stick. A dark handle had been worn into the wood by my hand, and I sneaked the stick down the first ledge of a ravine. The dry watercourse bored off the mesa and dropped away. It reclined into the mesa. First I could not see the surrounding canyons. Then I could not see the mountains. Finally I could see only the sky directly above.

Acacias grew from the cracks. Also called catclaws, they are notoriously hated and feared. Upon the sharply angled limbs are numerous namesake claws. They curve into barbs, tearing skin upon contact rather than merely stabbing at it. As I walked the ravine, there came the scratching chalkboard sound of catclaws grating against my clothes before they ripped and locked into my skin. Each time that I passed without proper caution, I ended up carefully withdrawing each claw from my body.

Dry, dead grasses wrapped between the clawed branches and cactus pads. The lower the canyon dropped, the more plants there were. The drainage came to a dense rock and quickly narrowed. There was no longer room to bypass the plants. Paloverde trees held out sharp green spikes. Even the jojoba bushes, into which I plunged up to my neck, were sharp. Balls of cholla cactus, with a hundred barbed spines, lay scattered in the vegetation. Dots of dried blood tracked across my forearms.

There were boulders plugged between walls. Handholds, dangling drops, not enough of a crack to hold a boot tip. I trusted too small a crack and slid off the handhold. I pounded onto the next ledge. There I was, pretzeled. Parts of my body would have bruises like smashed apples tonight.

I stood, shaking my head, then pulled my walking stick out and helped myself down. The plants closed up the canyon. I walked to the edge of a small pour-off. I was about to put my foot over when a large snap of motion came from below. Every possibility hit my mind. Bighorn. Javelina. Bear.

Mountain lion.

Five feet in front of me. The cat was in the air before I could jerk in any direction. In a quarter second it was all color and shape, moving fast, and my blood locked onto my organs as if I were flash-frozen. I couldn't tell which way it was moving. The tail was out. It unraveled before my face for a third of a second. That is when I was certain it was a lion. I was fixed on the tail, and it was fat like a jungle snake, its tip black. It told me that the cat was leaping head-long away from me.

Then the back paws. Toes spread from pushing off. Among the brown hairs and worn black pads, I thought I saw claws. Cat claws. A wave of air struck me. It tousled my bangs. The scent was strong, like a thousand words coming at once.

The mountain lion collided with vegetation below. There was a thrashing, and the animal was swallowed. Last to go was the tail. The sound went on for a few more seconds, dry grass and thirsty bushes crushing like wadded newspaper. Then the sound ceased. In the thicket of desert plants, the mountain lion stopped. I listened. There was no motion.

My hand was very tight on the walking stick. My right foot was still just above the ground, caught midstep over rock and sand warm from the body of a mountain lion. For quite a while I stood there. My mouth dry, the canyon five feet wide. Barely the length of the walking stick turned sideways. I listened for the animal's breathing. It was in there. I turned around for a moment, looking upstream at the walls, thinking about climbing, thinking about falling. I looked back down. "I'm coming down," I shouted, and waited. My words floated in the air, and the lion watched me from somewhere below. "Do you hear me?"

Perhaps I had cornered it against a dry fall in the canyon. I could not see far enough to tell. I held my walking stick out so that at least there was an object between the lion and me. I sank my chin into my chest, hiding the open flesh of my throat. What good this would do, I didn't know. I sent out secret prayers that the mountain lion would take to magic and slip into the ether, the only way I could see of getting out of this canyon.

I pushed my way into the acacias where the mountain lion had disappeared. My eyes were shooting around, looking for another set of eyes. The animal is *Puma concolor,* meaning "cat of one color." The buff, dry color of leaves. The genus *Puma* is a scientific name change that occurred in the 1990s. Prior to that it was *Felis,* the genus of house cats and other small cats. Now the catclaws were all over me. Everything rustled against me as I passed. I looked for a place where an animal could walk without making sound, where it could slip through. There was no such place. It was close by.

Around here a mountain lion will weigh eighty to one hundred pounds. The unusually long tail is sometimes 40 percent of the total body length, explaining why it was still impressed into my mind. Springing off of their hind legs, they can jump eighteen vertical feet. I measured the space with my eyes between myself and all surrounding blind spots.

Cats are deceptive, looking as if they may turn the other way before they suddenly vault. They do not want company when they find you. They are strictly solitary animals for most of their life. Their ability to wait and attack from behind without sound weighs heavily. They have attacked people who have been crouched, or small, or running the other way. Even in zoos they sometimes charge at the cage when children come by. Parents are often asked to hold their children close as they pass cages, to break up the image of fast little kids making random movements. Sudden motions, some researchers believe, are required to stimulate a cat's attack mechanism. They have stalked people for miles. One woman survived an attack and escaped by foot on a road. The lion shortcut the road several miles farther and killed her from behind.

I postured by forcing my chest out and jacking up my shoulders. My eyes were wide, showing a great deal of white. The walking stick was pushing ahead of me. The arguments were with me. The mountain lion would not fight here. There was too much risk. I was an unknown, and the injury I could inflict in my struggle could drive a crease into its ability to survive in this desert. At the same time, it is the mountain lion that has become most likely to make a meal of a human in North America.

I ran fingers on the ground, and even they made noise. No animal could move through this without sound. I said this to myself out loud. It could hear my voice. One step ahead of me.

Walking through here, I was communicating my presence down-canyon. The mountain lion now knew everything about me. It was Barry Lopez who wrote that predators carry on conversations with their prey. This language defines the outcome of a hunt, whether the prey is prepared to die or not. For Lopez the hunt is not merely a weighing of pros and cons but a dialogue that has evolved along with teeth and digestive tracts. The animals speak with one another through stares, body movements, scents, and gaits, turning both the predator and the prey into a single society. Now part of this society, I feared that I was speaking in tongues, sending down things I didn't want known.

There were climbs below. I furtively glanced at the walls. They were sheer. When I began climbing, my breath was loud, punctuated by strong heartbeats. Sweat collected around my body. So busy looking over my shoulder that I hit a loose rock and fell into the acacias. They were all over me, and I slipped through with a grating sound, a piranha attack of catclaws. I lost my stick.

"Goddamn it," I muttered, grabbing blindly at the plants. As fast as I could, I gathered my bearings, looking for the animal. Above, below, to the sides. I squinted through the crossed understory shadows, looking for *concolor*. The walking stick was caught and I pulled it out, shoving it in front of myself again. I was now panicked, thinking I'd fallen into the place where the animal waited. My breath tripped. I waited. Nothing. I would not move, would not make a sound. The muscles tagged to my eyeballs were tight.

I once talked to an old man in Belize. We had just come from a dance, and he was telling me that I should never go to a dance where the drum is made from jaguar skin. "There will always be fighting," he said. "Always hot and angry."

And I once spoke with a zoologist who told me that adult mountain lions sometimes require a diet of one deer per week. *That is a lot of flesh,* I thought. They will hunt anytime, equally as capable of taking an animal down during the day as at night. You will see the eyes of a mountain lion flash green in your headlights as you drive down a back road. The green is a light-reflecting membrane that takes any reflected, lost, or wandering light and turns it back for a second go-round in the retina. Lions then have the advantage of being able to hunt by starlight, or in the shadowy bottom of a canyon.

The idea that I had passed the mountain lion kept striking, and I quickly looked behind. But there was no room in here to pass. Fear rode my back like sweat. How much fear can one release into the world before it finally takes form, before it gains strong legs and canine teeth, hard and sharp like white steel? I tried to disassociate myself from the fear. I rattled through facts about how a mountain lion should be long gone by now, but my back was too wet with the fear already.

I moved branches away with the stick, checking before I stepped ahead. There was a pale light between plants. It was a clearing in the canyon. I pushed my way through, into the open. I was off of Black Mesa. There was no mountain lion. Not possible. I swung around with an impaling fear from behind. No mountain lion there. I looked at the ledges up high. Then I swung around again and looked into the open.

It was one hundred yards ahead, watching me as if it had been waiting for my exit. It began walking slowly away, and even from here I could see that its paws were very large, like heavy socks. It did not move with the jerks or stiffness a deer might use. It walked as if it were one continuous muscle, with everything moving at once, slowly and methodically. At the top of a rise, it stopped and looked back.

Mountain lions are psychological animals, preying on the mind with secret cat eyes. They know that they still dominate, that they cannot be cornered without ripping their way out. They know that they are still the heart of fierceness. Being pack animals ourselves, we humans have some alliance with other pack animals, like wolves or coyotes. When I see a free wolf, I feel as if we could sit down and talk, given that the details have been worked out. Not so with the cat. The cat speaks in symbols.

I glanced behind to the ravine. There was a hole in the plants. Prior to my arrival, it had not been there. I felt as if I had just stumbled through, pitching and crashing. I thought of mountain lion feet, the ones I saw splayed in front of my eyes earlier. Eighty pounds had been stalking through here lighter than my finger can run across the ground.

A recognition passed the distance between me and the mountain lion. It gave me the stare of a cat, disinterested but true. It then turned and stepped away, as though made of sand, slipping back to the desert.

I I

There is a place above the desert in Arizona where chasms are stacked within each other, where moss- and fern-guarded holes release waterfalls out of cliffs. Forests have quilted the ground with wet sycamore and maple leaves. The walls are steep, and on this day were shrouded with a passing storm that sat like a heap of torn rags over the canyons. Three of us crossed at the waterfalls with hands outstretched so that nobody slipped a thousand feet into rock and mist.

We had left camp behind for a daily exploration of the canyons, and we had gone too far. Now with minimal gear we realized that if we kept this route we would not make it back to camp by dark. We were looking for a cliff dwelling of the Salado people. It had been abandoned maybe seven hundred years ago, left high on a canyon wall. I once encountered it on a trek into these canyons, startled to find it hidden between waterfalls and cliffs. It lasted well through time, its location known to only a few, and it was full of broken pottery and deep grinding stones for corn. In a moment of catching breath and wiping away mud, we decided to keep moving toward the ruin. We had come too far to turn back, and with blind words chose to explore cold, hunger, and a long night without proper gear. This was January. The canyon was dark.

We ate wild miner's lettuce because there was no food in our packs. Narrow slots of cascades took us up and we tangled through raspberry bushes and tough, looping grapevines. There are only a few places like this over the desert, where the exposure of the canyon keeps out the light. Springs feed relic climates of deciduous trees and thick herbaceous plants. In a recess below a fat, angled oak was a skeleton. I slid to it through wet leaves and landed with muddy hands deep in damp, stinking fur. It looked like the remains of a mountain lion kill. This was the perfect place, the hideout. A place that forces one to look over the shoulder, expecting to see the eyes in the forest. Lions haul their quarry to secluded locations and devour them in solitude. They bury remains in leaves and finish the feast later.

The others came across the plush floor of leaves. "A deer?" someone asked.

"Looks like it," I said. I found the skull and dug it from the leaves. In my hand it was wide, too wide for a deer or a bighorn sheep. I spread my palm for a grip. I shook it loose and brought it to my face. Canine teeth were locked like ivory spear points in combat. It was the skull of a mountain lion. A female skull, just smaller than a male's.

For a time there was quiet. Someone said the name. Mountain lion. As if it needed translation because it was too wild a thing for us to find.

The skull was primal, from an animal that should have gone extinct with all other beasts too fierce for creatures of our age. The four canine teeth were too large, too long, as if overkill was in the design. A forty-year-old woman was fatally attacked by a lion one recent year. She was partially eaten, then blanketed with debris. An autopsy determined the final blow as a three-millimeter puncture to her skull. Her damaged skull was then handed over to a dental forensic team whose measurements showed that the teeth had been acutely sharp—a young lion—and belonged to a narrow bite—a female. The information sent Fish and Game hunters out to kill a young female mountain lion in the area. The one they shot and carried back produced flesh from beneath its claws matching the woman's DNA. People called this justice, that the lion had given itself away in its own bite marks.

To get a firm three-millimeter punch into a skull, the canine teeth have to be sturdy. The canines of the jaw we found were rooted deep, with about three-quarters of the tooth sunk into the bone so that it could not be pulled free. The points on the teeth were flat where they had once been sharp. She was an old lion when she died. She had come to this place for this.

Her sharp claws, curled round, were lined up to the small toe bones where even knuckles were still in place, where she nested into her last view of the canyon. Her skeleton had probably been exposed from the flesh for a year. The smell was strong, decomposing at a steady rate, with wet-headed mushrooms appearing between scapula and spine.

The jaw was hinged tightly into its skull to increase biting leverage. The bones forming the widest part of the skull, the zygomatic arch, were opened exceptionally wide where webs of muscle once connected skull to jaw. Animals with instantaneous jaw force—snapping turtles, alligators, and mountain lions—have enlarged zygomatic arches for intense crushing power. There were deep dishes in the bone to anchor muscles across the skull. The purpose: attack from behind, clamp onto the spine at the base of the prey's skull, snap the spine. The top few vertebrae were the target, housing respiratory and motor skills that cease instantly when the cord is cut.

For animals that work alone, as mountain lions do, the faster the prey is immobilized, the less the chance of the predator being injured by a struggle. So the skull is shaped like a fist, eliminating the snout for a more precise, efficient impact. Quick, shifting bites with reduced numbers of teeth track the spine and find the area for incision. Bone is rarely ever broken. Rather, the teeth slide between vertebrae and open the spine surgically. Cat teeth are heavily laden with nerves so that the animal can actually feel its way around the spine. Each species of cat has a precise width and positioning to its teeth, designed to get into the vertebrae of specific prey, with bobcats taking rabbits, and mountain lions taking deer or elk. Behind the canines is a gap so that the teeth can sink all the way to the gum.

Her collarbone, buried midway in a heap of fur, was small and sliverlike, designed to handle crushing impacts against stationary objects. The mountain lion body is built for point-blank attacks. It can outrun a deer for only a few seconds, so its physiology puts all resources into a single pounce. This style of hunting has created an animal of total stealth.

During the last Ice Age, the mountain lion was a small predator on a stage of terrifying animals — now-extinct saber-toothed cats, short-faced bears, dire wolves, scimitar cats, and American lions. Although it was as capable of quick killing then as it is now, it was more likely to be killed by something bigger about twelve thousand years ago. It adjusted to an enigmatic means of survival, much like the Asian leopards do today, living in the shadows and not following trails or streambeds, avoiding larger predators. It grew quick and efficient, silent and observant. Skills were impressed so hard into the genes that the lion today adheres to the stealth it learned in a world of lumbering carnivores. It is taking the stage finally as the last big predator, as the few remaining wolves and large bears are pushed out. So now the biggest, most dangerous animal is also the quietest and the hardest to see.

We tied the skull carefully with taut blades of bear grass so the lower jaw would not fall out. I kept it in my hand to take it to a better time and place for recording these zygomatic arches and canine teeth in my journal, momentarily disturbing a lay of bones cast in death. I carried it on, through faint animal trails that may have belonged to the mountain lion herself. I set it above me in shelves of roots when I climbed, picking it up from behind, then moving it ahead and climbing again. Sunset held the sky at the rim of the gorge, but here it had been dark for many hours. As we breathed, cold mist fogged around our faces. I climbed and moved the skull ahead of me. Each time I looked up, reaching for a handhold, the shape of the skull worked itself into the fear at the pit of my soul. I gripped a rock and pulled my body up, bringing my face to the face of the lion.

I cut more bear grass and tightened the jaw. It wanted out, to fall away from the skull as if the compulsion remained, built into the bones. Most cat jaws open seventy degrees, an impressive gape, but still smaller than the extinct saber-toothed cats' spread of ninety degrees.

Cats arrived at the end of the dinosaurs, long before the saber-tooths. The high metabolism of mammals required ten times the food of comparably sized reptiles, so the new animals ate either a lot of plants or a lot of each other. The stereotype of bloodthirsty dinosaurs pales before that of the bloodthirsty mammals. The original mammal was an insectivore, so the move to eating animal flesh came quickly.

With the abundance of meat, it would have made sense for numerous herbivore species to evolve into predators. Instead, carnivores specialized so quickly that nothing could compete. Scrupulous body designs of the new predators culled out anything that tried. From there it was give-and-take. Predators perfected attack techniques. Prey returned with highly developed herding networks, camouflage, speed, and avoidance senses. Advanced musculature altered the skulls of the predators. Slow herbivores became lithe, alert ungulates. Predator and prey leapfrogged through evolution, refining each other in the chase, whittling each other down to specific forms and movements.

It was the cat that came out of all this, perhaps the finest carnivorous product to rise from the symbiosis. It was the prize model, the clandestine design that, in the early Oligocene fifty million years ago, changed the hunt. Hunting by stealth, they became specialized for a life of killing and eating meat, often taking down animals larger than themselves. Necks shortened and strengthened to absorb the violent action of the head and teeth.

Once they were separated by their hunting techniques from all other predators, felines made a radical split. The split began with dentition. Animals evolving toward wolves, raccoons, bears, and badgers had teeth designed for crushing. These were all-purpose omnivore teeth, for meat, insects, and plants. They retained the flat grinding molars of herbivore heritage, as is the case with the grizzly bear, which fills 90 percent of its diet with vegetation. The cats, however, grew highly developed cheek teeth (lower molars) called carnassials, used for shearing flesh. Their mouths had only two purposes: grab and tear.

While dogs and bears worked and reworked their bodies and skulls, dividing into a cornucopia of species, cats honed the original form. A trademark of something that works well, the cat body has hardly changed since its inception. Like with today's cats, their digestive systems could handle only flesh. The lesson of the cat is that if you are to become a full-fledged carnivore, you have to commit everything to it. A house cat fed vegetarian food will shrivel and die. The cat's digestive system is short, able to break down the simple energy of meat, not the rough proteins of grass, leaves, or roots. Shortened intestines allow for swift, unencumbered motion, whereas excess entrails would gather in the body like a surplus coil of rope. The cat's intestinal tract shortened to only four times the length of the body while other carnivores retained guts up to ten times their body length. This allowed cats to compact their bodies, better for the attack.

Sixty-five million years of chiseling and redefining the predator.

Bones and organs sculpted to perfect form. Stalking skills and the stiff passion for hunting packed into the mysterious cords of instinct, building a clan of animals designed only to kill. Here was the result. The skull of a mountain lion in the vines. She had probably grown too weak to hunt. She had climbed into the brush, curled against soft leaves, and died. I held her skull close, under my arm so the jaws dug into my ribs.

We were deep in the gorge walls when we found the cliff dwelling. It was clutched to a ledge — a round tower with a square building to the side, rubble leading to where other rooms once stood. It was an ancient place, like something in a myth at the far end of a journey.

We crossed beneath a waterfall and entered the dwelling. It was three levels tall, filled with stone-lined windows and doors and solid, heavy timbers. Mortar in the walls betrayed the prints of ancient hands and fingers. Amazement slipped from our mouths, but in breaths, not words. I set the skull with the knots of bear grass at the entrance and ducked into the doorway. Cold air pushed through the mortared openings. I had on a thin coat with two shirt layers beneath. I folded my arms and shivered.

We moved into darkness, and the canyon closed to the sound of water and careful footsteps working from one room to the next. Final, dull light sifted through openings. It hung in the still air beneath the latticework of ceiling beams. There was discussion of solemnity, of respect. There was a need for shelter through the night and a need to live sparingly. The woman, with few hushed words and mud on her face, talked of how one should behave in here. The man who showed us plants to eat said we must be careful not to touch walls or the fragile doorways. We made agreements, then there were no words at all. We chose our own rooms and curled into sleep.

Strange dreams stayed on the tip of my mind. Cold stalked through the rooms. It elicited cloudy breath and the pulling in of arms and legs to contain body heat. I scratched the dust on the dwelling floor, as if it might conjure warmth. I was balled up, looking through the crossing beams of the next floor, to the level beyond that, made of a star-and-ink sky. My clothes were frigid where they touched skin, and my feet turned numb beneath the hard leather of boots.

Sometime in the night we became too cold to remain still. We found one another, moving between doors, whispering one another's name. We huddled together and shivered as if trying to shake loose our skin and muscle to leave only bones that feel no cold. The morning was far away, and constellations moved across the open ceiling. We crawled to a corner and slept, thronged all over one another like mountain lion kittens in a winter hole.

In the dark, the man dreamed that a mountain lion was stalking between rooms. In the dream there was nothing to be seen but starlight taking the form of a mountain lion as it saturated the inside of the ruin. The dreamer remained still, knowing that any motion could catch the lion's attention. The dreamer heard the breathing of the lion and felt her in the room. And it is true, the dreamer was not asleep while this happened. The dreamer's eyes were open, struggling to see in the dark.

In the cold blue of dawn there were no mountain lion prints in the dust to verify its passage. I do have my suspicions.

III

A mountain lion is at the water hole. I am one day by foot from the New Mexico border into Arizona's remote Blue Range on another trip. It is a male, well over a hundred pounds, lapping water from the edge. It does not know that I am here. I come on it from behind, staring a beeline down its long tail, which is laid flat against the ground. An early-morning breeze moves in my direction, taking my scent behind. I nearly tear a muscle in half, letting down a sixty-pound pack and rolling it to the ground without making a sound. I am motionless beside the pack, focusing binoculars to get a good look.

The mountain lion has been in battle. A long, old scar follows its right side, accompanied by a few other scars around the body. The males are territory defenders. They will fight over land quicker than females and come out with ragged ears and torn skin. It looks healthy, though. Its shape is impeccable for a strong, agile lion, hunched to the water so that its shoulder blades form shields around its back. When it stands, it makes a careful visual sweep. I am blending into my background, and its eyes swing by mine, not lingering on me at all. It is keyed to motion and scent, and nothing registers. I look like a rock, a stump, something simple and expected. Even so, a shiver pounces down my back. The lion walks away, into a mesh of junipers that leads into the ponderosa forests and the high desert beyond.

The wind shifts a few times, distributing my scent all over. I wait for several minutes, then walk to the water to get a good identification on fresh mountain lion tracks, to take measurements and write it all down. I kick rocks as I go, making plenty of noise. If I know the mountain lion, it is half a mile away by now, getting well out of my range. I don't see it anywhere.

At the water are many tracks in the mud, like sentences overlapping, getting all the words mixed up. I move to kneel and get a close look. Before I am on the ground, I scan the perimeter with a rigid movement like a cautious deer coming to drink. At first I see nothing. Then it is there, behind me. It has circled to my back. Eyes are in the shadows of a couple of low junipers, thirty feet away. From them I can outline the quiescent body of a mountain lion curled to the base of one juniper.

I move slowly, deliberately. The lion is probably startled by me. It may be hiding, like a rabbit that is nearly stepped on before it leaps away. But its eyes are not frozen like a hiding rabbit's, and its body is not bunched, ready for a line drive in the opposite direction. I am being observed.

In suburbs and parks, where lion space is being compressed, the mountain lions can be aggressive around people. Attacks are up.

Most of these have been at the edge of city sprawls and around frequented campgrounds and trails, especially in California, where we are forcing ourselves deeper into the land.

The mountain lions have not learned, like the wolf, to get the hell off the land or, like the coyote, to eat poodles and drink out of street gutters. They have an odd, powerful dignity that does not understand the endless catches and snags of the human race. That is why they are still at the fringes, still fighting. Close encounters in the deep wilderness are of a different category. This is their territory, and the strange behavior of a confused mountain lion at the city limits is rare. I feel safe enough here at the water hole. I am dealing at least with precepts I think I understand.

Certainly, mountain lions are known to take down animals six, seven, and eight times their own size out here. A midsized female made a documented kill of an adult bull elk. Concerning humans, lions avidly and skillfully avoid them. In this high desert there is none of the strain a mountain lion must face when pressed against cities and parks. Here, there is no Montclair, California, where police and wildlife officials approached a perplexed mountain lion beneath a car in a shopping mall parking lot, deemed it to be dangerous, and shot it. Or Mendocino County, where four picnickers grappled with a young, attacking mountain lion and killed it with a twelve-inch serrated kitchen knife, one of the people losing a thumb and another receiving a four-inch puncture wound. Here, there is land that follows the rules of wind and the presence or absence of water, a land this mountain lion understands.

I watch the lion, taking advantage of my proximity to study its features. I am expecting it to bolt at any second, to dive into the woods and vanish. *Remember this*, I think. *You will never be this close again.*

Instead of running, it stands. Without a pause for thought, it moves out from under the shadows so that both of us are in the same sunlight. We make clear, rigid eye contact. It begins walking straight toward me.

My heartbeat lodges into my throat. My adrenaline dumps. All of it. No dilemma in the lion's eyes; it stares me down as if I am prey backed against a water hole. Even with a slow, lucid gait, it is quickly in my world. It looks up at me from under its brow so that its head is down and its eyes are shelved by a shadow. A stalking stare. The distance is closed in seconds.

This cat is going to attack me. I pull a knife off my right hip. It has a five-inch blade. One claw against eight claws; hesitation against instinct. The advantage is not mine.

It keeps walking, focusing straight on me, not stepping left or right of its line. Its motion is sleek and exact, revealing that it has no intention of stopping short of me. I have understood that in the presence of humans, animals flee. It is a quick and certain instinct, and when I have appeared they have all done it, the chipmunks, bears, cats, grasshoppers, lesser nighthawks, tree frogs, crabs, and ravens. I am a human, for Christ's sake, *Homo sapiens*. Regardless of this fact, the mountain lion sizes me up and down, closing the space between us. The face says nothing, while the tail twitches like a lie detector.

A powerful voice in me says, *Run, before it gets closer! Find shelter, safety, hide!* The voice wants the lion magically gone, it wants to flee to my pack and hunch into a tiny ball. The lion is pushing my button, scrambling the innards of my instinct. Never have I felt *fight or flight* like this. My only choice, the message going to the thick of the muscle in my legs, is to run. Get as much space between me and danger as possible. The animal is too big, too wild. *I've got to get out of here before it's too late.*

What I do, instead, is not move. My eyes lock onto the mountain lion. I hold firm to my ground and do not even intimate that I will back off. If I run, it is certain. I will have a mountain lion all over me. If I give it my back, I will only briefly feel its weight on me against the ground. The canine teeth will open my vertebrae without breaking a single bone, like thumbing between pieces of paper.

Some of the larger animals push their faces toward an attacking lion. It can't get anything at the face. It has got to have a clear shot at the neck, from behind or the sides. It tries to intimidate and push the panic button with this kind of doubtless approach so the prey will turn. When the prey runs, the kill is sealed.

The mountain lion begins to move to my left, and I turn, keeping my face on it, my knife at my right side. It paces to my right, trying to get around on my other side, to get behind me. I turn right, staring at it.

Earlier I would have raised my arms and barked at it, but the lion had come too fast. Now any motion could snap the space we have. My stare is about the only defense I have. People working alone in the mangrove jungles at the mouth of the Ganges River in India sometimes wear the mask of a face on the back of their head. John Seidensticker, who studied the social organization of mountain lions, suggests that humans began to stand upright in order to more vividly show their faces to aggressive cats and to appear less like four-legged prey.

Most of my body has stopped. All that is left are my eyes, my right hand with the knife, and my ability to turn. The lion comes left again. When I rotate, it stops walking. It has got me in a stationary, tight stare from ten feet. Its nose is moist and pale. Its short, clean hairs follow subtle gradients between brown, tan, and white. The cat is so uniformly sculpted that I can see in its face where bone gives way to muscle. A few long, wiry whiskers splay to either side of its nose, bending down slightly. Its face is narrow at the snout, then much wider around the cheeks at the jaw muscles. Eyes are made of gray and green, and that is where I see all of the energy, bound up and ready to flush into the body for one quick jump.

It is too close for me to follow the prescriptions of brochures and field guides, or the wise words of those few who have been stalked. All the rules of mountain lion confrontations are out. Its tail briskly paints the air, the way a house cat's tail flicks before it leaps at a robin in the yard. The tail moves faster, betraying the cat's intentions.

If it jumps, the knife goes into its rib cage. All my energy will be in the thrust. The lion may reconsider after that. But what shape will I be in after the single blow its entire body is built to deliver? Fifty million years of evolution to make an animal designed to kill on the first move. It could be that I will get in a good knife jab, but what will its jaws do around my face and throat? What will its claws do, dug into my stomach and my back? I've had a house cat shred my arm before. A four-pound cat. And mountain lions are known to come back. They do stalk. Will I be holding my skin together with hands and bandannas when it finds me again? If I am crawling out of here, it may come back for me, finding me before I reach New Mexico.

It is looking for the approach. It looks one way, just a couple of inches to one side of my eyes, and then it looks to the other side. I won't give it leeway, moving my head to keep its eyes on mine. There have been cases in which a lion cleared twenty feet in about a second when eye contact was broken.

It steps to my right, coming clear around, and I synchronize myself with it. It is not focused on my knife, my body, or even my eyes. It is moving intently at some point through me, inside of me, perhaps the single point where life itself is seated. It has happened so often that a mountain lion has launched straight at a hunter or a field biologist who has a sidearm leveled at its head. The mountain lion does not stop and is shot point-blank, dead. Why is that? A coyote or a bear will know when a person has a gun, and will often behave much differently. But the mountain lion is a creature with too great a nature to see a gun or a knife. It is so focused that the rest of the world goes silent. When a lion is killed, it is a strange death, like something stolen from an animal that should be impervious to weaponry, like the Ghost Dancers who died believing that bullets could not find them.

The distance between us increases slightly. The lion walks toward the water hole. Until now I haven't had the room to take a good posture without triggering an attack. It is customary to throw your arms up and make noise when encountering an aggressive animal at a fair distance. Or to put your hands in your pockets and flare out your coat, making yourself look a hundred pounds heavier. It is an old bluff trick. Usually works. Now that it is fifteen feet away, I lift my hands in the air. All the way so that my knife is an arm's length over my head, looking like something too unusual and unknown for a mountain lion to bother with.

It doesn't work. The mountain lion swings back and comes straight at me again. My arms drop. Fast. Right to my sides. Ice comes down my back. The lion stops there, close again. I have never been watched like this.

It begins a long, winding route, still trying to come from behind. It covers a great deal of space, going back and forth. There is a seamless continuum from the surrounding world, through the lion's eyes, into its heart, and back to the world. I am somewhere in there, holding steady like a rock planted beside the water hole. It watches me closely as it leaves. It walks into the forest and I no longer see it.

I stand for a few minutes, staring at the forest. No thought can be boiled down from here. There is nowhere else to go. I have reached the hard, palpable seed of life. The image is now permanently formed in my mind. I can see how the mountain lion will be posed, suddenly in view anywhere around me, its tail weaving an intricate pattern, spelling secret words in the air. I have seen how it can walk, how it can turn, how it can stare. I have seen its parade of muscles. Now there is only the forest. Then I let go. My fearless eyes come down and fear spills all over the ground at my feet. My hand goes limp around the knife butt.

I had probably baffled its attack pattern. Nothing was right with me. I didn't run. I didn't have a horizontal backbone like a deer or an elk. I was an unknown. If I had come minutes later and not seen the lion, I would have walked to the water hole and gotten on hands and knees to look at all the tracks. When I saw fresh mountain lion tracks, would I have begun to turn to look behind just as it made its midair sprint for my back? Was it in the shade, waiting for something slow and edible to come down for a drink? I keep a close watch, but no feline shapes come through the forest.

I never saw that lion again, although for the next week of hiking alone, I could see it all around me. I could see it out of nowhere. I slept half awake. When I came to water, I gathered it quickly and retreated. I kept my eyes trained into the shadows, waiting, seeing a mountain lion wherever I looked. It was in shapes between trees and on open rocks in clear sunlight. When I saw that it was not really there, I barely nodded my head and relaxed slightly. An odd disappointment came over me then, because in the moment that we faced off, I had been picked clean of my questions. At the edge of a water hole, in the Blue Range of Arizona, I had been in the presence of the absolute.

Puma concolor

DOG

He appeared like a vision in boulders above our camp, suddenly standing there with a rifle in one hand and a pistol on his hip. He wore leather gloves and chaps, and even had spurs on his boot heels. Two dogs came to his side, a trail-worn dingo and a mangy, curly-haired mutt the color of hay. Four of us looked up from our morning tasks and stared at the man and his dogs. We were foul from many days in the deep country of the Sierra Madre in northern Mexico, faces powdered with sweat and dirt.

The cowboy, a middle-aged caballero, regarded us for a moment as if coming upon an encampment of cavemen, a primitive and ugly sight to him in the bottom of a soaring, nameless canyon. He called down in Spanish, demanding to know what we were doing here. In fact, he knew exactly what we were doing. Several nights before we had stopped at his small ranch house in the pines of western Chihuahua and spent the night with him, explaining at the time that we were hiking into the deep barrancas in search of wilderness. He had been polite but thought us little more than wandering fools. Now that he saw us in our element, he really thought we were fools, our camp pitched in a wild nest of boulders where a canyon puckers into a row of tight cliffs. We called back up with waves and smiles, but he did not smile. He slung his rifle and began the laborious climb down to us. We climbed up to meet him.

He was not happy to see us here. He said so in his quick, rural Spanish. It had taken him days to track us down. He had to abandon his burro to get in this far to find us. Why he was looking for us, he did not say. Maybe he was bored, or he was truly concerned for our welfare. He could not understand what we were thinking, coming so deep into a place where wild animals stalk the shadows. Were we idiots? We kept smiling at him, explaining that this is exactly what we were looking for, a place that belongs to animals more than to people.

The flat-headed dingo hardly looked at us, as if we were stupid cows, beasts not even to be considered. The mutt, on the other hand, came licking and nosing under our hands and knees. The caballero snapped at his mutt, forcing the dog to cower and slink back. The caballero squatted onto his boot heels, his hand on the stock of his rifle. He did not like the wilderness. We knew this about him the moment we met him. He was a caballero by profession, not by choice, and he had no love for wind, or rocks, or loneliness. He armored himself against the wilderness. He asked where our guns were, and when we told him we had none, he closed his eyes in disbelief and wiped an exasperated hand across his face. *No guns?* This was worse than he thought.

While he explained to us the myriad perils of the Sierra Madre, the jaguars, mountain lions, and rattlesnakes, I noticed his mutt staring at me with damp, pleading eyes. Where the dingo looked like a good Mexican work dog, self-assured and capable, the mutt looked like a softhearted house dog that got lost one day and found herself here, in hell. Her eyes said, *Please help me. Take me home with you. I am trapped with a madman.*

I imagined this was not an easy life for a dog in such isolated country, working alongside a grouchy caballero, ever aware of the presence of large wild animals lurking in the woods beyond. I tried to look away and hear what the caballero had to tell us, but the mutt was staring right at me, insisting I address her, damn near scratching a secret SOS into the dirt with her paw. We were a ray of hope for her, strangers with welcoming smiles, but there was nothing I could do for her. I looked away.

And what is this? The caballero demanded, pointing at a sleeping bag rumpled on a narrow, high ledge of rock across from us. *Who sleeps there?* My wife said that it was she, and the caballero snapped an incredulous gaze at me. *Your wife? You let your wife sleep there?* I told him that I have little control over where my wife sleeps. Besides, we found the canyon floor to be completely infested with scorpions. My wife was the wiser of us, taking her camp a little higher up. *Scorpions,* the caballero said, *were the least of our worries.* Then, in a theatrical move, he swept off one of his leather gloves and threw it into a bush. *Aya!* he shouted. *This was all we would find of her in the morning. Her hand in a bush.*

We all stared at the glove in the bush, its fingers curled. The caballero told us that there were big cats about and that they would eat us. Only days ago he had lost a cow, his animal eviscerated, intestines strung out. *They do not even eat the meat,* he said. *They just kill for the love of killing.* He said it again and again: *Mata, mata, mata.*

The glove hung limp in the bush.

I looked back at the mutt, whose eyes said, *See?*

The caballero felt responsible for us, as if we were still his guests though it had been days since we stopped at his house. He explained that there was a cow camp a few miles back, a clearing in the trees with a stagnant water tank nearby. We should be safe there. We told him we would think about it. After enough talking, he left. His dogs followed him, the mutt looking forlornly over her shoulder. A few minutes later the mutt came running back to us as if launched from a starting gate, her tongue flailing in the air like a kite. Her eyes were bright with joy. She had jumped ship. This was her one chance to escape, and she was taking it.

The dog was ours, but we could not keep her. We had miles to go, weeks into the wilderness. But one of us started secretly feeding her cheese. After that, we couldn't get rid of her. When we picked up our camp, packed everything onto our backs, and started into deeper country, the mutt followed. But the travel was too difficult for her, boulders the size of cement trucks leaning against one another. She was no good at climbing. She started yowling and barking to get us back, her pathetic voice echoing along the canyon. We all looked at one another, assuring ourselves that it was best this way. Soon she would register the reality of the situation and go home.

The mutt did not go home, however. She kept trying to follow us, and she kept failing. We handed packs across ledges, rising along a canyon wall, every move weighed out, our progress inchingly slow until we found a place to set a night's camp on a broad ledge. Getting out stoves, heating water for dinner, we listened to the mutt weep like a siren far below. Night fell, and she would not shut up. There were jaguars and mountain lions about. We'd seen fresh kills, bloody remains of deer. Apparently, next on the menu was this dog, its voice crying out to everyone, *I am scared and alone!*

We finished our dinner, scraping spoons inside of pots, any conversation halted by the mutt's forlorn serenade. We all waited for a horrible sound, yelping and meat ripping, and then silence.

My wife looked at me in the dark. "Someone should go down there," she said.

Go down there and what? I wondered. *Go down there and bring the dog back,* I supposed.

"I'll be back in a little while," I said. "I'm going to get that goddamned dog."

I took a small red light—the only illumination I had with me. I preferred to rely on my own night vision in the wilderness, but between my native abilities and the little red light, I could hardly see a thing. The way down was not easy. I teetered along ledges and boulder tops, all the way listening to the mutt's whimpering and bawling.

When I reached the canyon floor, she went inexplicably silent. There was not a sound at all. I swallowed. I had not heard a yelp, any evidence of attack, but maybe it happened too quickly to make a sound. My red light made every object look like a ghost, tree branches and boulders hunkered around one another. I pushed through a vault of darkness, turning slowly to cover my back, checking over my shoulder.

"Pup?" I called quietly.

There was no response. I stepped cautiously forward through fallen leaves, panning my light, looking for a grisly dog carcass, a basket of warm ribs. I widened my eyes, working them hard, involuntarily breathing louder. I reached down with my free hand and pulled a knife from my belt. I unfolded a healthy, five-inch blade and held it to my side, point down, fingers tight on the grip, ready for a sweep, a plunge.

"Here, pup . . . here, pup."

My voice sounded scared and alone.

"Where are you, pup?" I sang. "Come on, where are you?"

Excited voices came suddenly from above in the cliffs and ledges. Someone was shouting my name as if calling from the sky.

"She found her way to camp!" my wife shouted. "The dog's here! She made it!"

I stood very still, feeling a tang of adrenaline in my blood. I had stepped into a trap, one baited by a sorry mutt that was now safe and wagging its tail with my companions.

"Are you there?" my wife called. "Hello?"

"Yes," I shouted back. "I'm still here!"

"Did you hear about the dog? It's here!"

"Yes!" I called, irritated, nervously backing away, setting my steps as lightly as I could on the crackling eggshells of my fear. I crept out of the canyon floor, pointing the knife in front of me. I scrambled up over boulders and along ledges until I reached camp, greeted by a smiling, foolish dog.

We had to get rid of the dog. We were in the wilderness, after all. We did not want this anchor hanging around our necks. In the morning two of us started the ten- or fifteen-mile trek back toward the caballero's house. We coaxed the dog with smiles and happy calls, excited claps and whistles. The dog bounded along with us, snapping gleefully at the air as if in a field of butterflies.

Soon, though, it figured out what we were doing. From then on, the dog would not move. I strapped my arms under its belly and carried the unwieldy creature a short distance, where I hoisted it up to my companion over a boulder. Every step we took was cumbersome, the dog limp, helpless. We made a leash out of parachute cord and dragged her through the dust for miles. I hated myself the whole time.

Finally we reached an isolated ranch house, but the caballero was not home. We were all frustrated and tired, dog and humans alike. We laid the mutt like a sack of grain in front of the door and untied the strangling parachute cord. The dog crossed its front paws and dropped its head, ruined, condemned. It burrowed into its own misery and did not follow us as we turned back to our camp.

Getting rid of the mutt left me with a feeling of relief, but there also came a sense of inexcusable betrayal. I have often felt the case of domestic dogs piteous. They are half-breeds, part wild and part tame. We have bred them into subservience and strange proclivity. The obsession a Lab has for a thrown stick or ball seems perverse. Deliriously high-strung terriers and neurotic, boggle-eyed Chihuahuas are sometimes frightening to witness, as if born from a demented experiment. What on earth have we done? Should any creature be so excited at the sight of a leash? There is a reason humans and dogs came together in the first place, an ancient partnership of mutual protection, a ritual, a symbiotic dance created between two species. As I walked away from the ranch house, I thought that dogs at least deserve gentle, receptive masters to care for them. They should belong to houses and yards they can guard with dignity. The cord I tied around the mutt's neck as I dragged it away must have burned terribly.

Who was I fooling, though? I had no better rank than a dog. I too was once primitive. My kind climbed trees to sleep and threw stones to kill their food. Now we are near-hairless monkeys fitting ourselves into pants and shirts, our feet sweating in leather shoes. I find myself no less confounded than a domestic dog, half of me willing to bow to culture, the other half wanting to return to the wild and fill the rivers of my senses.

The forest deepened around me and my companion as we fled. We moved swiftly, easily dipping under tree branches, flying over boulders and exposed roots, leaving the mutt far behind. I forgot about its demoralized state. Our vision became sharp, muscles whip-snap quick. Our hair stiffened and our nails grew horny as we loped and snarled back into the dark Mexican woods.

Canis familiaris

RACCOON

July. A twin set of freeway lanes hugging the sedimentary face of Utah. Roan Cliffs, Book Cliffs, Sego Canyon. The top of the desert. A sky so blue and hot that it kneaded the geography below. The bridge over the Green River was hardly necessary where the river braided across cobbles.

I drove past the sign that read NO SERVICES NEXT 106 MILES. Air coming through my open window was blast-furnace exhaust, straightening my hair and splitting it at the ends. The interstate rose to the foot of the San Rafael Swell. Sandstone slabs a quarter-mile long angled against one another like toppled stegosaurus plates. Steep canyons crowded between them. At eighty miles per hour, I worked through my typical interstate thoughts. I wanted off this road. My eyes were all over the hot stones of the San Rafael, into shadows among the canyons. I imagined hiking routes from between the shimmering bug guts on the windshield. It would be a long drive, here to San Francisco on business. I took the next exit.

REST STOP.

The decision to stop and the flip of the steering wheel were so sudden I nearly plowed through the vacant median. At the far end of the asphalt parking lot was an outhouse, bleached by the sun. I parked, pulled on hiking boots, slung two quarts of water over my shoulder, and walked northeast, beyond the barbed wire fence.

The tilted sandstone block of the San Rafael Swell is riddled with slot canyons, propped up on edge where the earth broke its own back. I picked one canyon, hiked up its steep grade. *Water,* I thought, *find water.* I would be out only for a couple of hours, but it was an enchanting thought, finding water in this desert. This was the deepest of summer, when the boulders and cliffs held their warmth through the night and the few inches of annual precipitation were a memory so faded and warped by ripples of rising heat that they may as well have never fallen. Rust and beige hues of stone led upward. Deep round potholes had been drilled by floods, scoured clean and rubbed out like mortar bowls. They were dusted with sand and occasionally draped with a tapestry of dehydrated algae. Water had not been here in four months. The potholes had, in fact, stopped pleading for rain and had simply died.

A dragonfly, ruby-colored, droned up the canyon, hovering above an empty pothole as if thumbing through a compound memory, checking all the old spots—the place it was born, the dry holes with the shriveled cattails. The presence of a dragonfly, the only other moving, living creature out in the day, was startling. A dragonfly meant water. I could hear its hum fading off. Then I caught something, a scent of algae, a deep moldering smell of life, decomposition. Water. More dragonflies shot up the canyon, so I followed them, coming over the lip of an inset pothole.

Below the rim was water. A cavernous hole had collected enough of a flash flood to cradle it into summer. The water was a soupy emerald green, the color of life crowding into a smaller and smaller space as vapor lifted invisibly off the surface. There was more life than water. The walls into the hole were sheer, falling a smooth ten feet.

At the back side, in the shadow of the overhung rim, a bank of mud was exposed. On it, curled into a ball and studying me without motion, was a trapped raccoon. It watched intently as I paced the edge. It had fallen in while reaching for water, and there was no way out. One night, probably, it had climbed as close as it could, drawn by the cool, virescent smell of water. It was maybe a delirium of this dry year, a relentless gravity that compelled it to reach too far and tumble into the hole. Now it conserved energy, refusing to move, enduring a drawn-out, bitter death.

I looked along the canyon. There were two more holes. In one floated the carcasses of an antelope ground squirrel and a cliff swallow. The swallow's wings were spread like those of a drowned angel. An odd, tragic end for an animal of flight. I came to my haunches and stared at the raccoon. Around the bathtub ring of receding water were fine claw marks. They covered the circumference. No way out. I thought of how it would die, how in a month there would be a heap of bones scraped clean by ants and wasps.

I gave the situation some thought and used a couple of small cracks to lower myself into the hole. The water rose to my waist. Water striders skated to get away. They could not get far. The raccoon was ten feet across the pool, backing into the wall, growling. I slowly waded over.

"Hey, little guy," I said with a smile, as if talking to a stuffed animal, working in my mind the logistics of saving a raccoon and getting out of this hole with it.

It stared back.

I was bigger, stronger, had eaten more recently, and at least knew I could make it out alive. But the raccoon was smaller, quicker, and had nothing to lose. The raccoon recoiled and snapped at me. I had removed my shirt. Now it had two targets. I tossed the shirt at the raccoon.

There was an eruption like a spring-loaded kundalini. The raccoon snarled and bit into the shirt while I pulled fabric over its head, trying to cover it from two angles. With one hand I held its skull. With the other I clutched the scruff of its neck, hoping to immobilize it as if it were a cat. It was only then that I realized I was gripping a twelve-pound carnivore. They capture and eat cats. And rabbits, birds, small dogs. They do not lack in strength, agility, or fierceness. Cornered, they are unparalleled fighters. Its head weaseled out of my grasp, and I jumped back. It dug its teeth into the shirt and jerked it with breakneck snaps. It dropped the lifeless object into the mud as if presenting to me the mangled body of my compatriot.

I backed into a squadron of water striders that had converged on one of their own dead. I grumbled, slithering my hands in to retrieve the shirt. I tried again, but the raccoon grew angrier. After two more attempts, I was backed against the wall. Not as simple as I had thought.

A distinct black-and-yellow mud dauber wasp entered the hole, dangling down to the island. It landed without recognition from the raccoon, who was focused solely on me, and flitted about the bank. It scraped up a chunk of mud and fashioned it into a ball with its front legs. I could hear the scratching sounds as it gathered more layers, then flew out of the hole with a ball of mud. It knew nothing of the ongoing confrontation.

While the raccoon scowled at me, I gave it serious thought from across the water. I should not have come in here and interfered. This was none of my business — and now my fingers were going to get bitten off. I could use sweet, gentle words, but they would mean nothing. I knew a man who could talk a rattlesnake into submission, then pick it up with his bare hands, careful not to squeeze on its slender bones. I don't know what words he used or how he formed his voice. I could just as well recite poetry to this raccoon as croon to it that I was there to help.

Wedging with soaked boots, I climbed out and hiked back to the truck. Let the thing die. Mud and water slopped off as I circled from the door to the tailgate. *Things live, things die,* the most simple of thoughts. But I had already started something in the pothole. My presence was not unnatural, was not an interruption. It was, in fact, the same as anything in the desert—a dragonfly or a flash flood or a season of hot wind and no rain. Rethinking, I dug into my possessions, coming out with a box of leftover pizza and a tan sheet used to cover the truck's bench seat. I folded a slice of pizza into the sheet and picked out a pair of leather gloves. I carried my array of supplies back into the desert. When I reached the hole, the raccoon and I spied each other cautiously. It lowered its head between front paws as if wishing me away.

Armed with leather gloves, a shirt, and a sheet, leaving the pizza up top, I slipped into the water and moved across. The floor of the hole was a nest of fine, thick mud, with points of a few large rocks sticking through. I shook the shirt in the air, and the raccoon growled. Then I tossed it over the animal's head. There was a catapulting leap. In its sudden blindness I rushed in with the sheet. The raccoon lunged at me through the shirt. It ripped into the sheet, twisting it up. With a shot of adrenaline, I surrendered my grip and stumbled back.

We glared at each other from opposite sides of the pool. It remained crouched over my sheet, wadding it into a muddy, wet mass. Every time I reached for it, the raccoon snapped back. The fingers working the sheet were independent, shaped like human fingers. I have watched raccoons manipulate two unlatched padlocks on the back of my truck with such fingers, slide both the locks out, open the hatch, and crawl inside. The first raccoon from North America to be studied in the Old World unlatched its cage with its fingers in 1747. It escaped from naturalist Carolus Linnaeus's study in Sweden and was killed by a neighborhood dog. Ten years later Linnaeus published his name for this creature in *Systema naturae* as *Ursus lotor. Ursus,* meaning "bear," and *lotor,* meaning "washer," referring to the raccoon's habit of dipping objects, especially food, into water to then be rotated and fondled in its hands.

A quarter century after the raccoon's daring Swedish escape, a German zoologist named Gottlieb Conrad Christian Storr removed the genus *Ursus* and established its current name, *Procyon lotor*. *Procyon*, the name of the double star in the constellation Canis Minor, roughly translates to "before the dog." Regardless of the name change, the raccoon is a closer relative to the bear, as Linnaeus had noted, than it is to Storr's dog. This was what I was trying to grab, a small bear. It was robust and decisive, but it was dying of hunger and exposure. I climbed out, broke two dead branches from a juniper, and returned, using them as tongs to draw back the sheet.

The raccoon snarled. I charged several more times as it hissed and pounced, and together we rocked the waves. I was covered with dark, stinking, organic mud. Shaking and nervous. The raccoon was soaked, much smaller and more bedraggled now that its fur was matted. We were anxious and tiring, and the animal could not back any farther to the wall. Although certain death filled the hole like the smell of fear, some genetic demand, an unknown and untamed drive, kept the raccoon poised. Life at all cost.

I focused on its eyes, the white hairs around them making them look larger than they actually were. I focused on that drive. I rushed the raccoon, dove on it with as much force as possible. My palm wrapped over its head, stuffing it down. I could feel the shape of its skull, the round of its eyes. The sheet was torn and the raccoon poked limbs through the openings. I wrapped the raging bundle and staggered across the pool with it tucked under my arm. Claws scrambled, ripping the fabric. It snarled and twisted. I slipped on the buried rocks and landed with my face against the stone wall. Fighting for a hold, I hoisted the animal into the air.

There was nothing to brace against. The walls were curved and smooth. I held the raccoon high against the wall with one outstretched Statue of Liberty arm. Still I was two feet short of the top. There was no way to let loose. Twelve pounds of incensed carnivore would crash incisors-first on my scalp. I grunted and jammed my soaked boots against opposite walls. No traction.

I kept scrambling, going nowhere, sweating and mumbling through my teeth at the raccoon. In sex, in violence, and in desperation, we humans are most like the raccoon, most like animals. My life is often spent in stories and intentions, but now it was my gritted teeth, my face against a rock, and another animal trapped in the water hole with me. I dropped my arm back and I swung. The raccoon and the wet sheet spun into the air. They sailed for an instant. They floated. I waited for the pile of mud, raccoon, and sheet to glance off the edge and crash down on my head. Instead, smacking the sandstone with the slap of a waterlogged towel, they stuck. The raccoon was motionless.

I climbed out and lifted the sheet back, exposing a stunned raccoon. I tossed the pizza slice at its feet. For a while it regarded me. Notoriously intelligent animals. I could not help wondering what it was thinking.

Pizza. It was considering pizza. The scent of food. Between adept fingers it clutched the slice and brought it to its mouth. The chewing was meticulous. The flatness of its eyes, the intensity of its stare, spoke of a lack of pretense, a look of purity. I breathed heavily, emotions riding my veins like a drug. The raccoon ate, keeping me in full view. Human and raccoon, two different animals hunched before each other.

The raccoon rose and slinked up a rock. It straddled the spine and vanished down the ravine to the other side. I have wondered where it is raccoons disappear to in this land of naked stone. Miles of exposure. When I looked into the ravine, it was gone. I returned to the rest stop, where my truck was parked alone. I was heavy with the stench of mud, wet fur, and fear. With the tailgate pulled down, I sat and stripped off my soaked boots. They slapped the asphalt and I tugged on dry shoes.

Procyon lotor

CAT AND MOUSE

In March, preceding the season of ice and mud in the San Juan Mountains, I walked into a meadow between Horsefly Peak and Dallas Creek, dragging behind me nineteen shaved lodgepole pine trees. Twenty-five feet long. Two at a time. I also toiled across the meadow with a hundred-pound bundle of boat canvas, dropping it every nine feet, falling over it, getting up again, hauling it another nine feet. In a very particular place I lifted the lodgepoles, locking them into one another, and built a tipi. The meadow around it is an open bank of grasses spanning between ponderosa forests. At its edges the elk and deer congregated, walking cautiously through ecotone shadows, listening to my laboring groans.

The meadow leads south and east, into walls of young, seditious mountains that erode in radical crags like candle wax. Wind channels along this meadow, brushed off the mountains like a shrugged comment. The grass bends beneath its words. When the ponderosa pines are weighted by snow, the wind selects a few and hurls them to the earth, snapping roots in frozen soil like cracking fresh carrots. In the winter the drifts range freely over the meadow, building gentle waves as capricious as dune sand. In this part of Colorado, March is the season of avalanches. On a day between storms I draped canvas over the skeleton of lodgepoles and pulled it tight, pinning it together with rods of wood above the door.

I moved here from the town of Ouray, twenty miles away, where the sun had been reaching my window just before lunch and stuffing itself down between thirteen-thousand-foot mountains by early afternoon. I had been living in the cold top floor of a house on Main Street, rented to me by the county judge. My job at the time was the writing and publishing of the local newspaper, and the top floor was all I could afford. As I had been warned, the electric baseboard heating of my apartment failed severely through the winter. I was later told that every newcomer to town gets stuck with this top-floor apartment. Surviving a winter in the apartment was a sordid initiation, and its residents have consistently fled come March or April, as if we were the butt of a nasty local prank.

So I got out of town, building a tipi because the apartment was too cold. Because my truck was continually being buried by the work of the town snowplow. Because I had lived inside straight walls for long enough. I hauled a woodstove to the tipi and heaved my belongings inside just before it snowed again. When I showed up a week later at the hardware store to buy a cover for the stovepipe (extending from a hole in the canvas just above the tipi door), I smelled of smoke and I was groggy from a night of little sleep.

Working behind the counter, Jack Scoggins took a sniff and, with his slow, guttural voice, said, "Woodstove back up on you in the wind?" I grunted and shoved a wad of bills at him.

Slowly, pieces of my life came together. I built an entryway of moss rock and laid sturdy carpet over a plywood floor. From the nearest road I hefted pieces of ancient furniture and arranged them around the woodstove, adding to them an oversized down quilt I made while I was in Ouray. The quilt pinpointed home, and much later, when I traveled for years on end, the quilt was boxed up so mice could not get to it. Its patterns would backdrop my dreams like a nesting instinct.

I carried in a solar panel and leaned it against the south face of the tipi, powering my computer, a radio that picked up the two available stations, and a handheld food processor. In the summer I would use a solar shower outside and dry off in the sun. In the winter I used a ceramic pitcher and basin with warm water and a towel, and when I washed my hair outside, it froze within seconds. Blisteringly bright days followed the monumental storms, melting four feet of snow within hours, flooding the meadow. I once sat on my bed, my feet dangling off in rubber irrigation boots, and watched five inches of water flow steadily across the floor. (By the next summer I had moved the tipi to higher ground, out of the floodplain, to just inside the forest.) Snow rattled against the white boat canvas in storms, a gracious sound that covered me like a protective blanket, sealing me around the warm woodstove and burying the door while I slept.

There were winter months of struggling to keep water from freezing. Eventually came the realization that it was not possible to keep water fluid between October and April, especially after retired gold miners in town told me I had to sleep with it in my bed. The night the air inside reached twenty-seven below zero, I kicked the water bottles out of bed and let them fend for themselves.

The world on the high mesa was sly. It was constantly trying to get at me in an underhanded way, throwing impossible variables in my face — frozen cans of tuna fish, bumblebees nesting in my bed, and windstorms that turned the canvas into tall ship billows on nights I truly, truly needed to get just a little sleep. I sorted these problems out, of course. I didn't eat tuna. I was stung repeatedly by the most god-awful insects you have ever heard of.

But there was one thing I couldn't figure out. I had done everything but kill myself and still had no solution. Mice. Deer mice. *Peromyscus maniculatus*. With their wiggly little noses and faint whiskers, with their evening scampering and fanatic fascination with wadded aluminum foil keeping me up all night. Damn them all. I've always had an envious view of mice, the dormouse, the church mouse. Their world is in secret cabinet passageways, an underworld of snug, wool-lined cradles and escape routes behind the radio. At night the entire church, the entire house, belongs to them alone. As a child I longed to be a mouse. I would have a blueprint knowledge of my house that shamed anyone's clumsy trudge down the hallway, anyone's hiding of birthday presents or fumbling around in the closet for shoes.

Now they were the underground mafia. They challenged my every move. Their shit lay like confetti. They ate holes in my best clothes.

"Take the ones you've killed," a man told me. "Scatter their bodies in a circle around the tipi. Let 'em rot real good, and nothing will come near your place."

Thank you very much.

Another man suggested I get a shotgun. *What for?* I asked. He just grinned.

I did have a ridiculously huge Guatemalan machete. I languished in bed on lazy mornings and whacked at the mice as they scurried across the floor. The machete was the closest weapon on hand, and I kept it next to the bed for just this purpose. I never managed to kill a mouse with the machete. The floor was well scarred, though.

Following an unusually wet season, the rodents prospered in the Southwest. The problem was that this year the mice were doing something new. They were killing people. To the north and south of me, people were dying from a mysterious plaguelike virus emanating from mouse droppings. Flulike symptoms, they say. An impossible fever, loss of bodily control, fitful, horrible nights, then death. No way to stop it. In Utah a twenty-six-year-old woman died within six days of sweeping out her mouse-infested garage. The hantavirus, it was called. The mystery deathblow delivered by our tiny, scurrying cohabitants. Neighbors were afraid to clean their traps for fear of touching the creatures. I was thinking to myself that if I'm sleeping, eating, and sweeping my floor in a world of mouse droppings, certainly I would be the first to go.

So I got a cat. He went out there raising holy terror among all creatures. Mice, ground squirrels, chipmunks, birds, rabbits, voles, lemmings, and shrews. There was a perimeter I called the Zone of Death that the cat cleared out as a non-native predator, and even the coyotes did not come as close as they once did. The mice took refuge in the eye of my cat's storm, within the tipi. There were places to hide in here, places to build nests out of my wool socks, and I was certain that some sort of deal had been struck between them and my cat. He had been ambushing rabbits twice his size and stashing them under my bed. Bold little bastard. In the morning I could hear the vicious ripping and tearing, the crushing of bones just beneath my head as I lay snug against my pillow, gritting my teeth.

I knew when he brought one. Rabbits have an extraordinarily foul smell after they've been disemboweled. The worst things I have ever smelled, as a matter of fact. I had to wrap my face in socks and bandannas, barely able to breathe as I collected the pieces with my bed pulled back. My shouting was muffled. The cat was frustrated with my lack of respect for his quarry, and he usually attacked me in my sleep.

I took the cat in because tipis, by design, are no good at keeping mice out. I sat at my desk and wrote, and they lined themselves along the shelves, or on the arms of the rocking chair, balefully staring at me with their tiny eyes. They moved now and then to better their view or to scratch behind their ears. When I got up they leaped over one another like popcorn, and every dark place in the tipi was filled with the sounds of running mice. They don't hibernate. Instead they gather up food and warmth into a nice secret cache and rely on it through the winter. That food and warmth belonged to me first.

I tried to accept this behavior as one of the bizarre aspects of tipi life. At first I refused traps, and moved litters outside that were born in my bed while I was away for a few days. I harbored the thought that it was I intruding on their land. It was a bleeding-heart-liberal thought that I eventually abandoned. I once caught a mouse by hand and tossed it into a small paper bag. I took the bag outside and gave it a rough shaking, with the mouse banging around like the ball inside a can of spray paint.

"I want you to leave," I whispered with my mouth next to the bag. "Do you understand? Leave and tell all of your friends. I want all of you gone." I rattled the bag once more. Then I dumped it out. The mouse hit the ground running and scrambled back to the tipi. Now that they were killing people and making noise through the night, now that their populations had hit record levels, I was feeling differently. I looked at my cat, pointed to the mice, and yelled, "I want them dead, all of them!"

The first feline to come through had been a wild barn cat. I picked him out of a litter found by a woman who works on a nearby ranch. The kitten had never been touched by a human. She lured it over with food, and as soon as it was close enough, she grabbed it. The kitten went berserk. There was blood and screaming. The woman had the raging thing dangling by a single leg and it took two of us to stuff it into a cardboard box. Brothers and sisters watched with horror and backed into the shadows. As I drove up the switchbacks and washboards, I heard possessed, unnerving sounds growl out of that box.

I hiked to the tipi and placed the box on the bed. I had a new water bowl and a few cat toys, all spread over the quilt. I had cleaned up the place so it would at least look like a nice home. The kitten slowly lifted its head out. It surveyed the place from the box, then ran away like a weasel, darting out of my home. I never saw it again.

The second cat, the one that stayed, came from a shelter. He rode the dashboard back, and when he was introduced to the tipi, he stared at me in a distracted way that already suggested his territory was established. He took well to the tipi, and I explained very carefully to him that his duty was to kill and eat mice.

The cat shortly became bored with the sheer number of mice involved in his occupation. He let them roam freely while hunting out there instead of in here. He liked the wide-open spaces, the challenge of wild hunting, the breeze through his arrogant little hairs. In the winter he hunted at night. If he had been chasing an animal and missed, he would press his ears back and approach me with malice, avoiding my eyes. In a typical incident, he eased up to my ankles and pounced on them from behind. I kicked and scrambled. He hissed and drew blood. Just as I struggled to pry him out of my flesh, he popped loose. Instantly he returned to everyday life, nosing through a bowl of dried cat food, while I was left gasping on the bed, shouting, "Bad cat, very, very bad cat!"

In the mid-1700s, the poet Christopher Smart, confined to a sanatorium, wrote with a queer love about his cat, Jeoffrey. He ended his seventy-four-line work with

For God has blessed him in the variety of his movements.
For, though he cannot fly, he is an excellent clamberer.
For his motions upon the face of the earth are more than any
    other quadruped.
For he can tread to all the measures upon the music.
For he can swim for life.
For he can creep.

I feared that I understood Mr. Smart, that I watched my cat too much, bonding with an animal that would as soon eat me. In the winter he would often return not long after the fire burned out and burrow into the bed with me. He would be frosted with snow, and I would go suddenly stiff as ice-caked paws padded across my chest. In the morning I would say with a calm, quiet voice, "Sazi, start the fire. There are matches, there is kindling. Go ahead, give it a try." But Sazi would remain under the covers through the morning, only to come out when it was warm. He expected to be petted, with those half-closed, contented eyes, lounging with an obscene lack of decency on the quilt.

The rodents had meanwhile figured out zippers, Tupperware, hanging bags of food, cardboard boxes, and pans with lids. The cat ate a few now and then, maybe to prove something. The mice lived good lives regardless. Soon they would be able to make effective assaults on the dry pasta I kept in an ammunition box outside. It was a war.

The cat was heading out for nightly hunting raids, while the most fertile hunting ground remained inside. One time, in fact, he returned from a hunting escapade missing most of his tail, a story that only he can explain. Inside the tipi I heard the familiar scratching sounds of a mouse in a bag, so I snatched the thing closed and set it on the bed next to the cat, with the opening facing his terrible claws and teeth. The mouse shot out, and they stared at each other. The mouse ran the other way until it met me and I shooed it back to the cat, who was trying to get some sleep. There was an insignificant pounce. The mouse escaped and the cat curled back up.

I loved my cat, of course. I was able to unload heaps of unconditional affection onto him, petting and scratching, kneading his worthless hide with all the fondness and frustration I could muster. And the very second I tired of it, in the roar of his purring, I could stop. He did not seem to care. He either fell asleep, watched me, or left to kill something. And he waited for me at night. When I came home late I would always see his head, peering through a hole he had carved in the snowdrift that leaned on the door. We were companions of some sort. We stalked deer together in the summer. I would be down on my stomach, crawling along, and he stayed with me, dropping back so as not to startle them.

But the mice, Sazi. Eat the mice.

I had a few extra dollars while at the grocery store, so I purchased new mousetraps. My first catch was divided into two equal parts, both unflattering to the original animal. I carried the thing out under a night of intense starlight and, holding it by the tail, tossed it into its afterlife. I waited with terror when I heard the mice approach certain areas because I knew what awaited them. I whispered to them to beware, to go home, but, like my cat, they did not understand. At night the snapping jolted my dreams. The brutal noise was followed by the desperate sound of tiny scrambling feet. Then silence. I squirmed deeper into the blankets.

Snap. Shuffle, shuffle. Silence.

All night long.

The cat and I had many fruitless discussions on our differing viewpoints on what to eat and not to eat. He ignored me. The cat and mice were in collusion, plotting my demise. The mice wanted free rein of the tipi, the cat wanted the forest to himself. The mice were tired of traps, the cat was tired of being lectured to in some unintelligible language, then being thrown out the door into the snow. In the end, we all knew who the victim would be.

Felis catus
....

Peromyscus maniculatus
....

JAGUAR

In shadowed undergrowth I hear an animal moving clumsily through rickety branches. I stop and peer ahead, thinking, *Bear. No. It has to be human.* No one else travels with such a heedless gait in the wilds, dry branches breaking underfoot.

This is a piney, almost tropical mountain slope in northern Mexico, where I have been walking with a companion whom I have not seen for a few hours. We got split up in the undergrowth this morning, and I figured we would not find each other until tonight, back at our camp.

In the havoc of vegetation before me, I am just able to make out my companion's pack and his burnished hat brim ducking into paths cleared enough for javelinas or coatis, but not for humans. He has no idea I am here. I imagine exactly what he is thinking. He feels alone right now, wandering through his own tangled, private wilderness, nothing to answer but his every footstep and the haywire branches in front of him.

The second I am sure it is my companion and not a bear, a grin comes across my face. I slow myself and study his movements, thinking that if I am stealthy enough, I can sneak up and scare the crap out of him. I'll leap on his back from out of the shadows. This is how he and I travel together, testing each other, watching for tracks, alert to the smallest flit of wings or snort of air. If one is so careless, this is his chastisement, a prank, a delightful moment of terror.

I skulk off to the side, reading the steep, mountainous angle under my boots. I plant my palms across my thighs as I steer through the brush. My mind is set on the slow, persistent task of paying attention, losing sight of my partner but staying with him, listening ahead for tendrils of sound, his hard boot soles landing stride after stride. The terrain makes it difficult. Gullies lead in and out of one another, and down their embankments I have to slow even more so he does not hear me sliding after him. I go to my hands and knees, bowing under branches where something the size of a large dog has been clearing its own habitual path. The animal even left some tracks. Though they are little more than scuffs, I can see it was here recently. But my thoughts are not on animals. I am fixed on my companion walking at the edge of my hearing, his sounds coming from a faraway room.

I follow him through pines, brown-bark columns of old growth leaving little space to pass. He leads me out of the woods and onto a steeply pitched incline covered with oak brush and knee-tangling manzanita. I damn near have to walk like a snake to keep quiet, shoulders swerving around twigs and crooked limbs, one hand touching ground, the other lifting a branch out of the way. For a moment, I lose him, but soon pick him up again. His walking has changed. He is quieter now. Maybe he has spotted an animal, a white-tailed deer, perhaps even a bear, and he is stalking it for a better look. I have to move even more softly, stepping on the outside edges of my feet, rolling to the ball, half hovering, half moving.

High grass and Apache plume obscure my vision, but I am getting closer, now able to hear his every footfall. I can almost see him, my ears forming an auditory vision of his headway. I have to stop from smiling. I feel like a master tracker, expert trickster, just about to make my kill, ready to rush forward at a blinding sprint and dive onto my companion's back. His shriek will be well worth the effort.

Though I cannot yet see him, I know he is fifteen feet ahead of me. I calculate that I can be on him in three seconds, hardly enough time for him to turn and get his brain focused on me flying at him. My muscles tense and relax, tense and relax, looking for the window, the right moment to bolt.

Then I hear his voice. He is calling from far away. I freeze. Ahead of me, the sound of walking ceases. I stand up straight, head barely clearing the brush, and I can see my companion about four hundred feet up the slope from me. He is shouting about something he found, a huge, angry rattlesnake. He wants me to come up and see it, biggest rattlesnake he's ever encountered.

Still, I do not move, and a single question crystallizes in my head.

If not my companion, then what am I stalking?

As I add up sounds I had been following, the realization comes quickly. I was tricked off my companion's trail and was now following an animal with soft, even steps, four legs, not two. Weighs about as much as a grown man, but is not a man. How could I have missed the cues, stillness and shifts? I am following a jaguar.

My companion must have spotted me some time ago, watching me as I pushed my way through scrub. I shout up to him, "Listen, can you have a look around me? Do you see anything else, any animal?"

He is quiet for a moment. "No. Just you. Wait a minute. There's something in front of you."

My eyes throttle the brush. Nothing is there. Not a flick of fur. Not a sound.

"How close?" I call desperately. "How close is it?"

"There is a huge, pissed-off rattlesnake in front of me. You really should see this."

"How close?" I demand, trying to keep my voice calm.

"I can't see it."

"Where was it when you *could* see it?"

"There it is again. Something big is moving in the brush." His voice sounds startled, letting go of the rattlesnake entirely.

"Where is it?" I call. "Is it moving toward me?"

"It's coming around your side."

I crank my torso, looking both ways, seeing a hundred jaguars, seeing nothing.

"Which side?"

"Downhill. No, wait. Now I don't see it. It's ... it's gone again."

I wait for my companion's next words, and my focus fills the space around me, my entire body electrified, as if I have become nothing but a single sensory organ. Jaguars are different from mountain lions, much heavier and more aggressive. They attack from the front rather than from behind, tearing out your throat with their teeth.

"I can't see it," he calls again.

Time escapes me, turned into vigilance so taut that I cannot think a single word. I am breathing through my skin. My hands are out, floating around me, fingers extended, ready to do what, I do not know. I sense the big cat's body through the air, its hind legs bunching at the ground, ready to leap. I look so hard into the brush that I no longer form the image of the jaguar in my mind. I see only color, light, shape. It is as if a blindfold has been taken off of me. I am suddenly seeing the world for what it is.

"I see it," my companion shouts. "It's way out ahead of you. It's moving down the slope at a pretty good clip. You're all clear."

Shadows like veins cross my hands and boots. My face feels hot. I refuse to move, knowing that when I do I will have to laugh at myself, expert trickster, indeed. I will have to walk to camp, build a fire, tell a story. But none of this happens yet. I do not even lift my hand to wipe fear off my brow. I stand still, remaining in the esteem of the jaguar just a moment more, even after it is long gone.

Panthera onca

Aves

BALD EAGLE

I

Three thousand feet above the earth, we are returning from a logging camp, third stop of the day. Our last landing was at a curve where the right float had to touch the sea first so we could swing into the cove without hitting the rocks. Half our landings on the coast of British Columbia are like this, doglegs and half-cocked approaches. As we fly, each pocket of turbulence knocks the plane like a hail of stones. This floatplane is something like a flying tractor, a de Havilland Beaver built in 1947, one of exactly 1,692 constructed in Canada. No other country tried to build anything like this. The single engine is a Pratt & Whitney, 450 horsepower, good for ponderous flight with heavy loads. Better and slower than anything built since. The engine is spoked with radial cylinders like a pinwheel. A monstrous cowling swallows the front of the plane, and the blades of the propeller meet at a smooth, round hub. It is one of the loudest engines to have been stuck on a plane, and you lose your voice by noon if you want to say anything to the pilot.

I showed up on the wharf one day outside of Bella Coola, moved in with my truck, and visited with the fishermen. Each day after that I walked to see the pilots, notebook in my pocket, taking pictures of them sitting on their floats. They enjoyed the photos. They bought beers for me and began telling stories. After a while they invited me to fly. My career became the unloading of equipment, the repair of gear, dipping hot tar into cracks on the runway for amphibious planes. It was cheap payment for rides to the end of the earth, and I took flights in exchange whenever I could get them. I had been doing this all the way north from Vancouver, meeting pilots, flying with them, taking pictures with an old Pentax. I went with them, men and women, eighteen years old to seventy-three. We transported supplies to the periphery of human reach, to the villages dangling off the islands and inland channels.

A pilot out of Nimpo Lake took me on a barrel roll down Hunlen Falls in Tweedsmuir Provincial Park in a red Beaver, and from then on rivets rattled like pebbles in his floats. We had deposited a canoe, one we tied to the right float, at a small mountain lake and took off with too much weight, barely clipping our way from the forest. Gideon Schutze, deaf in one ear, hard of hearing in the other, lit the engine of his Cessna 285 on fire on our way back to Williams Lake, burning hairs off my right calf when flames came through the open door. He somehow cut the flames at the control panel and grinned at me, saying, "That's the wrong way to take off." One night, with a glacier pilot in Squamish, I got too drunk to stand; the next day, with iron hangovers, we spotted and mapped forest fires all day in heavy turbulence. These people live on impassioned fear. The farther into the bush you travel, the stranger they become.

The back of the plane is empty now. Supplies have been delivered. We are twenty miles from the fjord that haggles into the Coast

Mountains to the government wharf where my truck is parked. The land below is a churn of ocean and peaks. It is the unknown. Waterfalls are like white string clippings scattered on the mountains. They run for maybe two, three miles down chutes, vanishing in the thick of the forest. Where they reappear, they intoxicate the ocean with green glacier water that hugs the towering flanks of mountains. The ocean turns smooth and green as an emerald.

Last night there was a drunken birthday party for one of the pilots. We roved from the Legion Post in Hagensborg to the Cedar Inn Bar in Bella Coola to the government wharf, driving fast, truck after truck, headlights to taillights, spraying gravel into the forest. The drinking did us in. Neither of us is thinking straight today. The pilot, Rob Goguillot, is squinting. He is a tired man; five solid weeks of flying supplies. He has quit twice this year and sheepishly returned to be rehired each time.

He has crashed one plane in his life. He will admit that. Because of it, I trust him. The pilots in town say it will happen at least once, so I feel an awkward sense of safety with a pilot who has gotten it out of his system. These bush pilots thrive on strange adrenaline, telling stories that I first thought had to be lies and now accept as the way of things.

Rob once tapped on my shoulder and pointed down to a yellow spot in a valley between peaks. The compartment fills with a deafening radial engine blare, so we talk with gestures. I had shrugged, not understanding. He swept the plane down to show me what it was. In the valley was a single yellow wing belonging to a small Cessna from the Wilderness Air outfit in Bella Coola. There was no plane to go with it. I looked at him in horror. He grinned, almost proudly, and pointed at himself. It was his wing.

He had lost power and swiveled the plane into the rocks. The wing sheared off along the way. When they found him, they said, he was sitting on the tail with his passenger, both of them drinking beer. At the mobile home in Bella Coola where the pilots gather, there must be fifty photos on the bulletin board. They are all of wrecked planes: planes towed from beneath the surface of the ocean, planes with trees crashed through one end and out another, planes upside down, sideways, bent in half and nose-first in the ground, planes with blood and strewn gear, planes without wings, without tails, without propellers, without floats, planes lying in boulder fields and forests, planes gutted by fire.

On today's flight, Rob jostles my shoulder and points down. He puts his hands together and makes the shape of a bird, wings flapping. I press my forehead against the door window and look over the right float, to where he had pointed.

Spread like a map of feathers is the wingspan of a bald eagle twenty feet below. It does not appear to be moving. In fact neither of us appears to be moving. It is the earth that is sliding by. With a tailwind we must be going fifty-five or sixty miles per hour, both of us. But for all the racket this plane is belting out, we are hardly overtaking the eagle. Rob steers us over so that we are now aligned with the eagle, flying across its back.

The eagle is riding the air. Perhaps it has been doing this all day without budging its wings. I can see the pattern of feathers, where the pointed primaries are diagrammed into the round secondaries; where the fan of covert feathers holds everything in position. The feathers do not vibrate, even as the eagle hits the same wind that tips us back and forth. The wind coming through a split near the door is making the sound of a thousand pounds of air shoved at once through a keyhole.

I had been watching bald eagles for weeks. From my tailgate at the government wharf, I counted, in one sitting, thirty-five bald eagles on the wharf pilings. They squabble and screech like bad wheels on shopping carts. They badger each other over who gets which piling because only one and a half bald eagles can fit on a piling at once. This means that massive wingspans are arched around each other, and sudden flight strikes the air as the one with the lesser wingspan or the less grating voice is forced to leave. There are so many they are like seagulls, dots of white heads all over the forests.

I had never seen this, the open wings of an eagle in flight. Not from above. The bald eagle flies with level wings, flat like a mesa, like a dancer caught midair with her arms pointed to either end of the stage. The arms, the fine bones, are nothing. It is the feathers that matter, opened to catch the ocean below. If you get a close look at an eagle's primary flight feathers, you can see that the front of the feather is much thinner than the trailing side, giving it a sharp, narrowing appearance. About three-quarters of the way to the tip is a notch that nearly terminates the trailing vanes, allowing them to separate. They are called emarginate primaries, spread perfectly from one another in order to move independently. They work the air bit by bit with the efficiency of long, narrow fingers. There are, in fact, five on each wing, and they splinter so that I can see the ocean between them.

Look at the bones of a bird, and although quite distorted, they will match a mammal's skeleton. The wings anatomically correspond exactly to each human bone from the arm to the longest finger. But in birds, the forelimb is compacted and simplified so that the wrist, hand, and fingers are fused into a single elongated bone. Bones are nearly hollow, supported with light interior struts. The entire skeleton is welded up, redesigned from all other animals; a skeleton that, in some birds, weighs less than its feathers. There is complete redistribution of weight, taking the crushing end of digestion away from the mouth, where there would be heavy teeth, and putting it into the gizzard, at the center of balance within the body. Muscles are aligned to control feathers independently. The respiratory system can propel it to an altitude of thirty-six thousand feet, where no other animal could even take a breath without slipping directly into unconsciousness. It is fair enough to conclude that one of the more structurally advanced animals on the planet is the bird.

This one is glancing up now and then to see our whimsical

monstrosity of aluminum droning over its head. We are rocking like a train about to derail, entering and exiting thermals and downdrafts that outline the islands and their mountains. I can see no disturbance from the eagle. It has not changed course. We plummet ten feet closer to the eagle, then jerk twenty feet up. The eagle is watching the ocean three thousand feet below. Watching for salmon. I look past the eagle, to a stretch of ocean deep in the fjord. From here I can hardly see the waves.

Eagles have been known to dive five thousand feet without a single change in course and, at the end of that dive, hook into a salmon below the surface of the water. What a human can see at twenty feet, an eagle can see at one hundred eighty feet. Some smaller raptors, if they please, can read the print of this book from two hundred feet in the air. A human has about two hundred thousand visual cells over every square millimeter of the retina. An eagle has more than one million. So I imagine the eagle is riding the updrafts, so high that its shadow won't hit the earth, looking for fish about the length of my forearm thousands of feet below.

I think about opening the door. I have been around a door opened accidentally on a small plane in midair, and everything gets blown out. I still think about opening the door, even if Rob loses the paperback he has positioned on the throttle. I will open it and leap out of the plane. I will spread my arms and flatten them against the invisible horizon the pilot is always trying to adhere to. But I won't use equipment. I will use the eagle as reference. I will fly. Of course I will. I have three thousand feet to fly. To do it well, like the eagle, I would need wings one hundred seventy feet wide on this heavy, unwieldy body, and chest muscles six feet thick. I will glide alongside the eagle, then I will turn and breathe the racing air, and I will descend rapidly to earth.

It is the wish to be an animal again, to have the eyes that I have lost. No presuppositions. Just sticks and stones. I want something that is gone, something unacceptable, irrational. Where it is known when to sleep, where to seek food, which direction to turn. Where it is understood, without quarrel or reason. I want to lose my fingers and plans and I want to fly.

Rob adjusts the knobby instruments, made of the same hard, matte-black plastic as rotary phones from the forties, and we angle off. I look at him with impatience. He shrugs. With the third and final run of the day complete, sightseeing is not on his agenda. The plane does not have the same destination as the eagle. With a gut turning dip through an open space in the atmosphere, we veer southeast toward the government wharf. The open wings of the eagle remain unchanged, and the margins of its feathers blend into the shape of a large raptor in the distance. Then it vanishes at the angle on the plane where Plexiglas meets aluminum.

II

I am alone, although maybe ten minutes ago I could still hear voices. We intended to part for only a few minutes, each person taking a better route to our beach destination, and now we are separated. There is mud on me, smeared from crawling and pushing. Sometime today, if we keep our directions straight, we will hit the coastline. There we will regroup and tell stories about the forest behind us.

Two hundred inches of rain descend upon this island each year, sometimes two hundred fifty. It is one of maybe a few hundred islands straggled along the west side of British Columbia. Fog hangs as if the ropes and pulleys holding the sky have snapped. The rain is a shield of gauze. Before it gets this far down, the drops are broken up, spread across broad leaves and hemlocks, and drizzled to the earth. I have been sorting through mounds of louseworts, wood nymphs, and goatsbeard. There is a documented half ton of dangling mosses and lichens in every acre of forest canopy up here. The bigleaf maples have sent roots out of their branches into the soil and epiphytes that have gathered there, sometimes a foot thick, turning the canopy, fifty and one hundred feet high, into a second root system. Fallen Sitka spruce, like massive, overlapping arms, are being digested by ferns, mushrooms, and liverworts. When I inhale, beads of water collect on the inside of my throat and lungs. I have pushed into a clearing below the locked canopy. A boggy circle is bridged by fallen trees, like the inside of a palace overgrown with foliage. Mist clings to the ground.

The sanctuary is deep with gray and green. Beards of lichens hang from the Sitka spruce. Four of the spruce are standing dead, surrounding one another, leaning in to whisper with the slow insistence of old men. I slip out of my pack and sit on a fallen tree. The seat is cushioned by several inches of wet club moss. At my feet are butterfly shapes of vanilla leaf plants and dark dabs of bead lilies. The rain must have stopped out there. Maybe it stopped three days ago. The drops are only now subsiding. The ones still falling sound like water in a cave.

I wipe my forehead with my sleeve. Above me is a ruffling sound, like a pillow being fluffed. I look up and water spatters my face. A bald eagle is perched on one of the dead limbs, beneath the domed ceiling. It is shaking out its feathers and watching me with a sideways glance.

There are more eagles. Six of them, sitting in the dead Sitka, feathers puffed. The eyes are on me, inviolate stares from the head of the canopy. Another shakes out its feathers, opening a dark, robelike wingspan, then closing and settling. They seem to be waiting, maybe for the storm to clear, or for hunger to send them one by one back to the world. My addition is no more than someone else waiting. The eyes eventually roll off of me and concentrate on a forest that betrays focus.

Look too long at one thing in this forest, and you will never return. All the careful maps one gathers in the glove box, all the directions to and from places showing where we are and where we have been, all are broken down in this forest. You cannot be lost here. It is a ludicrous thought that there is any way at all. I see why the people of these islands paint and carve the way that they do. Their stylized bears and dogfish, their fantastic totem poles and white-button blankets, all have the essence; hands and faces embedded into the wings of sinuous ravens, eyes hidden among the fins of killer whales. The forest is, without a doubt, eternity.

It must be an hour that we sit, the eagles and I, before I hear voices again. People have found one another. I can hear laughing. The shore must be close, and they have found some route. The voices draw me off the fallen tree. I shoulder my pack. The eagles are unmoving in their shrine, feathers rolled out.

Later, we are near the village, on the beach. Someone has a crab and a pot of boiling water. We have to tear the crab apart while it is still alive and stuff it into the pot because the creature won't fit whole. The first thought is that this is inhuman. Then I imagine an eagle jerking apart the fine, strange organs beneath the crab's carapace, while the crab vainly struggles. We are cracking red shells, drawing out the white, fresh meat. What happens next is that a bald eagle appears from the dark of the canopy and flies over the shore. We can hear the deep thump of its wings, and suddenly I jump and run after it. One account is that I am running in circles with my hands to the sky. Another is that the crab has made me suddenly ill.

What I had seen was one of the round black feathers loosen from the inside of the eagle's wing. It is a short, dark feather with white down at the base, the kind that cups air, holding the bird to the sky. I run after it, following it through the ripples the eagle has left behind. The feather drifts over the sea, and I run into the water. I am running as if the sky has just caught fire and I am trying to catch the very first ember. The feather comes back to land and I am beneath it, with cupped hands.

It settles in my open palms, gentle as something that is not even there. I bring it to my chest so a breeze will not steal it. I unfold fingers and look into the hollow formed there as if I have taken hold of a piece of flight and wildness itself.

When I look over at all the crab eaters, they are blankly staring at me. I grin and gesture with my hands that I have caught the feather. They force strange smiles with meat in their mouths and gesture back with their crab legs.

Haliaeetus leucocephalus

PEREGRINE FALCON

There is a kind of rock called Wingate that appears in the deserts of Arizona and Utah. It is made of sand and ancient wind. Standing several hundred feet tall, it is as solid as brick, forming red buttes and fencerows of cliffs that tower over the earth. You can look into its cayenne-colored face and see the remains of an ancient sand dune sea, layers of sand feathered across one another by Jurassic winds. It is a formation with wings.

I enjoy walking where the high Wingate comes to an edge, leaving me thrust into the sky. Sometimes I balance on its ruler-thick lip and hold my arms out at my sides, listening to wind booming across the sandstone face below. Today I am walking to the end of Bighorn Mesa in Utah, out toward a tip of Wingate high over the looping course of the Green River. Wingate buttes stand at every distance, vertical striations of shadows dominating whole horizons, the earth below buried in shattered cliffs like fallen cities of stone.

It is a beautiful day, teetering on the fulcrum between winter and spring, and I walk with a wool cap pulled over my ears and light gloves with their fingertips cut off. Subdued March light brings out desert colors, a cool pastel landscape of rock and sand. Low, wet clouds ramble across the far slope of the San Rafael Swell. The island of the Henry Mountains is buried in storms, a final good snow, one last bone thrown to winter.

Bighorn Mesa comes to a sudden edge. Broken red towers spindle hundreds of feet downward. Wind rises up sheer cliffs like a water-fall in reverse. My face enters this wind, moving over empty space where a bird of prey vaults skyward from under my feet. It comes out of nowhere, born of smooth sandstone, as if I interrupted a myth in progress. I am startled to see such abrupt motion this close to a fall, and I almost swallow my heart. But the bird unfolds with such grace that I am immediately stilled.

It is a peregrine falcon, a cliff diver. Not once does it flap or even budge its outspread, silver-gray wings. It merely cups the wind with them the way you might hold a glass ball in your hand. The wind brings the falcon up to me, lofting it over the abyss. I lean toward the bird. I can nearly touch it. I can reach out my hand and graze its ranks of checkered feathers. For a falcon it is large, but the clean-ness of its shape makes it appear moderately sized, its wingspan no farther across than a yardstick.

Wearing an aviator's cap of dark feathers, the bird looks over its shoulder, flicking a glance at me. The expression is not infuriated, as I would expect from such a territorial animal as this. Instead, the falcon sets me with an easy stare, as if looking over the top of a book to see who has come through the door.

Fastest bird in the world, capable of two-hundred-mile-per-hour dives, this one is motionless in the air. It is an axis around which the world seems to turn as I stare back at the gleaming point of its eye, the desert dropping and spinning around it. I could fall for it, lean out too far, hoping to graze my fingers through its wings as I plummet off the Wingate. I nearly become part of the myth, barely remembering to keep my feet on the ground.

Where I live in western Colorado, a cliff stands over my house, and every year two peregrines return to nest in its soaring heights. From February to August they cut through my sky like scythes. I have watched their quick and baffling maneuvers drive off kingly golden eagles, turning the eagles upside down with talons thrust out, the eagles snatching nothing but air, never coming close to grabbing the assailing falcons. More than once I have watched them team up to kill a white-throated swift, driving the small bird to exhaustion, swerving and stooping in tandem before finally popping it out of the sky as if in target practice. In their spring season of mating and reproduction, they scream from sunrise to sunset, patrolling their territory at blinding speeds, raking their voices down the chalkboard of the cliff.

In winter I have followed peregrines south to find them in the desert of Mexico, where they travel in groups of six, eight, eleven. They practice aerobatics in gentle, hot winds over dunes and barren ridges. I have come to know peregrine falcons as perfectionists, birds constantly practicing their art. They take the lives of other birds midair with a two-hundred-mile-per-hour touch, blowing out their small lives like candles. No other bird has ever struck me as so excruciatingly precise, a seamless weapon, no gap between the purpose of body and the purpose of mind.

Many people imagine what animal they might be in some future life, and it seems everyone wants to be a bird—as if birds held the monopoly on human afterlife, ready at any moment to vacate their bodies and let us crawl inside. Who, though, considers how that gifted life will end, how a bird dies in the wild? For brevity, I choose the peregrine falcon to kill me should I be born a bird. I have watched them kill and have crept close to their eating, seeing them tear meat from small, limp bodies, blood-studded feathers flustering to the ground. It does not seem like such a bad way to die, taken into yet another body, made finally pure.

The peregrine floats in the air just beyond arm's reach. It looks back at me with such equanimity, such singularity, that I am emptied, contentedly bankrupt. This must be what it feels like to fly for the first time, to actually open up and soar, exchanging gravity for faith.

I hear the warning moan of a second peregrine nearby. There is a nest in a crack I cannot see, a mate brooding over a clutch of smooth eggs. The low voice says that my time is over and it would now be polite for me to back away. I do. I slowly step from the edge, returning to the earth, where I can no longer see the floating falcon or the cliff cascading below. The world around me folds back into its neat little boxes of dimensions and nearby distances. Broken red rocks appear at my feet. Once more I am an ordinary, living man, no longer eolian, no more a creature of wind.

Falco peregrinus

HAWK

I t is the morning following a heavy snow, when two or three small clouds are the only ones left, snagged on the mountains. Colorado does this with sunshine. It will sock the mountains with a blizzard overnight. Then, like a magician pulling away the veil, the next morning arrives with agonizingly clear sunlight. The curve of the planet becomes a refractive lens of snow.

In the tipi I am forgoing the woodstove and heading straight for my snowshoes. I push a small opening through the door with my hand, then force my full weight against the canvas, busting a hole into the snowdrift. Just in front of the tipi, I dig out two wooden snowshoes strung with animal sinew. I am wearing a long, heavy leather coat that drops to my ankles.

The snow is thick. The snowshoes cannot get hold of it, and I plod into the meadow. Even with sunglasses I have to hold my hand over my eyes. The ponderosas are hung heavy and buried. Mount

Sneffels, a fourteen-thousand-foot peak named after a Jules Verne escapade into the center of the earth, is striking into the sky. The bare black facet of its avalanche-riddled north face is the only thing that absorbs, rather than reflects, sunlight.

This is January snow. It is perfect for tracking, cold and dry so that it will record the detail of animal prints without crumbling. I am following rabbit tracks, heading into the meadow. I am going print by print, trying to decipher the concerns of a rabbit here around sunrise, leaping into an untouched world. The marks are casual, small, and not aiming at anything in particular.

Then there is a new print. It is about three and a half feet wide, a fan pattern spread where the next set of rabbit tracks should be.

Hawk.

There are three distinct patches of white fur, and the rabbit tracks have broken out. The rabbit is racing, sending sprays of snow behind its long hind feet. The wings hit again. Tail feathers and spreading wings outline themselves perfectly. It must have been dark under there, like the inside of a packing crate.

The rabbit, I do not know how, has gotten out. It is bounding for the mounds formed by shrubs beneath the snow, but there is no protection. I am moving as quickly as my snowshoes will take me, following the action. The hawk has swiveled as if on an axis, sending itself around by sweeping its tail. The sweep has flung snow clumps to the south. The rabbit has made an all-out dash, beelining for the forest where the tipi stands.

For a while there is no sign of the hawk. It is in the air. I know what will happen. Rabbit tracks lead out, one print, two, three, then the hawk's.

This imprint is the deepest. It is a pattern that, hung on a wall, would be revered as art. No one would say, "Ah, hawk wings." It would be called an ancient Native American design. It would be called postmodern something or other. It would not be called the first sign of hawk, last sign of rabbit.

The rabbit tracks never return. There is a blank space that is followed by the next hawk imprint. The wings are inset with hard blows. The hawk is narrowly contending with gravity and weight. The next print is lighter. In the center are the drag marks of a rabbit's hind feet. The hawk is pushing off of the snow to become airborne, more successful with each slap. The prints go on, becoming fainter and less defined. They point out of the meadow. At the far end the snow is pure, and vacant of memory.

Buteo

....

NORTHERN SPOTTED OWL

We moved fast. If I said anything it had to be swift or I lost my breath. Three people moving quicker than a walk and hardly slower than a run to make miles into the temperate rain forest of the Olympic Peninsula. We would have been stirring dust, but it had been raining on this dark northwest corner of Washington for six months.

At first the trail was eight feet wide, firmly beaten to resemble asphalt. We were at the trailhead, not far from an Olympic National Park ranger station, so it was *supposed* to be eight feet wide, lined with cut logs, posted with informative signs. I followed Gay Hunter, a biological technician for the park and a marathon runner. A sixteenth of a mile, and the trail narrowed, manicured by a few thousand shoe soles a week. Half a mile, and we crossed the creek, starting up the west side on switchbacks. The forest thickened as if flour had been added and the place was brought to a boil. The trail two miles in was sealed with ferns and alders, and the mud sucked at our ankles. It was no longer the trailhead, no longer a popular destination. I tried to get a look at it, at the drapes of moss and buried layers of fallen and standing cedars, but I had to keep up with Gay.

In my thumping backpack were canisters housing twelve mice. The mice would be dead by midafternoon, their spines torn from their bodies, their skulls cracked open. Every piece of them would be eaten by the owls. Behind me was Dr. D. Erran Seaman, wildlife ecologist and head of the park's Spotted Owl Project. We stopped for a brief lunch, sharing homemade bread and cookies. In that time, between bites, I got a look into the forest. It was made of ghost shapes — trees grown from upturned roots, grown out of fallen timber suspended off the ground by other logs, grown out of contours beneath the moss where trees toppled long ago. There was, in fact, no earth under our feet. It was a matrix of dead trees. It was more time than it was matter.

As quickly as we stopped we were in motion again. From the darkness came the complex organ-grinder music of winter wrens. They darted away, chattering as they fanned through the trees. They were tiny birds for all of their sound. Erran believes that the winter wren has the largest ratio of voice volume to body size of any bird. The high-pitched whistle of a varied thrush daggered through the forest ahead of us.

We kept on task. Four miles, and the forest hung across the mountainside like a tangled fishing net. Hemlock, silver fir, western red cedar, a thicket of salal underbrush, deer ferns, sword ferns, and wild ginger. Waterleaf, red huckleberry, fairy lanterns, and the Nootka rose. Flowers called elegant rein orchids grew at the bogs, "elegant" being an apt part of the name, *Habenaria elegans.* Fat, spiked leaves of devil's club, *Oplopanax horridum,* draped the floor. The canopy was one hundred twenty feet high. In some places the forest reached thirty and forty stories tall.

It was old growth, however you measure it, whatever definition you choose. It would take at least three hundred years to make a forest like this. A rare fire may come through, leveling the place, and the firs will be the first tall conifers to return. A couple of centuries later hemlocks will grow in the accumulated duff and shade of the firs. Cedars will then appear. The forests will build layers, canopies one after the next, each with its own ecology, like different rooms of a tree house stacking to the crowns of the tallest red cedars. In each bit of life here is a cunning attentiveness to detail. No envelope is empty. No streak of sunlight in the hole of a fallen tree can shake life off its back. These things do not clumsily scramble over one another for dominance. They carefully wind their ways into position, taking thimble-width ecosystems for all that they are worth.

No matter what is said, regardless of propaganda coming from any side of any issue, an old-growth forest is different. It has become a body. It has developed organs and arteries. There was no way to put together what we saw here. All we could do was move through at a brisk pace, focused on one thing only: finding the northern spotted owl.

I was invited along as a helping hand on the project, an extra set of eyes in the forest. Gay and I had once kayaked together off Dungeness Spit in the Strait of Juan de Fuca, and we had floated side by side, in thick fog, talking about the fate of the owls in the park. "I would like to see one someday," I said.

"They are out there," she said. "Just hard to find."

She is an athletic woman, sturdy and focused. It was good to move behind her, trying to keep up, with Erran close at my heels.

When I first saw Erran, we were at a community dance in Port Angeles. All I remember was him in the motion of promenades and swing-your-partners, sweat coming down his face, and I could feel the shaking of the floor as he stomped. We passed for about two seconds, whirling around each other in a bath of fiddle music.

Time altered when we left the trail. We cut off where there was a fallen silver fir of a certain diameter recorded previously in Gay's notebook, and everything changed. There was no more speed, no more urgency. We descended the steep slope, crawling over busted walls of cedars. Hand over hand, we worked into the forest.

At the base of the largest Douglas fir, its ceiling spiked with witches'-broom, we divided and walked slowly. This was a nesting tree. Gay and Erran began their calls. Hoots and low moans. They were well practiced, not sounding human at all. Off the trail they were inching through the forest, sending out these rehearsed, careful calls, hunching below branches. I stepped through the ground litter, six feet deep with shattered trunks and branches, my eyes to the canopy. Thrones of shelf fungus had grown into the tree trunks.

The spotted owl is the wizard of its race, the dark hermit living exclusively in seclusion. The bird nests in only the places half-lit and locked up, the places digesting themselves as you walk. Of 130 nests studied on the Olympic Peninsula and in western Oregon, only a quarter were found outside of old-growth stands. The messier the forest becomes, tangled with multilayered canopies, standing dead trees, live trees with broken crowns, and a profusion of microclimates, the better the chances of finding a spotted owl.

There was a return call. It came from deep below us, down the incline. Its low voice carried through the web. The owl knew that we had come.

Erran signaled, waving his hand at Gay and me, pointing down the slope. "Male," he said. I started in his direction, sliding under a bus-sized spruce that fell during the winter. Erran continued his call, and Gay remained on an overturned tree with her binoculars. The call from below drew closer, but I could see no movement. I came to Erran's side and asked him where. He pointed ahead. It was difficult to see. When the owl moved its right wing, it was there, a smudge of shadow little more than a dark knot in the tree bark. "Hand me a mouse," Erran said. We were here to see what it did with mice, which would tell us whether this pair was still a pair and whether they had juveniles or not. I dropped my pack and dug a white mouse from a can. I held it by the tail and it fumbled between my fingers, up my wrist. Erran took it and walked toward the owl. Dangling by its tail, the mouse grabbed hold of a branch. Erran stepped back.

The mouse perched at the tip of the branch, poking its nose into the air. It was all new information for this mouse, just released from a metal canister packed with sawdust and other mice. It turned and sniffed the other direction. Wings opened from the canopy. The suddenness was alarming, how out of nothing came this broad sweep of feathers. It moved without flapping, ducking between hemlock branches. Talons stretched forward. The mouse was snapped up.

The owl settled in a tree, thirty feet above our heads. "Took mouse number one," Erran whispered back to Gay. Gay scribbled in her notebook. The owl glanced once at us. It was a fearfully dark bird. Brown wings verged on black, and the head was speckled with small, brilliant white spots as if he had been brushed by snow. The eyes were corridors, holes cut through space. He observed us for a time with these eyes recessed so far into their feather dishes that all I saw was black. Then he put his weight into eating, digging his beak into the mouse's skull. He lifted with his entire body, not just his head, and held the mouse against wood with his talons. The mouse tore like fabric.

"Put one out there," Erran said, pointing ahead, not taking his eyes from the owl. I pulled out another mouse and took it to a fallen tree. I set it into a mound of club moss, and for a moment the mouse would not let loose of my fingers. I walked backward.

The owl plummeted off the fir. It came down straight like a dead body. Four feet from the prey, its wings snapped open, stalling its drop. There was no sound. I could not move. Its talons worked like a mechanical trap. The owl snagged the mouse, and I was in the way. Wings took up all of my vision. They were hung tapestries, these wings, feathers spread to play the air. The owl swerved and the left wing dipped, drawing the right wing just above my forehead. The mouse swished over my eyes, its spine severed.

There are people who want this owl dead. Before I left for this owl study, a friend in Port Angeles said I should take a gun for use when I sighted "the little bastards." In 1991 a federal moratorium had been declared on the cutting of old-growth forest, deemed critical habitat for survival of the endangered northern spotted owl. Logging jobs were lost by the hundreds, then by the thousands.

Environmentally backed researchers from the Audubon Society put the number of remaining northern spotted owls at three to four thousand pairs in North America. At the same time researchers backed by the timber industry came out with double and triple those figures. Wildlife biologists who were more involved with the straight science of the matter could only shrug at the claims. There is so much uncertainty in projecting numbers onto the spotted owl because more than half the information is made up of extrapolations and wild guesses. This bird is simply hard to find. A six-year study on the Olympic Peninsula saw a population decline of more than 5 percent. A computer simulation of spotted owl demographics, based in part on this study, reported the following year that populations were on the rise. Erran knows of sixty spotted owl pairs in the prime habitat of this expansive park. The official number, he offers, is two hundred eighty pairs, based on conjecture about the inaccessible backcountry.

The spotted owl in its political costume is nothing more than a warning light flashing in our faces. Most factions of industry and environmentalism are pointing to the same flashing light and screaming about it, forgetting that it is the machine underneath that is about to explode. The owl is merely an indicator of what is happening to everything below, everything from flying squirrels to mill workers. Overlapping layers of issues and demands and resources and jobs and lobbyists and election credibilities and emotions have turned Strix occidentalis into an inferno. None of which has a thing to do with the northern spotted owl itself.

Back in the forest, the owl had taken four mice now, clamped down and hauled them off. We sighted the female, and he delivered the fifth to her. Watching the two interact around the mouse was intriguing. They shared whines and whistles, their wings fanned toward each other so that they formed an empty room between them. The mouse was grabbed away by the female's beak. The show ended. Everything was cached or eaten on the spot, which meant that there were no juveniles to feed. It was not good news, but both Erran and Gay were hopeful because the owls were at least here.

In the previous year not a single nesting owl had been sighted in the park, which is part of a much more convoluted ecology than we understand. We are still straining to read nursery rhymes while this forest is written in Latin. With long life spans, owls do not have to tumble headlong into reproduction, creating progeny at any risk as some animals must. A pair will make decisions based on complicated environmental patterns. A quarter of most owl pairs do not even reproduce each year; a quarter more will make a late decision, refusing to incubate the eggs, thus killing the embryos. There are even cases of fledglings born but allowed to starve. Losses could be cut at any point, with investments in the nest, its eggs, or its fledglings shunted to next year.

With adult pairs having limited but well-defined territories, it may be unsafe for them to fill the space with new owls. Parents do not want to be squeezed out by descendants as forests shrink, and they don't want to compete their children to death. The Olympic Peninsula has the best recorded survival rates for spotted owls, with slightly more than 80 percent of adults surviving each year. Juvenile survival, though, ranges between 14 and 41 percent, as they fan into the forest in search of new, unoccupied territories. Radio-tagged juveniles in the area must fly up to seventy-six miles from home in order to be successful. That is seventy-six straight miles, but because the owl reaches that distance by indirect searches, it more accurately adds up to several hundred.

The conclusion about the previous year's absence of nesting owls in the park was that they had gone solo, or at least had vanished into the deeper recesses of the park. Even with federal funding and intense backcountry investigations, the environmental differences between last year and this year were not conspicuous enough to record. A message that we cannot decipher was spread among the owls.

The species is designed to such a sharp edge that only a certain forest in a particular prime will do the job. That is why the spotted owl exists in the first place, to live here and nowhere else. It is one of the incomparable organisms that forms in a beam of sunlight from a fallen tree.

Barred owls have been moving into the neighborhood, following a path of forest disturbances from the north. The barred owl is a generalist, bigger and more aggressive than the spotted owl. It is of the same genus and eats about the same prey, but it is quicker to take advantage of shifting environments. Spotted owls have predominant tastes, specializing in flying squirrels, snowshoe hares, wood rats, voles, and mice. But barred owls will jump the gun. They will more readily eat beetles. Nesting sites for spotted owls have occasionally been overrun with barred owls.

A paleontologist once wrote that extinctions are "blind to the exquisite adaptations evolved for previous environments." The barred owl will move in because the spotted owl belongs to a forest that may soon no longer exist. The smallest, most explicit niches will always be occupied by some form of life, and even the most advanced species are often the first to go extinct. The last time species met extinction at the current rate was when, it appears, an asteroid collided with the earth and exterminated the dinosaurs. Survivors of mass extinctions are usually either primitive organisms or ecological generalists with broad habitat ranges. Or just plain lucky. An animal such as the spotted owl is designed for a small and particular niche, and when the place is gone, when the intricate, embedded layers of this ecosystem have been flushed out, the animal will die. We are now experiencing the earth's sixth major extinction, the loss of species ramping up year by year. Of those still alive, populations are decreasing rapidly. Butterflies in Great Britain have lost 70 percent of their numbers in the past twenty years, and along with them, birds have decreased by 50 percent, and plants by 28 percent. Every continent is experiencing unprecedented loss. There is no way of knowing how many species are missing altogether.

The earth will, of course, fill up behind us. A thousand unexpected species will appear as suddenly as weeds in a lot. You would have to split this planet into pieces to rid it of life. The pieces would need to be melted, vaporized. The rapacious advance of organisms and evolution will not slow at the removal of a Northwest rain forest. But part of the memory may be erased here. The complex genetic pieces, whose value and purpose we could not come close to understanding, would be nullified.

We left this site with the male following, diving between trees for a seventh mouse that we never offered. The only thing that I could figure was that the spotted owl had seen so few people and so few large predators that it had little protective fear. It kept on us until we reached the trail, and then returned to seclusion. The pace again lifted. Gay led several miles farther. It began to rain.

The canopy dissolved into the liquid gray of the sky, trees staggering up and losing themselves. Gay said rain in Olympic National Park comes in units of small, medium, and large. Easier for recording in the notebook. Clouds rooted themselves into the forest. There was a waterfall to cross. The trail became a clutter of mud and soaked, spongy logs. We crawled under trees fallen over the path, and through mudslopped octopus roots from a tumbled stump. Gay could not remember the location of the second nesting site, so we marched back and forth, looking for an oversized Douglas fir down the mountain. The owls prefer the Douglas firs, with their mistletoe crags and wickedly deformed limbs. It is the ideal tree for the nest of this reclusive creature.

Gay stopped, her neck craned. "It's here," she said. Erran and I looked straight up, and fifty feet above was the dark outline of a spotted owl halfway into the clouds. I stepped by Gay and whispered, "How did you see that?" She did not answer, tipping her head far back.

This was the male. The female was somewhere below, and although we heard her calling repeatedly, after an hour of hunting we still could not find her. This male did not take our mouse. He glided between trees, his voice growing irritated. I had to run out and grab the mouse back because he wouldn't dive for it. He watched. His head moved as if it had the fluid suspension of a gyroscope.

The female finally came. I posed the mouse on a broken branch and stood behind a tree, extending the branch from my arms. The wings opened. I tried so hard to watch, to witness everything, but when it happened there was too much to see. The wings made a show in themselves, startling how so much space could be unfolded from this compact body. And the talons spread. Four feet from my fingers, it hit the prey. There was no weight to the attack. There was nothing more than a tremble, the mouse's toes unpinning from the bark.

It happened again, the female coming around. I kept up with the branch, leaning these curious pink-eyed victims into certain death. Each time, I wanted to see everything, but all I got was wings and power. It was over in two seconds.

The owl came on silent wings, and the only thing to hear was the abrupt cry of the mouse and, later, the cracking of its skull. Owl wings are studded for absolute quiet. The leading edge of the primary feathers, which are the first to cut the air in flight, are made of softened, curved barbs bending to the wind. In one respect, this quiet allows the owl to drop without alerting its prey. In another, it limits the noise of rushing air so that its most notable sense, that of hearing, is not distracted. A barn owl was once placed in a completely darkened room and mice were ushered inside. Going on sound alone, the owl was accurate to forty hits for every one miss. The mice did not stand a chance.

The owl's hearing is not unusually strong; in fact its ears gather nearly the same sound levels as human ears. The difference comes in design. The eyes are embedded in facial disks of feathers that can be altered to change shape, deflecting sound toward the ears from various angles. The ears are positioned fifteen degrees off from each other, so slight differences in timing of sound hitting one ear, then hitting the other, register the location of the mouse. Internally, the ears are designed to read slightly different frequencies to deepen the owl's sense of three-dimensional hearing.

The owl's soft feathers do sacrifice a degree of flight performance in favor of silence. It would follow that if any owl species did not require this adaptation, it would discard these soft feathers, replacing them with more accurate feathers that rattle in the wind. In the case of the fishing owl, depending on anything but sound to locate prey, the feathers are rigid and relatively loud.

I was out of mice. The female had taken each of them and was waiting on a perch over my head. They had all been cached or eaten. We doubted that there were juveniles at this nest. The intricacies had again baffled us. Gay took notes from the trail. Erran kept his binoculars on the male. I stared at the female and she stared back. This owl had no idea what we were doing here, what was at stake. I tried to think of the owl not as a political image, or as the trailing end of her species, but simply as a bird of prey in a wet, dark forest. This owl would rip the life from an animal in less than half a second.

Gay was of course fast as we left. I was in the back, tramping through mud. Clouds shook down in the timber. There was a lace of mist. I stopped once. There was a sound from behind. The owl called. Another responded. I glanced through the woods. It was like looking into the bird's own wings just before the kill; dark patterns set one behind the next. Too much out there. I listened. The owl called again, a heavy voice shadowing between trees. They were still alive, that was all I knew about them.

Strix occidentalis

BROAD-TAILED HUMMINGBIRD

Quiet dreams are sunk into the pillows. The soft end of a quilt is bunched between my clutched fingers and my cheek. In these dreams I know that the sun is up. The tipi is absorbing light, spreading it through the canvas, then immersing the interior. But my knowledge of it is distant, like hearing my mother calling from very far away as I turn to keep playing.

There is a breeze on my face, as if someone is blowing on my eyelids. I barely let go of the dreams and open my eyes like carefully peeling the shell off an Easter egg.

A hummingbird is floating just above my nose. I am not breathing. I know not to move, even though the dream and the hummingbird have yet to separate. Seventy wing beats per second send a draft across my lips. With serious, black points for eyes, it studies me.

It is a broad-tailed hummingbird, a male with a throat the color of fresh raspberries, its back iridescent green like a metallic scarab.

The bird is barely the length of my shortest finger. Its curled feet could land squarely on a match head.

It flits away so quickly I see only where it ends up. The red wooden handle on the kettle. Then the red knobs on the antique cabinet. Red is the color hummingbirds go weak over. It hovers, investigating the red in the oil lamp. Its needle bill points long and thin to slip into the sticky recesses of a flower. It finds no nectar at the lamp, then suddenly appears elsewhere. A pile of red yarn.

It rises, making rounds through the elliptical shape of the tipi. Its levitating circles grow tighter near the top, where the lodgepoles come together. It then shoots out through the open smoke flaps. I can hear the fading whistle of it racing into the forest. That is when I breathe again and let go of the dreams altogether, slipping into morning.

Selasphorus platycercus

RAVEN

When the first raven came it was alone, a piece of blackness laboring across a cold dawn sky. I too was alone, walking on an early-winter morning in southeast Utah, crossing a hard desert basin studded with towers of eroded rock. Three companions of mine were somewhere within a several mile radius, but we had split up with the fading stars, not planning to find one another back at camp until nightfall. With nothing else but Jurassic sandstone to look at, the raven and I took an immediate interest in each other. The coal-colored bird turned its head midair, its powerful beak pointing at me like a librarian's finger. I stopped and watched.

It was a big bird, a sorcerer wearing sleek black robes, its two talons tucked against its body as if each grasped a marble. It altered its path slightly, making a jog around me, wings laid out as it banked twenty feet off the ground. It obviously wondered what I was, and what I was doing here, one eye tagging me as it circled. It was close enough that I saw clearly into that one dark eye, the one that observed me with incredulous focus, as if to say *You again*. Had we met before, glanced at each other between buttes, passed each other a week or two ago elsewhere in the desert? But ravens, they all look alike. You cannot even sex them without elaborate manual procedures. They stay hidden in their cloaks, notoriously intelligent birds, a shrewdness I could sense in this bird's stare. The raven swept close.

"Good morning," I called.

Startled, the bird flustered away from me. Its wings beat loudly as it let out a cough of a sound, a surprised *quork*.

The raven resumed its course. I watched it fly, projecting its path into an empty bay of cliffs half a mile away. I wondered what it was up to this morning. I recognize myself in ravens. The way they timidly approach unfamiliar carcasses, ready to fly at any second—a tug with the beak and a quick leap backward—is something I personally know. When I have seen their wild, screeching attacks on falcons or owls that could easily disembowel them, I have gotten behind them, up on my feet, boxing their enemies out of the air. Their unbridled orations, calling from cliff top to cliff top, are not unfamiliar to me. Down to their every gesture, ravens are rich with character, more so than most people. Their sentiments are not disguised. They are theatrical birds. Even quietly perched on a church roof or under the arm of a bridge, ravens are obviously brooding, grumbling among one another, plotting the end of the world.

This lone raven had plans this morning, oaring its wings through air cold from the night before. It had a destination. Perhaps there was an animal carcass to attend to, some dead, gristly heap of a half-frozen corpse belonging to a mule deer or bighorn. It was early in the day, even for a raven. Usually they are not up until sunrise, when they can glide above warming, south-facing cliffs, flying in pairs that seem comfortable together, old family friends, mates.

The raven kept a straight course across the basin, passing rock towers that stood like chimneys of houses burned down long ago.

There was nothing ahead for a raven that I could see, just vacant rock faces with no exit. I thought that it better start working to get some altitude, otherwise it would smack into a cliff. But the raven kept on, and without hesitation or even slowing its wing beats, it flew straight into a blank cliff. It vanished. I frowned, not sure of what I had just seen. I looked at the cliff the way you might tilt your head at a magician's trick. The bird seemed to have turned to solid stone.

I am always prepared for the impossible from ravens. Animals of omens and nevermores, they rule the desert, able to reach every crack and ledge while I am restricted to the ground as if wearing chains.

Of all bird species, *Corvus corax*, the raven, is considered the most ingenious. In one experiment with ravens it was soundly demonstrated that they have the ability to follow another's gaze — e.g., you glance at a peanut with interest, and a raven turns to see what you're looking at. This is a skill documented among only the smartest animals, especially those with tight social networks like wolves and primates.

Ravens are the largest of the corvids, a group of birds whose behavior tops the avian IQ test. The test is based on the number of novel feeding behaviors any bird species exhibits, derived from two thousand observations in the wild published over seventy-five years. Corvids — magpies, crows, jays, and ravens — employ more adaptations and innovations than any other bird. Ravens pull up baited fishing lines by stepping on the line, reeling in slack with their beaks, stepping on the line again, and finally pulling in the fish. They poke sticks into bug holes, bend wire to hook meat from between cracks, unzip backpacks, and open ice chests.

Interacting in hierarchical, packlike fashion, ravens are known to cooperate with wolves. They circle injured or weak animals, alerting wolves to the presence of prey. In turn, wolves tear open carcasses and leave bones to be picked. Ravens also capture their own small prey, clubbing mice with rocks or sticks, snatching up snakes and dropping them out of the sky, or pecking smaller birds into lumps of feathers and blood.

But do they fly through stone? Staring at the place where the raven had been, I stood still, mystified. I admit that for a second I thought it had truly transmogrified before my eyes. As I looked closer, though, I began to see the raven's hoax. A thin shadow line appeared near the bottom of the cliff among skirts of fallen boulders. The shadow was a canyon mouth, a narrow crack opening into bedrock, narrowest canyon I'd seen for miles. Ravens know every turn in this confounding country, arches and canyons, every trick of stone. This one had slipped through a back door.

Having nothing better to do this morning, I decided to follow. I walked across sand washes and brittle earth, and the canyon opened wider before me. I heard something to my back. I turned and spotted three more ravens as they dropped over a nearby cliff edge. They were effusive, chatting with one another in guttural voices as they passed into the basin's airspace. Two nearly touched wing tips, and the third lagged about twenty yards behind. As soon as they saw me, they went silent. What was I doing here? Staring at me as they passed, they vanished between overlapping cliff walls ahead of me, heading wherever the first raven had gone.

I follow ravens out here, almost out of habit. They lead me from place to place, vanishing in this Byzantine terrain, unknown cloak-and-dagger affairs taking them around a thousand corners. I see ten or fifteen ravens flying to the same point on the horizon, and I have only imagined what they are doing when they get there, these smart, scavenging birds, pickpockets and tricksters. Theirs, I imagine, is a secret union, a lost tribe of ravens hidden from the eyes of men.

The canyon turned out to be much larger than I had thought, its bookended walls rising three or four hundred feet. I walked inside, following a slim dry wash at the bottom. I began to shrink, my sense of scale recalibrated by fallen boulders as big as buildings. The passage skinnied down to a narrow space where yet another raven shot over my head, startled to see me, wings beating to get past. It swerved around a turn, out of sight.

The sky became small, canyon-tightened. I thought that soon I would come upon a handful of ravens picking apart a fallen bighorn sheep or some other piece of death the desert left out for them. I lightened my step so they would not hear me. But they did hear me. They knew I was coming, and they all stared down the canyon so that when I walked into view, I stopped in my tracks. Ravens were everywhere, a parliament of them convened on both canyon walls, shoulders drawn, wings pulled against their bodies. They were large-bodied birds, each silent, each perched on a ledge or boulder tip. No one moved, even to ruffle feathers. Speechless, I began counting, and stopped at fifteen, leaving most uncounted. It was a crowd. A mob.

Each kind of bird has a name for its gathering. Geese have "gaggles," seagulls "flocks." Ravens come in "unkindnesses." Until now I did not fully understand the meaning of the term. I swear they were scowling at me.

There is a folk poem that goes: *To see one raven is lucky, 'tis true, but it's certain misfortune to light upon two, and meeting with three is the devil.* In that case, what exactly was I looking at here?

After a minute of all of us doing nothing, I began moving toward the ravens, but very slowly. The nearest birds seemed to become agitated. A few hopped onto their toes and petulantly flexed their wings, which opened like huge hands, feathers spread like fingers. They grumbled and cawed, their tones crass, brought up from deep in their throats. I thought I could not possibly be a threat to them, so high upon their ledges. Why were they getting upset? But I knew why. I did not belong among them.

Voices turned rough and vulgar. They were talking, making some kind of announcement. I listened for words, any hint of familiarity, but all I heard was a darkening dome of sound closing over my head.

They began diving from perches, opening their deep black wings to catch the air. My pace faltered. Voices became riotous, even more demanding as ravens crossed the canyon back and forth, landing on the opposite side only to launch back into the air straight above me.

Soon I was dizzied by their cacophony, the air filled with wheeling ravens.

Ravens are mobbers. They frequently gang up on invaders, generally the likes of hawks, eagles, or owls, pecking the back of the head, getting in their faces and screaming. They even attack one another if a particular raven, or a minority of ravens, gets out of line. They are skilled at delivering torment, combining sound, motion, and direct attack with open talons from all angles to drive out or at least befuddle a trespasser. These displays lie within the context of sophisticated territorial boundaries ravens adhere to. The boundaries are layered between individual ravens, pairs, families, regional gatherings, and associated raven groups living nearby. They have hierarchies, tiers of organization: families, unions, gangs, and enemies. I was bumbling right into the middle of their assembly.

"Listen to us!" cried the ravens.

"I don't speak your language," I called out, exasperated.

Hearing my voice, the ravens became only more infuriated. I was disoriented, watching them dive around me, and I could barely stand. Flashes of sky showed through ragged wings. I stumbled and found myself on my knees in the sand.

"Listen to us!" they kept crying. "This is not your place!"

At least that is what I thought they were saying. What else was I to think? I felt something the size and weight of a pebble hit my back. I looked behind me. Another raven flew in, and with a quick motion, transferring a pebble from its talon to its beak, it let a small projectile fly into the air. The pebble barely missed me, leaving a dimple in the sand near my knee.

I stared up, astonished. I'd seen this before, a raven pelting me when I came too close to its nest. But there was no nest here, at least not one guarded by so many individuals. Something else was being protected in this canyon.

The only thing I saw out of place was a stone in the middle of the wash. It was the size of a human hand, and something about its placement seemed peculiar, as if it had been recently set down, not yet embedded into the sand around it. Under it was a feather. That was all that caught my eye, not enough to sway my attention away from the ravens. I stood and slowly backed away. It was nothing like fearing for my life. I did not even think about having to fight off these ravens bare-handed. Such an image was too ludicrous: me flailing bloody hands against them, picking up rocks and pegging ravens out of the air to save myself. That was not going to happen, I was pretty sure. But what did I know about the secret lives of ravens?

I kept backing away, and the ravens calmed a bit. Some returned to their places, voices simmering, until there was only light protest from under their breath. Others spiraled upward, rising like a swirl of black wind between the cliffs. Those who stayed groused their wings and neck feathers. They looked like judges settling into their chairs, eyes grave, heads turned toward me, waiting for my imminent departure.

I turned and walked out of the canyon through eroded stone gates, my face blank with confusion.

———

I was here with three other men. They were nowhere to be seen. We had been walking for twenty-some days together, and this morning we had scattered, looking for routes. I had to find them before nightfall. I needed to bring them back to this canyon and show them this spectacle, the place we had all imagined, a sanctuary of ravens.

It took about five hours to collect my companions. They looked like mad desert folk, bearded men wearing heavily abraded gear and clothing. Tidy as you might be, you cannot help appearing this way after enough time traveling in rock piles. I told them what had happened. There was no need for a protracted discussion. For those of us who travel in this desolate terrain, ravens have become gods. An observation like this is a breakthrough, a glimpse into a social animal world otherwise kept invisible from us. November sunlight slanted between rock towers, inclining toward evening, as we walked quickly to the canyon.

One man led the way, following my earlier tracks. He was a raven talker, meaning that over time in the wilderness he had acquired the skill of talking to ravens by using their own vocal styles. Not to suggest he understands them, or they understand him; I have seen him carry on fifteen-minute dialogues with ravens, imitating them, cawing back and forth. As I watched these interactions, it became clear to me that ravens have almost nothing to do with us. They live in their own raven-centered world, and come to speak around us only if we have food, or if we trick them into thinking we indeed have something to do with them.

The raven talker was the most curious of us. He got well ahead, disappearing into the canyon through boulders as tall as cliffs. When we came around a bend behind him, we found him standing still. Ravens were watching him. Exactly where I had left them, the ravens lifted their heads to see the rest of us. They glanced at one another with ticking motions, obviously concerned to see so many people in a place where they had rarely before seen a human.

The raven talker said, in English, "Very strange."

Looking up at the ravens, I wondered whether they recognized me. Among their numerous uncanny talents, ravens can pick out and remember individual human beings, knowing them even by facial features. A corvid researcher banding young birds in their nests on the MIT campus noted that he was frequently picked out from the campus crowd and was followed and even attacked. The ravens in this canyon had to know it was me, the one they had dealt with earlier, and this time I was back with reinforcements.

We continued into the canyon, and the ravens again unfolded their wings and began calling. They were more reserved this time, threatened by our numbers. Still, some stepped from their perches and swung through the air, flying from one wall of the canyon to the other. Irritated, gravelly voices called down at us. One picked up a pebble and, with its beak, tossed it in our direction.

Never had any of my companions, even the raven talker, seen such an unkindness. Their dirty faces tilted up, mouths hung open. We had found the secret place where ravens go, a party we were not welcome to attend.

The talker began snooping around. "Something happened here," he said. "The ravens are protecting this place."

I showed him the stone I had noticed earlier, the one capping a feather on the ground. He knelt at it, and we stood around him. He lifted off the stone beneath a siege of protesting ravens, and he picked up the feather. It was not a raven feather.

"Owl," he said.

It must have been caught in a rockfall or been brought by a small flood, the only way it would be deposited under a stone. But the feather turning between his fingers was clean. He looked up at the ravens, puzzled, and then looked back at the feather.

"They put it here," he said. "They stuck it under this rock. That's why they're here."

We scattered and began looking around, and quickly came upon more owl feathers that had been stuck in rock cracks and laid one atop the next on boulders. We called them out as we found them, five owl feathers, ten, fifteen. Not one was out of place, each carefully positioned. Those the wind might disturb had been put under rocks. Some had been furiously pecked apart, their quills turned to pulp. Some stuck out of the cliff high overhead, where they had been poked into crevices. This was not an owl losing some of its feathers. This was an owl losing everything.

I climbed to a ledge and found what looked like an altar, a stack of feathers, their quills shredded by raven pecks. I picked one up, and the ravens became incensed, driven mad around me. I looked up at them and said, as if accusing them, "What have you done?"

Ravens had mobbed and killed an owl. That much was clear. Ravens will naturally mob an owl. They do this because owls are raven killers. Ravens beat down the doors of their mortal enemies, and this time they managed to kill one, cornered it in this canyon, where they tore it apart. Then, like hanging victory flags, they cached its feathers all around.

This was speculation, of course, detective work. This mobbing-and-killing explanation made sense, but the feather-caching? I knew ravens cached their food, and sometimes did so in surprisingly methodical ways, but this was not food. There was no functional necessity I could see in this deed. It is believed that among corvids, caching behavior has actually led to larger brains. In order to keep track of where many items have been placed, parts of the brain—namely the hippocampus, which is directed toward spatial memory—have evolved to become larger than those of birds that do not cache their food.

Murder is known among ravens, meaning they sometimes kill without eating. This killing is often done within a social context. The esteemed and most eloquent raven biologist Bernd Heinrich has reported ravens killing their own kind, an act that Heinrich believes to be a form of social justice. In one case he documented four related ravens attacking and killing a lone stranger that was trying to eat their food. Even when the stranger prostrated herself and made gestures of subservience, perfectly willing to wait her turn at a site of ample food, the others did not relent. They killed her and pecked out her eyes. Ravens have rules and stigmas that maintain community order, and violating these rules results in reprimands, banishment, attack, or death. Heinrich wrote, "The extreme case, the murder, was thus a social—and hence moral—act."

Perhaps this is what we found in a remote, nameless canyon: the commemoration of a moral act. An owl had been defeated by a coalition of ravens. It was a long time coming. How they dreamed of the dreaded owl, at last torn apart by their black beaks. They enshrined the dead owl's feathers, and gathered, perhaps every morning, to remember what had been done.

With a clutch of owl feathers in my hand, I noticed my friend, the raven talker, deep in conversation on the canyon floor. He was throwing a volley of sounds at a single raven, who came back at him with equal vigor. The raven strutted, knocked back its wings, and flushed its throat feathers, and my friend did much the same. For a good half hour, the two kept up their animated display, my friend posturing on the ground, the raven perched upon a pulpit of rock above him. Enough was enough, though. This was their place, their kill. We had no right to it. We were strangers, and we had interrupted their ceremony with our presumptions and amazement. We replaced all the owl feathers and slowly backed away, allowing the ravens to settle. One by one, they flew to their perches and straightened their feathers, hunching their shoulders back into place.

That night we sat in the dark, no fire to light our camp, only a bath of stars. Stoves set aside, we ate dinner from battered metal pots and discussed what we had seen. For years we had wondered what ravens did behind the curtains, and now we knew. But did we really know? We agreed that ravens living in this desert probably formed long-lasting alliances. The same families may have been here for centuries, if not thousands of years. Knowing their tendency to have regional variations in behavior and vocalizations, we thought that these groups were probably insulated out here, becoming clans of a sort, each belonging to its own part of the land. Why not imagine that they had made covens of themselves, secret societies gathered inside lost canyons? Ravens, after all, can remember detailed events from certain locations. Researchers have noticed that when something catastrophic occurs in a nesting area, those ravens do not come back the next season. When a power line is cleaned of nests, the ravens will not return, even if they have been profitably nesting there for generations, as if the place fell under taboo. Most birds come back no matter how many nests they lose within the space of several generations. Consider woodpeckers dauntlessly returning to plugged holes, and swallows rebuilding nests knocked down season after season. Ravens know better. They have memory, history.

Questions arose between us. What did we truly know of this animal? What we had witnessed in the canyon could have been a hallowed death ceremony as much as it could have been a gang incident, Bloods driven to a frenzy over the corpse of a Crip. Or none of the above, an assembly beyond our imagination, something excruciatingly simple, bogglingly complex. We had only metaphors to work with.

Anthropomorphism is generally frowned upon. It is said to be improper to see animals the same way we view ourselves. We are asked to temper our language when speaking of animal traits, lest we call them by a name that is not theirs, forming words in our mouths that do not sound like a snake's whisper, a grasshopper's clicking. It seems just as odd, though, to sequester ourselves in a cheerless vault of sentience, sole proprietors of smarts and charm. Bees form a mind of a hive, don't they? Doesn't the bear dream when it sleeps, and don't grasses stretch with all their might toward the sun? Every living thing has the same wish to flourish again and again. Beyond that, our differences are quibbles.

I do not want to be a lonely species set adrift from all the rest. I want the ravens that we saw to have been performing a ritual, animals of sensibility. I envision a righteous murder performed by birds living in a moral universe. I yearn for them to have societies, secret handshakes and knocks, associations and enterprises. With our dinner pans laid down on smooth bedrock, my companions and I talked back and forth, and I wondered if the ravens were doing the same, somewhere, while bright and countless eyes of stars looked coldly down on us all.

Corvus corax

GREAT HORNED OWL

This was the full moon of high winter. It came when the season was at its deepest, in February, when the razor-blade cold of January ran into the hay-bale snows of March. Each full moon brings a different season to my tipi. Thirteen seasons a year. Seasons that have no names other than that of their moon. The November moon of the first strong snows. The August moon of hot days and thunderstorm nights. The May moon of mud and the last big snow. High winter, the February moon, was when you first wished winter would end and when you first knew that it would not.

In a blizzard, the full moon of high winter atomized through layers of wind and snow. It was a rumor, a ghost, a tease of moonlight that came when the big rags of clouds swept by and there was a thin place worn through the storm. The wind did not move in one direction. It was a madhouse wind. To ski through it, I had to lean.

When it shifted in the dark, when it thought otherwise and turned on itself, I nearly fell over.

I skied the meadow route to get home to the tipi. Snow piled up my shins. It was fresh snow, fallen only moments ago when the wind pushed it from one drift to the next. The ground was a canvas of blowing snow. Snowdrifts migrated back and forth across one another. I could not see the tips of my skis when they emerged. I could barely see my legs. Then it cleared and the moonlight was a wave, only seconds long. It ran across the white ground in a band, overtaking me, then moving beyond me. I made a rhythm, swinging ahead with the poles, planting, left leg up, then right leg.

I had been at the ski town of Telluride that night, dancing until closing at the Fly Me to the Moon Saloon. The lead singer for the band wore only jeans, and a pair of large plastic sunflowers to cover her breasts. For the entire second set the bass player performed lying on his back with his eyes closed. In the dance floor confusion a woman I knew only casually from the town of Ridgway either kissed my ear with great vigor or was knocked into me while trying to say something, and I was left here skiing, wondering which it was.

She had worn a flowered dress. She had blond hair and a very attractive face. I was trying to remember the chain of events and at the same time wondering how I could have been propelled out of a packed bar an hour from here, three-dollar cover, into a blizzard where I was now entirely alone. I stopped to adjust, reaching back to tighten a strap on my pack, clumsy fingers in mittens hunting a piece of webbing. Then I heard an owl. It was a great horned owl, and I cupped my ears to keep the wind out.

Its voice was like wood, like a heavy, well-polished oak. Three notes, the last descending. Then the long wait before it called again. Ten seconds usually for great horned owls. Sometimes fifteen. Even more rarely, twenty seconds before the next call. I waited for it, and when I heard it I cocked my head and listened through the wind.

This was the time of year that great horned owls mated and this was when they were most often heard. A rather bleak and difficult time for mating. Even in storms, the owls press on as if they are elevated beyond such conditions, which they may well be. I have heard the call on calm nights, often within hours of sunrise or sunset. It has always seemed abstract, as if it could be anywhere, emanating from all corners. This owl was somewhere toward the forest, maybe in the grove that stood alone in the meadow. Maybe on the snag tree that had grown a length of homestead barbed wire into its side. Maybe just at the forest's edge, where it could, on better nights, listen into the meadow for the footsteps of mice.

For owls, winter hunting is far less profitable than summer hunting. When conditions are finally favorable between blizzards, owls cache as many prey animals as possible, stuffing small bodies into tree knots and holes or in exposed litter on the ground. The prey animals then freeze and are left cached until needed. The problem is that a dead bird or squirrel at ten degrees below zero is too stiff for a talon or beak to cut and too large for the gullet to swallow. Try fitting a loaf of frozen bread down your own throat. The response of the great horned owl is to sit on the meat, to thaw it. A great horned owl has been seen huddled over the icy carcass of a red fox, its feathers puffed to focus body heat.

On nights like this, in a storm like this, a dead mouse will freeze within minutes, able to be snapped in half. The same for skin exposed directly to the storm. Blizzard nights are not as empirically cold as clear nights, but once the air gets into motion, the windchill can reach eighty below zero. The snow this time came from the north and then the south. It came with gusts working like fingers mending a basket.

West, south, west, south. Industrious wind, intent on getting somewhere.

North, west, east, north.

It moiled into the weave of my clothes, through my hat. I put my weight against it and it threw me. I stopped again and listened to the great horned owl. The voice was so calm I could sleep to it. Omen of death: sleep in the snow on a night like this, and you will die. Owl lore dates back thousands of years. The owl hoots and someone will die and you just hope that you are not the only one who heard it. The Egyptians said it, along with East Indians and most cultures of the Americas. Keep your children close when you hear the owl. Cross yourself.

I thought of death, now that I was listening to its voice. I thought of the harbinger, and tamped down my hat and continued skiing. The owl voice had gone to my side, and I figured the bird must be at the edge of the forest.

The full moon was deceptive. It was like a candle shown through a heap of wool blankets. It was almost enough to make me believe that there was light. With the roving snow, I could not see a thing. Ahead would be a forest. It was a firm wall of ponderosa pines, and I thought for a moment that I had swung wide and missed it. I kept skiing forward until I saw the first tree, four feet away. Sagging branches hit my shoulders, and I turned to follow the tree line. There was a false entrance. I had to remember this. It was an opening that looked like the right one and it led southwest. It had tricked me before. If I skied southwest I would cross nothing but mountains for sixty miles. I stopped and ran my hands through the air, feeling for the trees. Maybe I had passed the false entrance already. This could have been the correct turn. The more I touched and squinted and brushed snow from my hat, the more I believed that I was in the right place. I listened for the owl's voice. Ten seconds. Fifteen. Then it called. Sad, simple, deep. I turned and skied into the forest.

A year ago this month a man I knew only by name was lost on his way home, not far south of here. Friends dropped him off at the end of the plowed road where he began his walk. They say he had been drinking. Tracks in the morning showed a confident forward motion, a few stops and turns, then an increased gait. Within half a mile, his tracks were far from his home and they began a panic circle, tracing the edges of forests. At a certain point his situation must have become obvious. The patterns became pragmatic. He was making a grid. He was trying to find his way back. Glove prints were put down as he pushed his way through the snow. When his grid failed, turning sloppy, he pushed toward a creek and dug a hole in the soft, deep snow that had gathered out from the trees. The shelter was well constructed. Its entrance was dipped low from the room, then up to the surface so that insulated air would not fall prey to wind. It was a snow cave built by an experienced man, just large enough for his body, not so big that it failed to insulate.

That was where he was found in the morning. He was frozen dead. Too much time had been lost in the panic and the grid-walk. He had only the strength to dig a hole and die in it. Each year it happens, someone heading to a remote cabin is taken in the night. Sometimes tracks are left to be read, other times the person is not found until spring.

Blizzard stories.

"He was ten feet from his door and he froze to death, his hand reaching out like he was still alive," they said about someone a couple of years back, and I didn't know if it was true or not and I didn't know if it mattered. A car slid from the road, a Buick. Eventually it ran out of the gas that was keeping the heater going. Husband and wife and one young daughter dead. Their dog survived. No one had died yet this year. I yanked my mitten away and used bare fingers to scratch the ice off my hat and ears. I had not come through the small oak grove that hangs so low I have to duck. That was my marker, and now it was not here. The entrance was false. I had gone southwest. I was lost.

I pulled a corner of my hat to listen, and I waited. There was no owl. Not for twenty seconds. Not for a minute. I remembered the woman with the flowered dress and was now remembering that her arm had gone around my waist. I could feel her fingers. I was asking myself why I said nothing in return and why I was lost in the forest only an hour and a half later. I turned to find my tracks, and they were buried in fresh snow. I came to my knees, allowing one ski to drift back, and felt for the loose snow. It was all loose. I cursed and skied forward, the direction I thought would take me to the owl. The powder snow became deep. It came to my calves and then to my knees. It formed deep wells around tree trunks. I turned again, ninety degrees, and ponderosa boughs raked my head, spilling loaves of snow down my neck. Ninety degrees again. I waited for the owl. It was not there. A few minutes ago we were the only two animals out tonight. It had been enough to stifle the loneliness of the storm. Now I was the only one anywhere, beating my way alone through the snow.

I was far into the forest, so the wind was not as strong. Pillars of trees fell back on themselves. Layers of dark shapes in snow. I did not know which way to go. I stood limp. Ski poles hung from my hands by leather straps. I bit the corner of my lip.

I was not going to die tonight. In my pack was the avalanche shovel I used to either dig out the tipi door or dig out the truck. It could build a good shelter. But I would not need it. I was well dressed. The night was not bitterly cold if I avoided the wind. I could ski until I found the tipi. I was no good at building snow caves, but that did not matter tonight. If I needed to, I would pick a tree and ski circles around it until sunrise, keeping my blood moving, keeping warm. At the most it would be a very uncomfortable night, toes maybe lost to frostbite.

I was thinking of death again, though. A friend with whom I guide on the Colorado River had several encounters with great horned owls. Then, on a ski trip he was guiding, a ninth-grade girl plunged to her death. She died instantly. He stayed with her, trying to revive her until the helicopter came. Even months later, people cried, people who had not even been there. There were hushed words, spoken only in small groups, about the owls he had seen. About the great horned owl that perched on his tent one night. But it was only a story. We all see owls.

I skied a grid pattern, coming back on myself, and my tracks were gone. The snow built against me. It grew on me, trying to change my shape, trying to make my body soft and long like a snowdrift. The moonlight became frustrating.

On a backward sweep I heard the owl. It came like a foghorn. I pivoted off the sound, skiing fifteen seconds and stopping. Its voice was the patron saint of the terminally lost, telling me where the forest edge was and how far I had to go to clear the false entrance. Soon it was louder, and I tried to remember which tree was there: the tallest one where the hawks roost in the summer, or one of the old, flat-topped ponderosas that had stopped growing upward and now only grew out. Against the grumble of the blizzard, the owl call was perfect. It was so clean that it was stronger than the storm itself.

With the million and a half disparities between the owl and myself, it was good to have some grounds of similarity, the grounds of being out in a snowstorm together. The most compelling difference between us may be that the owl does not deal in notions, only in certainties; that I am able to question my very intentions and the owl is not. Go into a forest one night and listen for this austere voice emanating from every point at once; you will understand this. I could assume a great deal about the owl, the nearly three-hundred-degree range of its head movements, the fact that it could see eighty to one hundred times better at night than I, and what the animal might mean in symbols. At the same moment, the owl knows without doubt how soon winter will end, how to respond to subtle air-pressure discrepancies between the front and back of a wing in flight, and where exactly a rodent is nudging through the snow in absolute darkness. To know something rationally and to know something down to the root of each of your cells, these are different things.

With its call, I found my way to the meadow. I turned along the forest line and skied ahead. The next turn was familiar. The owl was behind me, and I cut back to the trees, hunching through the low oaks. Across a few openings and to the tipi, not visible until I was right on it. I pulled the shovel from my pack and cleared the doorway.

I planted my skis to the left of the door and groped into the snow with mittens to find firewood. Then through the door, into the dark tipi. I spilled wood into the corner where canvas reached the ground, and

I brushed snow off my legs with a whisk broom. I found matches and lifted the glass globe away from an oil lamp. When I sealed the globe down, the flame magnified. The tipi filled with shadows, and my breath drifted like smoke. I had tracked snow across the floor, so I swept it out. Listening for the owl, I could hear only snow and wind climbing the canvas. I lit a fire in the woodstove and fell into the rocking chair.

In the same regions that the owl is called death, it is also called wisdom, not that the two are exclusive of each other. The bird is deserving of as many powerful symbols as we can heap on it, although I doubt that it has taken time from its life to come throw symbols at me. Or even to show me the way home. Our paths had merely crossed in the storm, and for that time we were companions. I was sacked into the rocking chair, wishing someone would stop by to visit. But no one has come to the tipi since the onset of winter. Then I was pleased to be alone. In this kind of squall, wishes move like gusts. I was astonished merely to be alive. It was such an improbability in all the turn of events.

For me, storms like this are merciless. I don't know how to survive them or seek their soft spots. All I know is how to try to outrun them, how to tuck tail and head for home. Here was a wonderful home of canvas and lodgepoles, something outwitting anything the owl could construct with its three-pronged talons. But my skill felt falsely overrated out in the groan of the blizzard, when I could hear the owl's voice calm as a sigh.

Wind shuddered up the walls and snow began to melt in my clothes. There was a grace to this weather that was more easily apparent from inside. The brittle consumption of fresh wood settled into a long night's fire. I tilted my head back and thought of the great horned owl on its ponderosa limb, feathers fluffed right now to keep off the wind and snow.

Bubo virginianus

VIOLET-GREEN SWALLOW

E very day I walk to the water. There was once a stock tank here, shoveled out and reinforced by homesteaders who left their buckets and square nails along the forest. Now it is simply a pond in the meadow, heavily fringed with sedges, forgotten by livestock. Every day, even when it rains, I come down and leave my clothes in a pile, my feet gingerly sorting through the basket weaves of dead reeds. I slip in at the south end and kick off, propelling myself to the center. It is just deep enough. I have to maintain some momentum, otherwise my feet and knees drag in the dark mud. Frogs leap away, plunking like small stones to the bottom.

I come in the mornings or just after lunch. The world shifts and rolls, calling up weather, sending it away, and the pond remains. It will stay for another month and then will be dry for autumn. I am cutting wood for the winter. Sawing by hand through winter-kill aspens. Carefully stacking split wood.

At the end of the day, violet-green swallows come down and flash over the pond. It is an acrobatic performance, whirling and crossing; compact, iridescent birds diving for insects, and diving also for no obvious reason, above the water's surface. Their terse wings are like those of a plummeting falcon. I could sit out and watch them for days, if not for all the wood that needs cutting. The species is legendary for its aeronautics, with sharp turns scissoring holes and spirals out of the sky. I have heard hundred-mile-an-hour winds tune themselves through the wings of diving cliff swallows. I have nearly been smacked in the face by swallows who were using my head as a pivot point at mountain ridges.

There has been a storm. At the pond the violet-green swallows are turning the sky into a ball of twine. I am naked beneath the mountains, hands clutched to my shoulders in the breeze. Squalls break apart so that tracts of sunlight roam the ground and the aspen groves glow for two minutes, then turn dark. The clouds curl and cave in on themselves. I enter the water and drift at eye level with turquoise damselflies that swing between gritty horsetails. The damselflies land on my eyebrows and perch on my shoulder blades.

Above, the swallows wheel over one another. A delicate freedom is traced out by their motions. The liberation is so visible because they are working within the confines of specificity, taking tangible details of physics and building wings out of them. They have allied gravity and motion without dissection. There is nothing I can honor more than this. Seeing a swallow in flight is no different than placing your hand on a beating heart.

Fifty of them are working a cat's cradle into the air. The perfect reflection below makes it one hundred swallows. They parade and swivel off their tiny wings. There are no sudden veers to avoid collisions, and none of the birds are coming within a foot of one another. A web of flight regulations hovers above the pond. The law has been set. The curve of a violet-green swallow is reminder enough to heed everything. To cinch down your life and your body like a harpsichord string and pluck it.

Down here there is no sound other than the flutter of birds three feet over my head. With my eyes exactly at water level, I slide alongside swallows who drag over the surface, leaving a wake where they have troubled the water. Images of mountains wrinkle in front of me.

Tachycineta thalassina

BIRD

Walking with a friend in Manhattan, I brushed through a cool September evening. Yellow taxicabs pulsed beside us as thousands of people darted by like colorful reef fish. The air smelled of flowers and of dark subway breath coming up through grates in the sidewalk. We were out for a night's walk, street by street, angling south toward the tip of the city. There we would find the source of two columns of light beaming into the sky. The date was September 11, 2002, exactly a year after the World Trade Center towers fell into a smoldering heap.

It was hard to miss the lights, twin memorials rising side by side, their candlepower so strong they projected off the planet and into space. No matter where you stood on the island, they seemed to vanish at a point directly overhead. We were in no hurry to reach them, stopping at cafés and bars along the way until it was well after midnight.

The intimate stage lighting of the West Village gave way to broad, busy streets and huge, grimy buildings in lower Manhattan, where the congestion only increased. The conversation between my friend and me rippled and churned through a terrain of sound. The pop and clap of many footsteps blended into a thousand rumbling car engines. Sirens and human voices filled the middle octaves, while underneath was an almost audible groan of buildings straining against gravity.

Near Ground Zero, sightseers crowded among vendors and pickpockets. Though we were still a few blocks from the source, the two lights overwhelmed our sky like towering obelisks. When we looked closer we realized the lights were filled with movement. Countless birds raced in and out, bright, meteoric paths cutting into the sky. They must have been drawn by the light, pulled out of their nightly habits to enter this aerobatic flourish. As we walked closer the birds became more brilliant and numerous, a mass of charged, speeding particles. As each crossed into the light, it was suddenly branded white, turned into pure light.

We followed the crowd until we reached a battery of huge spotlights with blinding, electric-powered faces pointing at the peak of the sky. From here we looked straight up into twin pillars of illuminated birds, a dizzy field of motion that was doubled, quadrupled by the reflective glass of skyscrapers on all sides. I had to spread my feet apart so I would not tip over, disoriented by all the motion overhead.

Never had I seen such a gathering, plumes of birds billowing upward, multiplying upon themselves until they appeared infinite, as thick as Milky Way stars. They reflected so much light that their individual features were erased. I guessed them to be terns, flycatchers, whip-poor-wills, nighthawks, jaegers, and crows, interrupted by swerving raptors. I picked out some by their flight patterns: seagulls coasting back and forth, and falcons plunging through flurries of swallows. None could resist the light.

This must upend everyone's schedules, I thought. Daytime species would wake hungover in the morning, bewildered by the night's new sun.

"They must be feeding," I said, trying to find an explanation for what we were seeing. But few species of birds besides whip-poor-wills and nighthawks are night feeders. Those that I saw, perhaps the majority, were migrating, and the lights had apparently pulled them off course. September is prime season for migrators, and many travel at night, relying on stars and moonlight for orientation. Now they were fixed solely on these two lights, the axis of their navigation fastened over lower Manhattan. Many would probably die because of this, their energy diverted, wings exhausted. We were killing them.

My friend did not reply, standing next to me with a thin-strap purse over her shoulder, her head tipped all the way back. She had grown up in the city and called herself a New Yorker, with the cool omnipotence so many residents of this city possess, yet she had never seen anything remotely like this, a night sky peopled with birds.

Though many were killing themselves with exhaustion, I thought these birds must be in some sort of ecstasy, thrust so willingly in and out of the light. I wondered whether survivors would remember this night of illumination, whether the small avian brain has a place to hold an unconformity of this magnitude. Then I thought there must be no need for such memory among animals as swift and transfigured as these. This moment went beyond mere recollection.

I glanced around to see who else noticed this phenomenon. Most of the thousands surrounding me pressed into one another's backs, navigating a cluttered horizon of heads and shoulders. Meanwhile, only a handful of people were stopped. They looked like oracles, standing still in the moving crowd, their faces upturned. I craned my neck and joined them, my eyes climbing rungs of innumerable birds. We were the lucky ones. We happened to look up and witness an event so blindingly extraordinary that most people could not see it. On this night our world had a new axis to turn upon. We were ruled not by gravity or any other familiar law, but by birds.

Aves

....

Artiodactyla

MOUNTAIN GOAT

There is no trail into the center of the Gore Range in Colorado. A few tease the edge: the one to Cataract Lake, those up to the deep, glacier-hollow lakes above Boulder Creek and Slate Creek, and a trail that flanks the low, nine-thousand-foot country to the east. But none through the meat of the range. Come over the timberline summits, and below is the roar of cluttered waterfalls. Metamorphic blocks are crammed into the sky with the topography of broken beer bottles. There is a ridge forty miles long, running north to south, hardly ever dropping below twelve and thirteen thousand feet. From every angle it looks impassable, built of half-fallen towers and tightwire saddles. There is no desire out there, no passion, no deception. That is what is frightening. There is nothing you can do.

The Gore is a small range, its landmass dwarfed by larger ranges to all sides. For its size, though, it is mayhem. To walk into the center is all scrambling, climbing, and taking compass bearings on lakes that do not appear on the Geological Survey maps. The maps of the area have never been entirely correct. The USGS came back in 1983 for aerial photographs, printing corrections in purple, and still did not get it all.

If you want to reach each of the headwaters with time to rest, you will need two or three months and a good ice ax. If you find a pass over the ridge, which I have yet to see, it might make the walk easier. You may have to carry a seventy-pound pack in certain seasons, even if you eat trout from the creeks every morning. Those months will get you in. The rest is uncertainty. If something goes wrong, no one will find your camp or your body. The few people who have vanished are scattered out here. Their bones are dwindling shrines beneath spindrift snow.

I came to the Gore to walk alone for two weeks across the east side, working into the headwater valleys, to the last vertical fields of snow before there was only sky. I walked ten miles from the nearest trail. Ten bitter miles that became fifteen. I followed avalanche chutes below the crisscross of high ridges. Forests had heaved together, snapped into splinters. Aspens grew out of this, bent by the impact of winter slides, humped over from the busted lumber. The forests were steep and dark. I stumbled on the lattice of fallen trees five feet off the ground. The creek was mad, loud in the half-light of the forest floor. Legs bloody, grunting, cursing, hating everything. The muscles in my back spasmed. My knees were weak, jackhammering to keep my pack up. I could hardly see ten feet ahead, and I rarely took the energy to look up from the raspberry brambles and webbing of winter-kill trees.

This is not wilderness for designation or for a park. Not a scenic wilderness and not one good for fishing or the viewing of wildlife. It is wilderness that gets into your nostrils, that runs with your sweat. It is the core of everything living, wilderness like molten iron. At night I camped in a thin chasm, its roof linked with snapped spruce. The waterfall rebounded between knots of fallen timber and boulders. In the thickening of twilight the forest looked like collapsed scaffolding. That was when I was hesitant to move my camp any farther, when I was so deep already that I was afraid. I slept with my ear to the ground, and the waterfall made the sound of the earth ripping from its socket.

Dawn. I was up quickly, gathering equipment onto my back, moving upstream. Animal trails appeared momentarily, smooth traces against the grain of the forest. They always vanished within twenty feet. That left only the forest, the feet over hands to get through. There was a place where a glacier once flattened a stretch of the valley. The creek became serene and colorfully deep. I could hear again. I came to the edge and watched brook trout brace to the current. I slipped back so that they would not see me, so they would live as if I were never here. Farther on I chose a place carefully. A pool with sunken logs and small riffles upstream. With a collapsible rod I cast a line into the water. I took three trout from the pool and cleaned them in the forest. I cooked the trout on a smoky fire and I ate them with hard cookies.

Where the valley was flat the beaver had built dams. Over a few hundred years this work tramped the forest edges into broad, marshy pastures. For the first time I could see around me. The mountains, all of them without names, struck the sky. I kept walking. The flatness ended upstream with waterfalls; log crossings twenty feet above towers of water.

I spent time, days, working across timberline. Above the trees it was primarily rock and snow. Lakes appeared in the seat prints of glaciers where, when the Ice Age stepped back, the last of the glaciers cracked and rumbled their way to extinction, leaving cavities in the planet. Some lakes were half a mile long, others fifteen feet. I came to one, and deep inside, where blue turned to green, and green turned to black, was a clutch of dark boulders. With all of the shadows and deep fissures, the small lake appeared bottomless. Out of the center sat a boxcar boulder tipped on edge. I skirted the talus where glaciers once fed stones into the hole. It was not added to the map until 1987, when the USGS flew over for yet another look.

Peering into this deep second world from the tip of a boulder, I stripped my clothes away and dove. I was in the air for half a second, not really a dive but more of a leap, arms and legs out like a cat thrown from a window. Then I was in the water. At eleven thousand feet, with a permanent snowfield fingered down its south side, the lake had been frozen until maybe a month ago. I swam over the darkest stretch, where boulders hung below like sunken ships. Before my body crimped to a knot, I got back to a rock and crawled out. I lay there for some time, feeling out the smallest cracks in the stone. The sun dressed my bare back while startling beads of water found their way down.

I dressed and walked higher, water soaking into my clothes. Twelve thousand, two hundred ninety-two feet. What I found up here was wool. It was stretched on the stiff tundra grass like taffy. I pulled a snag of it from a low bush and smelled it. The scent was strong and dark like peat moss. The white wool sprang in my fist. Mountain goat. I looked around, scanning the cliffs with binoculars, but there were no goats to see.

I kept walking. Ptarmigans flustered out of my way. They are cousins to the chicken, and there was something in their bobbing strut that reminded me of chickens. But they are not farm animals, their feathers scribbled in earthy colors like paint spatters. They have the size of grouse and the camouflage of chameleons. I never would have seen them against the frost-cracked boulders had they not moved.

Pikas dispatched messages about my approach. They are squat little creatures, resembling noble-postured mice, related to rabbits, as much as ptarmigans are to chickens. They studiously perched on timberline rocks and sent dog-toy squeaks from rock pile to rock pile. I came to one, and the pika dismounted quickly. As it scrambled into the rock causeways below, I leaned over to sniff the perch.

The smell was woody and organic. To make sure I was not tricking myself, I smelled other places on the rock. They smelled only like rock. I returned to the perch and ran my nose over it. The pika barked from far below in its stone maze. They normally urinate at the same posts, and lichens will grow there, phosphorescent orange from nitrogen. This was not such a post. It did not smell of urine.

It was good to smell the fresh print of a pika on a rock. I took the tuft of mountain goat wool from my pocket and gave it a sniff. Indeed, the rock and the wool were not the same. Often I fear that I am losing the sense, that novels of olfactory signals are slipping by me, passing, in fact, my entire race. I smelled the perch again, leaning right up against it and pressing my nose to the rock.

In *The Wind in the Willows,* Kenneth Grahame wrote that we "have only the word 'smell'... to include the whole range of delicate thrills which murmur in the nose of the animal night and day, summoning, warning, inciting, repelling." Imagine reading a book with your nose. Having a conversation without a voice and without eye contact. We are far more packed with neural receptors for smell than for color vision or for taste, with the physical capability to sort through ten thousand scents at once. But few come to the surface. Few make it so far that you could even comment on their presence, could even know that they are there. Eight molecules are enough to send an impulse to your brain and alter your hormones, but it will take at least forty for you to take note. Without our permission, molecules snagged on our olfactory nerves can change the way we breathe, start and end fights, induce miscarriages, and cause our stomachs to rumble. The smell of a forest, its leaves shedding chemical ingredients into the air, pharmacologically soothes and cures ulcers. But we are still somewhat blind in the nose. A dog registers certain odors ten to the sixth power more faint than what a human is able to detect. Of the ten thousand scents the human brain reads, most of us can speak to only forty of them, identifying them correctly as strawberries or as motor oil.

There are people, though, accomplished perfumers, who can accurately name one thousand scents. This monumental gap between forty and one thousand leaves me believing that we have not lost the skill of smell, we've only forgotten. The nose of a perfume maker is merely well trained. Smell comes easy enough to the dark places in our minds, triggering covert internal responses. In women's prisons, uproars are often traced to the presence of a male, either as close as a visitor or as far as one man walking by the outside of the prison. Conversely, men's prisons often calm to the presence or the scent of a woman. This is something like male mice, who start biting one another and their handlers with about a 50 percent increase when given the urine scent of an aggressive male mouse. But when they are given a whiff of female urine, aggression drops by half.

There is no library of tactile sensations as complex. But if someone came to you with a sharp knife and gave you a choice between the loss of your eyes, your ears, your fingers, or your nose, which would you sacrifice? Light and sound enter the brain in an ambiguous rush that must be broken apart and deciphered consciously. There is no meaning to a word, spoken or written, until you've had time to spell it out and cross-reference it with what you know already. Smells, on the other hand, are dissected and routed molecule by molecule before ever reaching the brain, torn to small pieces of digestible information. Dive your nose over a bowl of steaming pasta, heavy with garlic, and the olfactory bulbs sandwiched between your brain and sinus cavity will take this wall of sensations and isolate each ingredient. Those ingredients will be divided even further so that you can instantly tell the difference between fresh or dried garlic. Smells are untangled as the constituents of a single scent take to their own paths of neural cells. One component belongs to one cell strand alone so that a single sniff can break into ten thousand signals. With this much information available from one sense, the potential for combinations and meanings becomes an exponential pantheon. All other senses are subordinate.

Become fluent with this kind of communication, building multi-dimensional images out of smell alone, and you are an animal, nose to the ground. Otherwise you put all of your weight on everything but smell, and the images fade.

The smell of mountain goats was all over. It was strong enough to rise to the top of my brain, and constant enough that even I could find it in small traces. It was hard to tell how many steps they were ahead of me. Only the flag of wool was left between rocks.

Mountain goats are white. As the writer and researcher Douglas Chadwick once described them, they are a beast the color of winter. Most of the year, their wool shag hangs low. Sharp black horns curve from their skulls. They are the sole animals of size to live here, occupying only the ragged places. Hardly anything will follow them into their terrain, places like this where cliffs stagger to razor-tipped ridges. Their primary predators are avalanches, severe winters, and rock slides. Many are taken by bad footing. Something to keep in mind.

The boulders were monstrous, rested into one another in ways that suggested they would not stay for long. Below, within the chasm matrix of overlying rocks, was the sound of a waterfall running in darkness. I dropped between cracks, landing in snow. The place was ripe with the scent of mountain goats. I found their scratched sleeping holes and their webs of shed wool. I lowered to the ground and sniffed the dirt. When I came to a rise, I lifted slowly, looking over the edge. They were still ahead of me, gone.

Moving faster. Lightning broke like glass across the ridge. The sky split open. I ran to the top, clipping the ridge so that I could look down into the next valley. Here it was a cemetery of peaks. They rose in quick crags—hard, dark stones grafted into one another. Lightning was still breaking. It was a localized afternoon storm. I got my look into the valley, into the topaz lakes on the floor. Then I was off the edge, trying to get out from under the lightning. Clouds rose and spilled their guts, water and electricity bursting out of the air. At this elevation the storms are concentrated and swift, here and gone. Not the closet purple of a storm you see from below, but a swirling white and gray as clouds pass at eye level, each strand visible with dime-a-dozen lightning bolts arcing from place to place. The storm struck one mountain and not the other. It raped summits with ice and wind and explosions. Then the storm roved to the next mountain.

At 11,700 feet, a crest ran northeast. The storm was gone. Several others promenaded behind it. A mountain goat lay dead across the top of the ridge. The head pointed north, almost due north. White clumps of wool trembled in the wind. At this point there was more wool than animal. It was probably a late-winter/early-spring death; its skull eyeless and its leather face drawn tight, exposing bone. Its dry skin was firm. This one did not pitch down a cliff to land here and it was not taken by another animal. I figured it was starvation and cold. Many new kids will not survive to their second spring. Even half the yearlings will probably die in the fierce weather. The memorable winter of 1977 killed more than half the kids in the Gore Range.

I slid a hand down each horn. They were unexpectedly smooth, ending so sharply that they pricked to the touch. Unlike bighorn sheep horns, they were not broomed and frayed at the ends, not belted with armor plates, not given an exaggerated corkscrew curve. They were like brand-new, polished leather scabbards. Around the exposed cervical vertebrae was a leather collar. It was a radio collar. I dug into the wool and found the ear tag: 212. DEPARTMENT OF WILDLIFE. GRAND JUNCTION, COLORADO. PLEASE NOTIFY.

Grand Junction was so far away. Far in all respects, nowhere near this ridge of the Gore Range. *Consider yourself notified,* I thought. But I would take the tag. They would want to know.

I later found out that a researcher named Anne Hopkins had collared this goat on a study with the Division of Wildlife. She was there as a student intern, and the goat, a one-year-old male, was born there to a transplanted family. He was part of an introduced band of mountain goats that Division researchers followed across the range, but this goat was never heard from again. Whenever a plane came by to locate local radio tags, frequency 148.750 was out of range, hidden somewhere in the rocks. This was the first spotting of No. 212 since Hopkins had tranquilized it five years earlier.

The animal died at the age of six, middle-aged, nearly at the top of the world. A few steps in either direction was a thousand-foot drop. I could not decide what to say when I left. It wouldn't be appropriate or it wouldn't sound right. So I said nothing and walked down the ridge, descending into a forest of waterfalls, where I set camp.

In the morning I climbed the next mountain over, preparing to drop into a new network of drainages. The peak took me out to a catwalk occupied solely by alert, studious pikas. From there was a rising plain of tundra holding several summits together like a web of muscle. I was in the center, nowhere to hide, when I saw the first mountain goat. Instantly I was on the ground. Somehow, two hundred feet away, it had not seen me first. The animal looked like an unraveling rag of wool, leaving bits of itself around as it scratched on the stunted bushes. It was molting its way through the summer. The staunchness of its body gave it the appearance of a linebacker. When it glanced in my direction, I forced my face into the tundra.

Undoubtedly it had seen a human somewhere in its travels. Mountain goats are notoriously curious. On mountain ranges closer to Denver, closer to trails and roads, goats crowd around one another, fumbling for hand-given potato chips, licking salt patches where people have urinated. Diseases flash through these populations like electricity. Social orders break down as herds gather around car windows for half-eaten corn dogs and mayonnaise-laden bread crusts. Areas that could hold no more than fifteen goats suddenly sport a hundred; in the winter, the stress time, there are no tourists to feed the hundred starving goats. Summer tundra is trampled to mud, and goats weaken, then die, in these boomtown environments. The Mount Evans west sector, most populated by people, has two hundred goats, the highest number in Colorado, as well as the sickest, weakest goat population in the state.

This was a Gore Range goat. There are few sanctuaries as intact for goats as this, and it would be better if I was never seen. Ironically, it was humans that brought this goat here. Every goat south of Idaho's Sawtooth Range was transplanted or is the progeny of a transplant. There are vigorous disputes about whether or not mountain goats were here to begin with. They may have been killed by gold rush hunters before they could be documented, or they may simply have faded on their own before any European got a glimpse. When notebook-toting naturalists first reached the higher, rougher topography in the late 1800s, there were no mountain goats.

The oldest record of a mountain goat surfaced only a week before my trek into the Gore, from a Denver Museum of Nature and Science dig in a cave not far south of here. It was a middle phalanx bone that took the goat back at least three hundred thousand years, probably further. Its southernmost identification was also a single Pleistocene phalanx, from Stanton's Cave in the upper stretches of the Grand Canyon. Information about recent goats, mainly sightings from the 1800s, is thinly spread. Lieutenant Zebulon Pike's expedition of 1806 turned up not a single mountain goat in Colorado. Commercial hunters flocked to the region in the coming years, but tales of mountain goats often proved groundless. One hunter came to "look upon all 'goat' stories with a good deal of suspicious reserve."

In response to drastic wildlife depletion, the 1887 Colorado State Legislature banned the killing of bison for ten years, bighorn sheep for eight years, and finally "Rocky Mountain goats" for ten years. Not long before this legislation, 150 supposed mountain goat hides were sold in Denver for fifty cents apiece; a written comment by the 1898 Colorado state fish commissioner said that "there were some Rocky Mountain goats in the state, but they were not abundant."

If, historically, there were mountain goats in the area, the turn of the twentieth century left few, if any. The then Colorado Museum of Natural History in autumn of 1900 sent a hunting party to Idaho to kill a mountain goat for its collection, having determined that in Colorado the species was "quite extinct." Evidence is sketchy, but it repeats itself enough to suggest that the mountain goat was native to Colorado not long ago. Alex Chappell, who studies mountain goats with the Division of Wildlife and lives at the southern foot of the Gore Range, has little doubt that they were here. He has compiled extensive historic literature on the animal and filed through the most obscure and disputable reports. If anyone knows where the goats have been, it is Chappell. His map titled *Pre-1900 Distribution of the Rocky Mountain Goat*, with shaded stretches in Washington, Idaho, Montana, Wyoming, and northeast Utah, also shows a single island in the middle of Colorado.

At the moment, the goats are doing well in the Gore Range. Since the 1920s about three hundred goats have been shipped into twenty-nine areas in western states, mainly for hunting. Some remained in hunting areas. Others, like the goat I was observing on the tundra, were dropped and immediately vanished into the deeper backcountry, the land of exile. It is here, in this mountain range alone, that the introduced populations are faring best and the goats are the most difficult to reach. The Gore's population began with sixteen and has now reached one hundred sixty.

I kept down, motionless, not wanting the goat to see me, not wanting to alter what was happening here. I slung my pack away, leaving it on the ground, and looped my camera on so that it rested on my spine. There was just enough topography for me to remain hidden. I crawled across the land, keeping to the tundra mounds as the goat worked west, stopping every few feet to snap grass off the tundra. I cleaved my knee against a rock. Fresh, luminous blood ran into the grass.

Then two mountain goats. The second was just beyond a rise. I stayed lower. A third goat appeared, hidden behind the second. It was young, probably an early-season kid from May. Its wool was white like shreds of typing paper, more brilliant than the discolored white of the older goats. Its motions were tinted with naïveté, a curious, uncertain gait of youth that was obvious from a fair distance, even in the energetic lowering of its neck to take a nip of grass. The other goats were plodding with age, already convinced of how to get from place to place.

For a half hour they led me west. My stomach and chest were raked through the shirt, swollen red from sharp late-summer grasses. The blood on my leg was dry. I closed on the goats, sneaking ahead with elbows and toes. They brought me to a lake, one depressed into the tundra, a hundred yards long. At one end was a wall of snowfields. At the other was an abyssal drop to the valley floor. A fourth goat waited by the lake. This one was hornless, the youngest. Its robe was pure. It was not moving with any cognition of gravity. Birthing season was May to June, and this was probably a late birth. Winter would be oppressive for this one.

I moved very slowly now, grinding on the earth, muscle by muscle. I hid my predator eyes with my arms and hands so I wouldn't give myself away. Every inch of forward motion was plotted, as I waited for their heads to drop to forage before moving. Sixty feet was as close as I could get. There was no more room to push my luck. I took photos, burying my head behind the camera, hoping the ratchet of the shutter was not too loud. I watched with binoculars, watched their noses, their eyes. I could smell them in the soil. Wool was caught on the tundra around me.

It was originally proposed by the Greeks over two thousand years ago that foul smells are made of ragged, hooked particles while those sweet are composed of smooth balls. In respect to the Greeks, the smell of a mountain goat is smooth and at the same time rough, combining rank and attractive scents at once, something akin to warm yeast. It is a steamy, soft smell impregnated with territories and maternal instincts. If I learn this well enough, drive my nose into this wool over and over, I may be able to tell one animal from the next. Even as it smells similar to a buffalo, like a bighorn sheep, like any wild, hairy ungulate, the messages inside tell of entirely deeper stories. There were enough flavors here to indicate estrus and age and imminent winter.

The wind shifted to my back. My scent fled with it, tumbling toward the goats. It was not something I could reach out and grab before it blew away, not like a sneeze I could muffle in my fist. I nearly reached for it, as if my hat had blown off. The youngest kid suddenly braced against its mother, and they both turned rigid. They were looking for me, but they couldn't find me. I was not motion. I was not shape. I was a dead lump on the ground issuing a troubling scent.

As quickly as it moved one way, the breeze moved the other. Even with the loss of my scent, the two were frozen. Their noses were up. They both briskly walked toward the lake, gaining on the other two, who had not smelled anything but recognized the concern. I was cursing to myself, keeping my eyes low against the tundra. I knew I shouldn't have come so close. There was a bit of circling and pausing in the small herd, and staring in my direction. The alarm wore off. Within a few minutes they forgot. One older goat dropped and rested on the tundra. That was when I backed out. Lift and crawl, backward into rocks until I found the depression of a dried snowfield. From there I hunched my way out, leaving the goats at the lake.

Namewise, this animal has gone through numerous scientific incarnations. It has been *Aplocerus montanus, Antilope americana, Mazama sericea, Haplocerus montanus,* and *Capra montana.* Common names have identified it as an antelope, a buffalo, a snow deer, and even a pygmy bison. The most lasting name has been the genus *Oreamnos,* developed in 1817 by Constantine Samuel Rafinesque (the species name was determined a year later by another naturalist). *Oreamnos* comes from the Greek *oreos,* mountain, and *amnos,* lamb.

Rafinesque's naming of the goat was more successful than his naturalist career. Rafinesque was a guest at John James Audubon's home when a bat flew into his bedroom window. Thinking it a new species of bat, he grabbed Audubon's violin and went after the creature, trying to kill it for closer observation. Startled and disgusted by this indiscretion under his own roof, Audubon cultivated a sneering dislike for Rafinesque. He later sent to Rafinesque several "creatively drawn" illustrations of nonexistent fish. Rafinesque classified the fish for Audubon. Audubon then presented this error to the world. Rafinesque was horribly embarrassed before his peers, and the credibility of his entire body of work was shattered. In the name of the mountain goat, *Oreamnos americanus,* Rafinesque's skill has at least outlived Audubon's malicious chuckle.

I found my pack and slipped around the abyssal end of the lake, scrambling in the balanced boulders so that I was below the goats. This route ran into a steep snowfield, out of which puppet strings of waterfalls descended into the valley. I had no ice ax, and this would have been a good place to use one. The drop was too abrupt. It brought the kind of fear that tastes like a swallowed ember, especially on the streamers of ice that would not even give way to a footprint. I moved off the field as soon as possible and worked farther west. In the patchwork of boulders I smelled goats again, the rich, musky breeze blowing east. That slowed me until I saw a yearling. I came down behind a sizable stone, pressing my back to it. The yearling walked slowly in my direction, dropping its head to graze. An adult appeared to its right. I pushed closer to the rock.

From the north came another goat, boulder-hopping off a ridge. You fall into some of these holes, and your spine gets wrenched into several pieces, yet the goat was dancing its way down, and I swear it did not pause once. It pounced across the tundra below. Another yearling emerged from a draw in the boulders. Now I was stuck against this rock in the middle of a herd. I couldn't get out from behind the rock without at least one goat spotting me. Its inflexible stance would send the message into the crowd. You cannot be subtle in a herd.

For distraction, so I wouldn't fidget out of impatience, I nudged a paperback book from my pack. The book was *Autumn Across America* by Edwin Way Teale, well read by many people, with "$2.95" scratched in pencil inside. I turned to the dog-eared page and started the third paragraph down. The closest goat was forty feet away, and I promised I would not look up again. I did not know what they would do if they found me. Females occasionally get angry. I recalled a goat study from this mountain range using words such as "extremely aggressive behavior characterized by high-intensity weapon and rush threats." Captured females tend to thrash and attack. Captured males go weak, often lapsing into a glassy-eyed stupor.

But I was not thinking too much about being trampled and jabbed by angry mothers. My effect on them, I feared, would be more pronounced than theirs on me. I just did not want to be seen. Teale was gathering ferns in the Northwest. I would go with the author and gather ferns with him. I did not want to be the obscene gesture in the goats' sanctuary, to get caught sneaking around the garden. It was not that I was poison, but maybe I was. It was not that I would break a sacred trust, but I might. I could no longer turn a page because one of the goats was twenty-five feet away. It was a yearling. I leaned my head against the rock and closed my eyes. The paper slipped from my fingers and I felt the flutter of several pages as the book closed itself. I listened to the chewing of tundra grass and I did not move.

I must have fallen asleep because the thunder came from empty space. I was curled against the rock, and when my eyes opened, hail was coming down. I could smell the goats, but when I peeked, they were gone. I curled tighter to keep the hail off of me. Lightning came down in the rocks with an electric-white flare. There was another burst, a shocking crack down the center of the sky. The sun was low, hazy through the strung beads of clouds. Storm-driven ice gathered in the cups of my clothing. I waited through it, wondering if the goats had found me, if they came up and sniffed the back of my neck while I slept.

When the storm rolled east, I walked out, shaking off the hail. The last few pieces of lightning were still close, and I crawled down in the rocks several more times for cover. I saw no goats, even with binoculars. I picked tufts of wool off the ground and kneaded them together, burying them in my pockets to keep my hands warm.

A ridge enclosed one of the deep valleys, and I walked its spine. Long shadows stretched from the sun, which had gone to the surface of the earth. Sometimes I could see the shadow of myself on the snow the next ridge over. Twisted alpine trees tucked against one another, driven as if they themselves were the wind, turned an astonishing red with sunlight. It seemed that I had been walking for days through a cave that now brought me to the other end, the place where the world is as vivid as a taste of anise. Gray stones counterbalanced the last cornices of avalanche snow. You could breathe the entire sky up here. As I walked along the high tundra, I nuzzled my nose into a fistful of wool. The smell was wonderful and clean, like that of newborn kittens.

Oreamnos americanus

PRONGHORN ANTELOPE

The pay for the work was seven hundred dollars. It didn't include film or gas or food. Because I was sixteen years old, it was much more money than I had expected. Seven hundred dollars to walk across a barren space in Wyoming, find an oil rig, and photograph it.

The oil company that hired me also employed my mother. It was her connection: at a meeting of geologists and management, someone said that the annual report could use a nice photograph, and she said that her son would be in Wyoming and that he had a camera. "Does he know how to use it?" management asked. "He's had it since he was little," she told them. So I came to Wyoming with a camera, driving a dirt road longer than any I had ever driven. Near the town of Lonetree, close to Robertson. Uinta County, the badlands of Wyoming, clay hills shaded with pastels. Lavender buttes and mauve washes. Southwest Wyoming.

The oil rig was in the open. It was white and red, towers and pipes and two mobile homes. Holding pools lined with black plastic. Parked trucks with Wyoming plates, streaks of mud up to the windows and stains of dog urine on the tires. At night steel banged on steel. It was the switching of joints, men in one-piece work suits slinging chain, hoisting pipes into position. There were spotlight beams that made the drill platform glow like a stage. Drilling mud exploded and hit the men in their faces. Their expressions did not change, jaws set, all their weight going into the machine. The machine groaned and spun its needle into the ground. Mud hurled in all directions as chains uncoupled. Grunts and commands were issued, no time even to wipe away mud or sweat. I dove between the men, taking pictures, keeping clear of the chain.

The driller, hands on the lever, was named Bobby B. Blanchard.

"You know what the *B* stands for?" he barked.

I looked dumb.

"Bastard!"

By the age of twenty-seven most drill workers are off the payroll. Hands go to the chains. Arms are taken down with drill bits. Burst metal robs people of their eyes. They all had stories, told later as they rubbed their necks and wriggled out of their suits. Drilling stories. The woman who lost a finger and said nothing until the chain was set. The man who got his head too close to the drill. They joked with me and showed me rope tricks, old drillers' magic tricks with nails and pieces of twine.

I walked into the dark clay hills, away from the rig. Tripod on the shoulder, bought at Kmart from the seven hundred dollars. I planted it in the loose, dry soil and photographed the Christmas tree tower of light. It was the only light anywhere. An island of light, and above were the stars. Coyotes howled in the restless sprawl of washes. A dark breeze. The muffled rumble of the oil rig half a mile away. The sound was alien. The earth is no machine. It makes no such noise. This was the sound that rumbles beneath prosperity. It was the sound of work, the labor of a thousand people, of businesses and cars and meetings compacted into a single oil rig running twenty-four hours a day with its five-person crew. Even on Sundays.

I rested on my back against the crust of the planet. Hands behind my head, I watched the sky and listened to the metal moan of the rig. Dawn came and I was awake, moving. Colored bands penetrated to the ground so that I walked across cured clay the color of the sky. Light changed quickly, too quickly for the light meter, for any piece of equipment to record. The light altered its shape and its voice. Time between the first thin light and sunrise was a quickening metamorphosis.

A herd of pronghorn antelope stood north of the rig. Fourteen animals. Their bodies were sleek. Color on their throats and breasts was a necklace work of tans, blacks, and whites. They were like gazelles, refined in muscular detail, with outlines striking against the horizon. They faced the same direction, as if the wind left them here momentarily. On each, male and female, was a set of short black horns. Those on the males were more ornate. They were different shapes, hooking inward or to the sides or down toward the skull, rooted just above the eye sockets, in front of the ears, where a bone core was encased in smooth black keratin.

A good picture, I thought, the lithe pronghorn standing before the oil rig tower. Snow covered Wasatch Mountains in the distance. The pronghorn watched as I shuttled my equipment. They appeared swift even in repose. I kept low to the ground, quiet in my steps. I came wide, hunkering in and out of the washes, looking up for only a second to see if we were aligned, the oil rig, the herd, the Wasatch Mountains, and me. They shifted and watched, keeping track of me. I hid in the washes. They knew where I was. Pronghorn eyes are seated farther to the outside of the skull than those of most prey animals, giving them wider vision in this open topography. The eyes are large enough to belong to a draft horse while the body is less than half the size of a small thoroughbred's. They are meant solely for an animal who lives in the open, in places where you can see from one level horizon to the next.

Moving slowly, I lifted the camera and reached ahead to adjust the shutter speed and aperture, framing the animals with the rig. Suddenly they were in motion. There was no acceleration. There was only speed where there had been stillness. White patches flashed from rosettes of short hairs at their tails. The panic signal can be seen for miles, and it comes with a glandular flush that sends a scent into the air. It means *run*.

They do not run like deer, who will gather speed with hesitation, glancing back, bounding, jumping and weaving between trees. Not like elk, the ones that crash and gallop, heavy and solid, moving toward a forest into which they can vanish. The pronghorn were gone with grace, sprinting into the open. They moved like birds, swerving together as they aimed for a single point. They are the fastest long-distance runners on the continent, some of the fastest land creatures in the world, clocked at nearly sixty miles per hour. They have been known to clear thirty feet without touching the ground.

I lowered the camera and stared as they streaked over the land. Only slightly startled, they were running at about thirty miles per hour. The ground was used only for propulsion, as a springboard. For the most part, they were in flight. Their bodies drop and carry so low that the center of gravity does not have to be shifted during the run. More energy is thus used for moving the legs rather than moving the center of gravity. Oxygen is driven into the blood and muscles at a rate that would cause a human to instantly black out. The general weight of a pronghorn equals that of a light human, yet the pronghorn's lungs, heart, and trachea are twice the size of a human's. Rarely will you see a pronghorn gasping for breath at the end of a run.

The gallop reduced to a lope within a quarter mile, and the pronghorn reassembled shoulder to shoulder. I moved back. This time I made a mile loop, disappearing into the hills and coming down where I could pin the herd between myself and the rig. When I came out of the draw and was hunched, I lifted my head slowly so as not to attract attention. The rig clanked and growled. They were switching joints again.

When I could see, when my eyes were level with the earth, the pronghorn stared at me. I crouched and shuffled, lifting the camera from its case. When I had it in my hand, I diverted my eyes, anything to calm them. Again, they burst away. This time they reversed their line and circled to where they first stood, a quarter mile back again. My camera came down to my waist and I huffed.

Their bodies are sheer thrust. Even their spines mobilize in order to streamline the running stride. Fast predators were the first to do this, evolving supple spinal cords so that they could outrun and outmaneuver everyone else. Most prey animals require stiff spines to support their weight, making them a bit more cumbersome but at least bulky in a fight. A flexible spine allows the body to contract and expand during a race, spreading the burden from the legs to the rest of the body. At its extreme, a pronghorn's spinal flexion is more similar to that of a cheetah than that of a horse. The design, though, is too much. The pronghorn's speed is overkill, outpacing all predators so well that there is no sense in a chase. The pronghorn was once hunted across Wyoming by the North American cheetah, which explains why the pronghorn came to run more like a cheetah than a deer. The two species nearly match speeds. Twelve thousand years ago the cheetah vanished from this side of the planet and the pronghorn survived. Embedded in the pronghorn's ability to run so outlandishly fast are the cheetahs in their memory.

Everything in their bodies is an adaptation to one piece of ground, to flat-out running across a terrain that never seems to end. Pronghorn have lived nowhere but here, western North America, which is rare on a continent populated by European and Asian descendants such as deer, elk, and bison. Their local history has kept the body evolving specifically to this one place, with expanded eyes, wind tunnel organs, and a running pattern that frees them from predators.

The zoologist George Ord was the first to catalog the animal when it was brought to him in the early 1800s by members of the Lewis and Clark expedition. No European had yet seen an animal like it in the New World. The scientific name, *Antilocapra americana*, means "antelope-goat of America," because Ord observed in the specimen characteristics of an antelope and a goat but knew that it was neither. Their genus, *Antilocapra*, belongs to no other species in the world but the pronghorn, endemic to North America. Since they are technically not antelope and their genus is solitary, the pronghorn is the sole animal of its genetic kind in the world.

In the past ten million years, the species of this now-small Antilocapridae family were comparatively diverse. Fossils have been found of four-horned and six-horned and spiral-horned North American antelope-goats. One of the early relatives stood less than two feet high. This elaborate genetic array whittled itself down in the past few hundred thousand years to only one species, the pronghorn, *americana*.

I walked farther back, several miles into the hills. For an hour I was lost. The hills flocked against one another, and I had to scramble to their summits to look around. Sunburned mounds fanned in all directions. I listened for the rig and heard nothing. There were no pronghorn tracks. Nothing alive. Not even grass emerged from the crumbled clay.

In time I found the drainage and followed it, coming to my original tracks and the scuffs where earlier I had tried to keep low. The pronghorn were already staring at me. There was a moment of equilibrium. I did not move, and the kinetic energy of their bodies held tight. I licked my lips and sent my hand into the camera bag.

Energy sprung loose. They galloped away. I glared at them. Later the drill workers would tell me that they stopped work and walked to the edge of the platform to watch me. Five men standing there, hands on hips, mud running off their faces, and some kid way out there chasing pronghorn around. "We were wondering what in the hell you were doing," one said.

When I walked to study their tracks, I saw a small shape left on the ground not far from where they stood. I walked slower. The shape was a young pronghorn. It was flat, its nose tucked to the ground.

The dark round eyes were the first marks I saw. Instantly I dropped to my knees and made myself look small. The herd closed itself into a circle and watched.

The young pronghorn was a newborn. Days old. It was motionless. This is the defense of newborns. The only defense. To survive by running at this age is impossible, so the infants keep still and low. There must have been some sort of hope from the herd, some wish as they stood against one another and waited.

Thirty feet away I photographed the fawn. I crawled on hands and knees. At twenty feet I lowered to my stomach, pushing the camera ahead. Soil broke around my body and I dug with the tips of my boots, inching ahead. The fawn did not blink. This was not a stillness like the holding of breath. It was a physical state, like hibernation. Its body was so flattened that the bones appeared to be broken, its joints shattered.

Pronghorn fawns spend most of their time alone, inert on the ground until they are strong enough to make a thirty-mile-per-hour sprint. It may take as little as three days to develop that kind of speed, at which point they can keep pace with mildly panicked adults. Still, they are not fast enough for a serious chase, so for eight weeks they keep to the ground. Within hours, sometimes minutes, of birth, they seek a hiding place, drop, and wait. The technique works. Wildlife researchers have observed standing fawns from a distance, but when they have walked down, startling the fawns into hiding, they have been unable to find the animals. A group of three observers walked the sagebrush for two hours without finding the fawns they had been watching. I once saw a set of photographs showing a Labrador retriever nearly stepping over a hidden fawn and never finding it.

On average a mother will keep several hundred feet from her fawn, trying not to reveal its location. She returns every few hours for nursing. The fawn curls to the ground when the nursing is over, and the mother quickly leaves the area. The difficulty for the hiding infant is that it is not able to adequately forage because it must remain so still. The energy it requires to grow and reach that thirty-mile-per-hour sprint must come from a mother's milk alone. The fat content of pronghorn milk exceeds that of any other North American ruminant, including deer, whose fawns are generally followers and not hiders. The milk has two and a third times the protein of cow milk and nearly four times the fat. Nutritionally, it is equivalent to evaporated milk.

With adults being so absurdly fast, the only real threats to mature pronghorn are illness and high-powered rifles. Population control then lies primarily with the young, and half of a season's newborns tend to get eaten by the next fall. Coyotes are the best at the job. They have possibly found a way to backfire the hiding scheme, stealing information from the mother that leads to her fawn.

The first hunting method is that the coyote sits and waits for the mother to walk over and nurse, revealing the fawn. However simple this tactic may sound, it is surprisingly ineffective. A fawn needs only small amounts of the high-powered milk, so nursing sessions are widely spaced. A coyote planning to sprint in and take a fawn after nursing may have to wait too long for the hunt, while it could be out scrounging mice. Taking pure energy usage into account, with a forty-pound coyote consuming a nine-pound fawn, the coyote who sits and waits will use more energy in the end than one who trots toward a pronghorn herd and noses randomly through the sagebrush.

The second method, which has yet to be fully documented, is typically ingenious and observant on the part of the coyote. Two researchers, Karen and John Byers, set out on the National Bison Range in Montana to watch pronghorn mothers and fawns. They parked on the road and kept notes from the front seat. Statistically, they found that a mother pronghorn will most often point her head or body toward her hiding fawn, perhaps to keep track of its location, using her body as a compass. Coyotes are notorious for taking advantage of such subtle hints, and they may sweep the corresponding area until finding the fawn. A 360-degree hunt around the mother is reduced to a 90-degree hunt.

On average a coyote needs to be within about six feet of the fawn in order to find it, so the tactic would weed out a great deal of unnecessary hunting. The Byerses calculated that a quarter of the expected energy could now be used by a coyote to make a meal. Mothers, they theorized, were inadvertently giving their fawns away. The hunting tactic is a good one, but no one is sure if it has been put to use by many coyotes.

This fawn on the ground adeptly followed the rules of the hide. It was doing everything possible to survive, which meant it was doing nothing at all. Its spine was nearly pressed to the earth. Legs were splayed flat, ears ducked against the neck as if there were no ears at all. Hair on its head was swirled into small, wavy curls, as if it had just dried from the placenta. The mother eats the placenta fast so the scent won't linger and draw coyotes. I clicked several more frames and pushed ahead. The camera was then left behind so that I could use my fingers to move. Within arm's reach I breathed so carefully that my lungs hurt. I held my breath when I was there, as close as I could get. The pronghorn's eyes were moist, hills reflecting in them. I could see my own face. I swallowed.

My right hand involuntarily moved forward. Middle fingers spread and reached. I thought that I shouldn't, that I had come too close already, but my hand was there. I was fundamentally drawn. I touched fur at its hind leg. The hair was as stiff as the bristles of a coarse brush. My fingertips barely moved beneath the surface to reach its skin.

In that second the fawn released a startled cry and leaped away. With knobby, unstable legs it galloped toward the herd. It did not have the gentle speed of its parents, but the speed was there, in the bones, waiting. The herd took in the newborn, absorbing it. I was left on the ground, belly down, my hand still out where we had made contact.

Antilocapra americana

ELK

My grandfather's were big, old hands. While he sat with the local paper, or thumbed through fresh jalapeño peppers in the Number 10 can with the label printed in Spanish, I read the lines on his hands as if they were words. I helped him with lumber, and he wrapped his fingers around a two-by-four in a way that still makes me look at my own hands and wish there was more.

Known him since I was born, got my elbows slapped by the man if I was propped on the dinner table. His voice was the kind that would seek out every lie you've ever told. He raised two children, both girls, and in places he became soft. I was born to his elder daughter, and he sang to me. I learned to sleep on his belly when I was tired. A judicious and spare man, he did not understand why I built a tipi in Colorado. It made no sense to him that in the era of productivity and success, a person would regress to such a hard and inconvenient life. I wasted no words with him and said that it was an important thing. So he gave me his coat. It had been necessary for his winters in Farmington, New Mexico, and in Denver. Living in El Paso now, he says that it would be better if I had it for the tipi.

It was a huge coat of leather and fur, and when I took it from him, my hands disappeared into the folds. The massive object draped over me, and I was a kindergartner clumsily fitting on Grandpa's clothes. I wore it in the way one would wear a buffalo robe. It descended almost to my ankles, and when he jerked the enormous collar, showing me how to do it, most of what made me physically recognizable was swallowed. The heavy-stitched belt bore a solid metal buckle that swung when not pulled up.

Before I pushed through the snow at the tipi's canvas door, I pulled the collar the way he showed me, with a good tug to cover the back of my head. The daily avalanche rode off the tipi face and was deflected by the collar. It spilled in a clean pile at my boots.

In the evening I jabbed split juniper onto the woodstove coals. The coat was slung over the back slats of the rocking chair, sealing out the cold from behind. Frigid nights solidified into mornings of ten and fifteen below zero, and the cold permeated the tipi's interior. Spread out completely, the coat covered my bed and held in whatever warmth drifted through the quilt. Ice crystallized on the fur where my breath emerged throughout the night. Curled together, my cat and I could hardly move under the coat's bulk.

The most physically notable thing about my grandfather was those large working hands. They gripped tools well. Good Missouri agricultural hands. I remembered this whenever the coat hung from my body. Like him, the coat was protective. No extravagances or unneeded loops or buttons; only what was required for the coldest of times. He was raised during the Great Depression, which does not produce a flamboyant posture.

When I traveled, the weight of the coat slowed my pace. There was not a moment that I was not aware of its weight. I responded by moving slowly. My steps were careful. Clad in lightweight, high-tech winter gear, I could bound through the forest, crashing into drifts of snow, snapping the fragile twigs below. Synthetic fibers rub like sandpaper, giving a brash sound. But with my grandfather's coat I moved with the quiet of an animal. It begged for such treatment.

Through the falling snow on a moonless night, I followed a familiar trail from the tipi into an open meadow, essentially blind. When I sank knee-deep in snow, I knew I was off my trail and I pulled myself out. I stopped suddenly to the sound of foraging elk. I had stepped into a herd of maybe forty of them. The sounds were hooves pawing through snow and mouths brushing down to dry browse frozen below. This was the herd that spent each winter here, attended by two local coyote packs on the rise toward Horsefly Peak due west and in the piñons growing to the southeast. I have followed this elk herd up Horsefly in the spring, through the iris blooms in the wet aspen groves. I have stumbled upon a motionless calf hidden in the forest. They rarely traveled far beyond the tipi this time of year.

It was a hard time for the elk, the middle of winter, when forage was deep beneath the snow. The frozen grasses they were able to reach were far less digestible and contained only a sampling of nutrients from those in summer. Calves born late in the season were now struggling. To keep warm, a five-month-old will expend nearly twice the energy of an eight-month-old, and when the predators come, or during fierce January nights, the energy loss is critical. Winter is a long, open time. The nights are as dark as the end of the world.

The elk that you glimpse in the summer, those at the forest edge, are survivors of winter, only the strongest. You see one just before dusk that summer, standing at the perimeter of the meadow so it can step back to the forest and vanish. You can't help imagining the still, frozen nights behind it, so cold that the slightest motion is monumental. I have found their bodies, half drifted over in snow, no sign of animal attack or injury. Just toppled over one night with ice working into their lungs. You wouldn't want to stand outside for more than a few minutes in that kind of winter. If you lived through only one of those winters the way this elk has, you would write books about it. You would become a shaman. You would be forever changed. That elk from the winter stands there on the summer evening, watching from beside the forest. It keeps its story to itself.

This winter night I pulled the coat tight and listened to the elk. The coat settled on me like ancestry. Snow built on the collar and I waited in silence. It was so cold and still tonight that my scent dropped to the ground and settled there. The elk called to one another with snorts and whistles, and I sensed that I was intruding on a conversation. I finally heard the breathing, hot air huffed into the snow. The shuffle of hooves working down to the ice grass. When I moved again they stampeded. Shapes appeared from darkness, quickly pounding the snow. The figures came at me, surrounded me, and were gone. I was left alone.

Old customs are easy to forget with the flashing of events in our lives. Easy to forget, like the heavy clothing we once wore to survive the winters. It is an old custom, the handing down of things. A good knife, a well-made pipe, a heavy robe. Tradition falls prey to constant change, and creativity becomes so revered that the past is a relic, only to be admired. But in this coat, I was held to the earth, pulled to the past by its weight.

Several nights later I write this story in the tipi. Glass oil lamps are on a handmade desk. A bright, flickering circle lies on my journal. There are shadows in the stacked books and warm bands of light and dark from the woodstove. I am writing about the elk and my grandfather's coat. I write these words, about his hands on a piece of wood, me sleeping on his stomach, the day he gave me the coat; about the night with the elk in the meadow. The cat is a feather of gray and white curled on the floor. He is freckled by shifting firelight showing through the woodstove vents.

I remember being out when I was eight or nine years old, walking in the mountains of eastern Arizona. I found a pair of elk antlers, shed that autumn. They were huge antlers, and you do not find such items at that age without thinking you've discovered something no one has ever seen. Stood on end, they reached above my forehead. It took muscles to lift these objects, and I groaned just to get one off the ground. Elk instantly transformed from pastoral critters of the meadow into powerful forest beasts. They could not be paltry animals with this kind of weight and size on their heads. The points were not as sharp as I thought they would be. They were rounded and polished from clattering through trees, from catching threads of lichens. The knuckled butts were hard in my hands, stained pink with flesh and broken veins. It is one thing to find the worn skeleton of an animal, but it is entirely another to find a sign like this left by an animal still living, eating, and walking the forest under dappled afternoon shadows. You touch antlers like this, and you have to look up, knowing that the animal is out there right now.

I was there with a neighbor girl, Paige. Paige and I carried the antlers home. It was like dragging whales through the forest. I did most of the work, so I pouted when Paige got to keep one of the antlers at her house. I had to have a good talking-to about sharing. It wasn't the same, though, having only one antler when everyone knows they come in pairs.

Over the years mice chewed at my prized antler. That is how I learned at an early age about rodents needing calcium and why the tips of old bones and antlers have tiny scrape marks. From then on I marveled at any bone I found scraped by mice and I made sure to point it out to whoever was nearby. I tied the antler up to the rafters in the garage to keep it safe. And never did I find a pair of antlers like that again. Never so fresh, and both of them side by side in the forest, as if they were waiting. And never ever so huge, taller than my body.

I sit back in my chair for a few minutes, close enough to the stove that my back grows hot. Now that I think of it, I can't remember what happened to the antler. It was taken by somebody, or the mice whittled it to dust. It perhaps vanished to the forest when it was no longer admired, hanging in the garage. I place my pen in the binding of my journal. I am thinking that I've got to go out to the truck, where I left a full grocery bag that wouldn't fit in my small pack and a book I wanted to read before bed.

I close the journal, tying it off with a leather strap. I seal the vents on the stove to hold the fire, and I pull on the coat and a pair of insulated leather army surplus mittens. From outside, the tipi is a glowing cone. The lodgepoles run shadows along the interior and are lit where they emerge into the stars as if there are footlights below. I leave the tipi and, wearing Sorel boots, walk through the forest.

The elk are in the meadow again, nosing through low places between snowdrifts. A crescent moon hangs over the Sawtooth Mountains, just off the square of Courthouse Mountain. Snow is blued by the thin light. Bundled, I listen to the elk, and the coat cloaks my figure. It has smuggled me back into the center of the herd. They come closer, pawing and huffing.

I often think of elk as the cumbersome animals. When they run through the forest, there is always the sound of snapping branches and hooves clobbering the ground. With deer you hear only delicate tromps as they bound away, their forelegs secured to their bodies more by muscle than by bone. Elk are stocky, their necks heavy and thick. On the highways deer are hit far more often than elk, because deer are constantly ready to leap. They dive into the road without notice. Elk are more likely to wander into your path, looking up as if startled out of important thoughts.

I was once driving Highway 550 into Ouray at two in the morning, tired and staring listlessly somewhere between my radio and the speedometer. Something passed my side-view mirror at seventy miles per hour. I looked up, and the highway was a chessboard of elk. I threw my weight against the wheel. The truck skidded between them, tires squealing and huffing smoke. I could see each of their faces, sometimes a foot away. One after the next. Not a single elk moved. If they had been deer—although the chances of finding twenty deer congregated on a paved road are slim—the entire herd would have exploded in every direction at once. There would have been blood and bodies, and my truck would have been crushed, upside down in the creek bed. Elk are of a different nature. Although they do run, and sometimes suddenly, their trots are distinguished and a bit ponderous, their heads lifted as they gallop. Deer are pieces of crystal ware; elk are galvanized-steel lunch boxes.

This night, the elk move in on me again, surrounding me without the slightest clue that a predator is among them. I am cringing at their approach, even closing my eyes.

It happens at once. One of them finds me. It smells me or sees me, and out of nowhere, everyone panics. The message races across the herd faster than a shout. Their sudden motion snaps into my blood. I am running with them. With the heavy buckle pulled tight, I race across the snow, chasing these charging shapes through the slim moon.

My knees are high, flexing through the leather, and I sprint without thought. As hard as I can run, digging into my muscles, driving snow up to my waist. I can see them, blue images in full gallop beside me. They are so close that I cannot stop running. Legs clatter past one another, the elk building speed against me. I push onto my toes, kicking over the deep snowdrifts.

The elk dive into the drifts, jerking to get from one leap to the next. In soft snow, elk go all the way to their bellies with their sharp hooves and thin legs. That is when the predators have the easiest time with them, running on the surface. The elk are quick nonetheless. I drive them into deeper snow and we both have to leap to get over the big drifts. That is where I break to my left and cut them off. I land barely on my feet.

Four elk have to rear back. The others veer. Back legs go out of control in sudden turns. Snow sprays into the air and lands on me. I see the antlers, and the flared nostrils sending out steam. There I hurl my spear, I notch my arrow. I make the motions.

When the din of movement has stopped and they regroup, I come to my knees, panting. The coat's shanks fold into the snow, and from across the meadow I hear the elk breathing hard. Most have made it to the forest, but those that were cut off are still out. They pace against one another, building a defensive circle, their heads tilted nobly into the air.

My mittens are spread on my knees and I struggle to breathe without pain. The elk press together, with faces and antler racks toward me. Even from here I can see the clouds of heavy, hot breath surrounding them.

Cervus elaphus

BIGHORN SHEEP

I

Three of them are behind the boulder. Made like windows, they are hollow inside, square at the edges. You can see clear through them. Compared to their bodies, their heads are nothing, their legs sticks. Idols, gods, remembrances, wishes: they were carved on the wall of this canyon a thousand years ago. Their disproportion and odd, hollow shapes must once have had significance. The bodies are wishfully large, sketched by Anasazi bighorn hunters who left their spear points and arrowheads here in the sand, as if to say *enough*. The people vanished from the canyons seven hundred years ago, leaving behind the desert bighorn sheep, both those carved and those living.

Draw a line from here in any direction for a hundred miles through southeast Utah. Walk that line, down the glass-smooth cliffs and through the embattled heaps of boulders. You will find the carvings. You will find hundreds of them as you learn to recognize the walls good for chiseling and the protective overhangs where people once gathered and painted ceilings. Out where there are only walls and spires, where there is nothing living to the horizon, there will be one boulder with a single bighorn carved into it, then nothing else for miles. There are those blatant on the scalloped cliffs and the few prudently painted on the back side of a stone, meant for an intimate audience.

I have seen them drawn in herds, long lines of ten, fifteen, and twenty. When the rock face turns, even where it falls back ninety degrees, the bighorns will turn with it, their carved bodies cornered in half. Their horns are always curled back, marking age, wisdom, and health. Sometimes there will be precise details telling of careful observation, such as the intricacies of a cloven hoof or the shape of the ears. There will be whimsical bighorns with a head at each end, and arrow-carrying hunters who wear the skin and horns of the animal. A line will show the trajectory of an arrow across a rock, leading from the hunter straight into the heart of the animal. There will be bighorns even older, six thousand years, painted with a red iron oxide so rich that it has become blood.

Like the petroglyphs and pictographs, the living animal exists only within the confines of stone. If the land lacked in severity, if it were not an upheaval of canyons and impossible turns, there would be no bighorn sheep. They range from the Arctic to Mexico, suggesting that biological environment and climate are not primary to their habitat. They thrive, rather, on arduous terrain. You will see them in places, walking on a ledge shored against a cliff seven hundred feet over your head. You will encounter their tracks when you are desperate for a way out of a canyon, when you are broken to pieces from searching. Follow their tracks. Their knowledge of the land is ancient. Bighorn sheep are not tricksters.

They are serious animals. There is far less behavioral diversity among desert bighorn than among mountain bighorn, probably because of the hazards of getting around in the desert canyons. There are few safe playgrounds here, little room for acting out. Desert lambs do not play as hard or as often as Rocky Mountain bighorn lambs. Desert bighorns reproduce earlier, climb earlier, and are prepared at a younger age to set out on their own. What has developed is an animal more apt to be still than to be in motion, an animal lacking in frivolity, knowing the routes from water to safety and back; an austere, armored monk of the desert. Although they tend to be more aggressive than mountain sheep, they are discreet with the broad behavioral repertoire of the species.

I follow a line from the square sheep petroglyphs. It takes me across the Colorado River, into the farther chasms. The red rock of the Moenkopi Formation is shaped like pillows and bulbs. Above are the boulder-strewn Chinle Formation and the magnificent walls of the Wingate Formation. The Moenkopi makes labyrinths at the foot of the Wingate.

At a bend in one of the passages are four painted handprints. They were left by the Anasazi, not far from cliff dwellings snugged against the wall and from shattered bits of pottery in the sand. Near the handprints is a white, painted bighorn sheep, three feet high. Its belly is auspiciously round. From this panel of paintings are higher benches and canyons. Ledges lead into one another, following smooth chutes of sandstone. It is a region that belongs to the precise, unadorned moves of the bighorn. Never think that there is a top to these canyons because they continue upward, and if climbing could go on for weeks, one would begin at three thousand feet and end at twelve thousand feet. I stop here, on the nipple of a dome, above a ring of canyons. It is a warm day in November. Nights to twenty degrees, days to sixty. I have been coming down the river in a canoe, and my camp is only a few miles away. There is a good boulder to lean against, and I watch from there.

Within an hour the bighorn comes. It is an old ram, a lone patriarch on a tour of the surroundings. He moves with nonchalance, the placid way animals move when they are alone. His lack of caution is startling. The ram passes below. I can see a coating of dust on his hairs from when, not long ago, he had rolled in a sand bath. As he steps, muscles waltz along his back, around his spine, shifting with each motion.

He circles the dome, moving to the other side, and I snake on the ledge above him. His horns are old, maybe ten years, coiled back to a spiral that becomes a full curl. Battles are marked on the flakes and rings. They are dark and heavy, like artifacts of warfare, some prized weapon carried through generations. There is a point between them on the skull and it has grown hard and round from head-butting in contests of dominance.

On my stomach, I crawl around the rim and rise behind a stack of boulders. Sometimes you will see bighorns in groups of lambs, ewes, and yearlings. Other times you will see a collection of rams only. Most often the rams are alone, wandering the canyons between mating seasons, familiarizing themselves again with the lay of the land.

Most bighorn routes lead to water. The Colorado River is only a few miles from here. Conservative statistics have them returning to water every ten to fourteen days in the winter, five to eight days in the summer. One large ram in the Mojave Desert was observed taking in nineteen liters of water at one sitting. Some reports suggest that bighorns are able to stay away from permanent water for six months, and a few researchers have suggested that bighorns of certain environments can survive indefinitely without ever coming to water. In the summer, free water may be replaced with water metabolized from forage or even water metabolized from the body itself. Metabolizing water from the body is a rare and complex process in which the burning of stored proteins, carbohydrates, and fats creates hydrogen. Respiration then introduces oxygen. Hydrogen and oxygen atoms combine within the body to form water.

Water is of little concern in the winter with a river nearby. The ram is nosing through the dry clumps of shadscale and blackbrush that have risen from cracks in the rock. Shadscale evolved to specifically defend itself against bighorns. The ends of its branches grow sharp so that they prick an approaching mouth, keeping the teeth away from its small oval leaves. The ram lifts its head from the shadscale and moves on. I am twitching. I want to remain hidden, to watch this ram candidly work its way out of view. There is a deeply satisfying sense to not being seen. But I have a childish itch. I want to be an insolent meddler. I want the animal to know I am here. I want it to turn around so that we can get a look at each other at the same time.

I fight it for a good while. The contentment that comes with this stolen anonymity is pure and sacred and unobtrusive. I want to do it, though. There is a devil in my ear. I cluck my tongue.

He stops and swings his head. His body is suddenly tight. He scans the rocks until he finds me crouched twenty feet up. At first he jumps away. Hooves clack on the sandstone. Then he rears around and stares. Not fearful, but suspicious.

I do not know what to think of this. He stomps his front hooves. I do nothing. He lowers his head and thrusts. When I stare blankly he grows impatient and stomps again. He is waiting, and I come out from behind my rock so that we can fully see each other. He stomps and once more waits, as if I am supposed to do something.

The best thing to do is to stay here and observe. Instead, I stomp my feet. I jab my head. He repeats his action and snorts with more energy. I do the same. Then he sits. Right there, as if on a whim. He drops down and faces me. Am I to take this as a challenge, or a slap-in-the-face sign of boredom with my presence? I stomp a few more times. He blinks and looks west for a moment.

Insulted and curious, I climb down. I want to get closer, to have a good look at this animal. There are times when I get too close to things I should not even approach. I can't tell you what it means. It is an errant foolishness buried like a dog bone in my head.

I reach the ram's level as he stands again. My stomach suddenly goes soft. I am meeting the eleventh-grade football player behind the school, the one who wants a fight and says he will be waiting for me. This fight, though, will not be fair. There will be no imposed rules of conduct. I want to look and he wants to fight. I am still in the rocks, ready to bolt upward. The power of a bighorn is certainly not something to underestimate. He snorts and lowers his head to show the lead of his impressively curled horns. We gesticulate at each other again. Maybe he is merely humoring me, luring me in so he can bust my ribs open with his head.

In 1984 a man was taking pictures of a ram near the Atlas uranium mill, just outside of Arches National Park. At a distance of ten feet, the ram took action and ran the photographer down, shattering his arm. The man slowly came to his feet, screaming for help. The ram charged from behind, hammering him squarely in the back. As two witnesses ran in and waved their arms at the ram, the man stumbled his way to his parked station wagon. The ram stood its ground and watched. Bystanders tried to help the man toward medical attention, but he refused and climbed into his car, which already housed his terrified wife and children. One witness said that he was visibly injured, that bruises had already spread. He slumped to the steering wheel and drove away.

There is a great deal of snorting and lowering of heads. I step onto the naked red sandstone. I am in the open and in direct line with the bighorn, too far from my ledges to get back, too far from the edge to take a running leap into an abyss, walking out on my own ridiculous cognition just to see the sheep. There is strange medicine between the animal and me. He tosses his horns into the air and snaps his head back. I am playing with a language I hardly understand.

An array of particular behaviors usually leads to a collision. The first is what I am part of now, the horn display, head-shaking, hoof-stomping, and huffing. Then come the back leg–kicking and the jumping. A threat jump often precedes a clash, as one ram leaps in the air with its hind legs still on the ground. This is usually enough to stop the fight, but the careful dialect of a bighorn, the point where confrontations end, is hard to decipher.

Bighorn sheep have no true territories, at least not ones defined by land. Groups and individuals within an extended herd occupy land areas that could be considered commons. Without particular territories to defend, aggression, particularly among males, revolves around group dominance. Horn size in itself often settles disputes. Rams with fully curled horns, usually more than seven years old, are the primary breeders in a herd, no questions asked. Nearly all courtship displays, which occasionally involve skull collisions, are performed by rams with a three-quarter or larger curl to the horn. The smaller and younger rams are left out, rarely even trifled with. One reason for them to stay out of the fight is that clashes between rams with different-sized horns consistently end after the first blow. A smaller, younger skull may not endure the impact of a large ram's horns. A mismatched joust can easily end with a dead or crippled bighorn.

Rams of similar horn size, when not fighting, tend to congregate. This reminds me of high school. Even when they are walking in lines, hierarchies are set up, as animals, both male and female, cut one another out and push ahead in line. The species is very intent on getting ahead. The old, big rams, more than any other, are the most concerned with status.

I once saw a Lincoln Continental that had been broadsided by a Rocky Mountain bighorn ram. The passenger door was caved in and the side-view mirror dangled. Before the animal was able to make another charge, the driver slammed on the accelerator and narrowly escaped having the door removed.

Now I can see the dark keyhole pupils in the bighorn's brown eyes. They are the kind of eyes, herbivore eyes, that seem to have no focus but are intent on something. I stamp and snort a few more times to keep both of us occupied, creeping toward the other edge to see if I can leap away. The drop is about forty feet. Midway between a suicide leap and a bighorn, I am wondering what exactly I was thinking by walking out here.

We are poised together, glaring and grunting. The decision comes in a second. The ram snaps around at once and walks away. He walks as if I had never been here, as if there had been no conflict. Without any sense of angst or speed, he leaves.

Startled, I call him back. I issue threats. He does not respond. I am no challenge. His ears do not even twitch to my voice. I feel suddenly tentative and ashamed. I had just finished a thorough conversation and I hardly knew what was said.

When an animal has been startled away, especially a bighorn or a mule deer, it will run a certain distance, then turn to view the intruder. This ram never even glances back, so utterly certain that I am a harmless, innocuous creature, that I have no ground to stand on, using his language as if I knew what I was talking about.

He returns to casual roaming. I watch him, alone. He disappears into the rocks and I stand on the open sandstone, stunned and fully aware that the canyon does not belong to me.

I I

Hand over hand we scaled into the Grand Canyon. We did not use ropes or harnesses, just bare hands and the edges of our boots, carrying gear on our backs, dancing across the tops of boulders, and skirting ledges no wider than a wedding ring.

Without benefit of manicured trails, two of us had come on a journey of a couple of weeks, old friends wandering the gray-walled bowels of the Grand Canyon. The work was hard, and I grew tired over the days. I felt a strain on my bones, my tendons taut as bridge cables. I was climbing a rock face that felt like a brick wall, negotiating nicks of handholds, when the weight of my pack became too much. Very slowly I began to fall, separating from the rock face like a gently departing kiss.

Time slackened. I looked over my shoulder about thirty feet straight down into the shadowy floor of a limestone canyon, figuring I would land in a pool of cold rainwater, and maybe I would break a bone or two on the boulders beneath the surface, but I would most likely survive the fall.

A labored breath escaped my mouth, all that I had left. At that instant my partner, who was climbing fifteen seconds above me, grumbled, "You've got to really want it."

Hearing the grit of his voice, knowing he had just climbed this very spot—and had done so without falling—I remembered why I was here. I remembered my ache to move and fly through this treacherous terrain, to become a lissome, capable animal. I sucked myself to the rock, the tips of my fingers crimping me back into position. My face pressed against cool gray limestone.

I really wanted it.

We did not stop to let out a breath or even glance at each other, not a moment to regroup. We kept moving, miles to go before we slept, days stacking on days, canyons building into canyons.

The inside of the Grand Canyon is not what it looks like from the rim. All the vast, visual grandeur you see from the top falls between cracks of hundreds and thousands of feeder canyons. Horizontal vastness becomes vertical declivity. Boulders the size of refrigerators choke narrow passages. Pieces of cliff two city blocks tall break off and lie like walls of collapsed temples. Taking rest in this geologic upheaval, we sat on a flood-polished edge of limestone as slick and silvery as dolphin skin. I picked up a rock and fiddled it between my fingers, appreciating the articulate range of my digits. I was proud of my hands. As long as I gave them my undivided attention, they took me far. My feet did the bulk of the work, but my hands managed finer details, picking out tiny, crucial holds, the pads of my fingertips used at times to support the entire weight of my body and gear. You travel on your hands inside the Grand Canyon. Flexing them opened and closed, I thought about how they are the one thing that conclusively separates humans from all other classes, orders, and kingdoms. Hands for making machines and threading needles. Opposing thumbs for grasping pens and paintbrushes, for counting coins, for absentmindedly toying with a stone to feel its every facet.

Of the creatures without hands—at least those my size—only a bighorn sheep could have gotten itself to here. Another traveler of sheer, rocky country, the bighorn was a constant companion, leaving tracks and scat pointing this way and that, showing crafty passages throughout the Grand Canyon. Four-legged and cloven-hoofed, they had this place mapped out. Given the same topography, though, I figured humans had a slight edge over bighorns. It is our hands. We can hang. Bighorns cannot. I believed I could outclimb a bighorn if it came right down to it. It became a competition on my part to see if I could reach where they could not. But I must admit that at times I've become lost, believing I might get pinched out on a cliff, and the slightest sign of a bighorn—a scrambling hoof scratch on rock or a single nut of a dropping—comes as welcome relief, proof someone found the way before me. Still, I bet I could best them if I really had to.

We moved into the floor of a narrow, cliffed-in canyon. The space was hardly wider than two of us walking beside each other. Paired cliffs to either side were not smooth like glass but were instead curved and undulated by erosion—bowed out, overhung, under-hung, broken into fissures and crags where pieces had fallen out, leaving boulders cockeyed in the floor below. The canyon was nearly a thousand feet deep, and its walls pressed us down the middle. Through veils of shadow we both had a sense not unlike claustro-phobia, a kind of enclosed vertigo, like looking up from the bottom of a well. We walked across damp sand and loose flood cobbles, our steps resounding along the corridor.

We rounded a bend and there stood a bighorn ram fifty or sixty feet away, body rigid in the middle of the floor. His horns wound around his head like an ancient battle helmet, pagan warrior. He looked at us with chilling confidence. He had known we were coming.

We both automatically dropped to a crouch, hands pressing into cool stones at our feet. We were hoping not to startle the animal more than need be. But startle it we did. Its head ticked back and forth, scanning its options, and suddenly the ram bolted straight at us, kicking up rocks with its hooves. Caught down on our knees, we were dumbfounded. This was not right. *What was happening?* The ram picked up speed, charging at us through a stone hallway, no way out.

About five seconds away, the ram lowered its head, concentrating solely on speed. I had encountered enough bighorns in my life to know things were not adding up. It had no reason to charge us. Thus, the forefront of my mind believed what I was seeing was not happening.

The rest of my mind panicked. I was going to be trampled, blown over. Three seconds away, the ram was committed. Even if it wanted to stop, it had no room or time to turn around. It would strike my left shoulder and my partner's right with the force of a car crash. Still we did not budge. We knew there had to be some other outcome. But we could not see what it might be.

Two seconds in front of us, the bighorn galloped through a spray of cobbles and sand, and I clearly saw the hard, bony rings of its horns, their surface dark and chipped like an old battle-ax. Alarms rang through my body. But what could I do? I certainly could not leap out of the way, not unless I sprouted wings or could climb like a lizard. *It was not going to hit us, was it?* I saw its eyes on either side if its head, dark glass balls in the canyon shade. I began to doubt my doubt. My partner and I were about to have our clavicles shattered, knocked out of the way like bowling pins.

With one second remaining, the ram veered suddenly into the cliff to its right. Then, he flew. He ran up the wall using momentum and impact, using cracks and aberrations in the cliff. His body spanned and recoiled with instrumental precision as he soared over our heads, hooves barely touching rock. In a single breath he bounded a hundred feet up, his body a pinball, bouncing, zigzagging between crooks and invisible textures in the rock. Pure thrust delivered him to a high ledge, where he stopped.

The ram situated himself, then cast an assured glance down at us. We stared up, our necks craned all the way back, mouths dropped open. I looked at the route between here and there but simply could not see it. No matter what latitude I gave my hands, they would be useless. I could not climb to him. This was one of his exits out of the canyon, one of the places in the map of his memory where he could escape. The second he saw us, he knew what he had to do. He just had to outrun us, cut us off, and in a breath he was out of reach on another level of the game. And, poor fools, we were left at the bottom of a hole. The ram watched us for a moment, then lifted his head and did not glance at us again. He was certain we could not follow him. He turned and walked along his ledge, vanishing into a network of passageways we could never see.

We eventually stood, dusted off our knees, and kept walking too. What else could we do but continue being the creatures we were? Slowly, we began moving again into the rhythm of boulders and outcrops, hands coming alive once more. We slipped into the deeper canyon, now with a changed sense of our place, humans wandering through the house of the ram.

Ovis canadensis

CAMEL

The sound of work was sealed within the cave. Rock picks and small tools clanked against the night-dark earth. Steel against dolomite. Headlamps swiveled, scattering light into back passages, illuminating small entrances to a hundred other causeways, a Minotaur maze of caverns. We were deep within the cave. To get here you have to climb down, get on your back, and squeeze through a toaster slot into a palace-sized room. Then you walk between fallen slabs of the ceiling to a place called the Damp Room, stacked with crates of equipment and specimens yet to be sorted. In the bottom of this cave was a camel older than the human species.

There were few voices. The excavation work was steady, taking us deeper into one of the continent's most important holes in the ground. Almost two million years ago it was open to the air, and through incarnations of ice ages and shifting herds of now-extinct antelope and short-faced bears that towered over grizzlies, it gathered the bones of the dead. Three hundred thousand years ago it sealed naturally, and until the turn of the twentieth century, when a group of miners broke through, no other animal entered. It is a time capsule, stacked to the walls with discoveries reshuffling our history of North America. We came with our screens and vacuums and plans and theories, looking for the past.

I found it just above a big dolomite boulder. It was four inches into the compacted dirt. Bone, a large fragment half the size of my palm. "Bone," I said, and all sound stopped. Four headlamps swung up to my position, near a duct to another chamber. I held the thing to the light. It was not obvious where it came from, if it was a piece of skull or of scapula. That was for later work, at the museum with magnifying lenses and fine brushes. It was from a large animal.

The bone was passed around as if it were a china cup. Each hand took it, turned it between fingers. Fine marrow sponge still clung to its back. It was a bone as fresh as last week. But it was older. It belonged to the camel, an animal that stumbled into this cave in the mountains of Colorado a million years ago.

Most caves have produced a handful of bones and only scant clues about who lived outside. This cave, at 9,500 feet, had us running with hundreds of small bones an hour. Few places on earth have produced the number of Pleistocene carnivores we found here. Wood rats hauled in most of the pieces, stacking their nests with the heads of wolves and striped skunks, the teeth of badgers. The oldest known black-footed ferret was deposited in this cave (more than 350,000 years old, while the next-oldest remains are closer to 15,000 years). We unearthed parts of a ground sloth, cutthroat trout, coyotes, foxes, extinct horses, and an extinct wolverine that has never before appeared in this region. Several thousand rabbit specimens were exposed, along with twenty-four fleas; twenty snakes; frogs; salamanders; and toads, and a snowy owl that today rarely travels south of Canada. Cheetah kittens came out of this cave, with mink and long-tailed weasels. A shy female student from Spain, just learning

English, found the penis bone of a badger and, having never encountered such a thing, took it to several stammering men who struggled to describe its origin.

I was after the camel. Its skull was just above my left shoulder, encased in white plaster. A one-humped camel, *Camelops hesternus*. The skull was too large for a wood rat to be toting around, so the conclusion had been that the camel fell into the cave and died here. The rest of the skeleton would be here. It was possible that other large animals fell through an ancient sinkhole and their bones were cluttered at the bottom where I worked each day. We had yet to find a saber-toothed cat or a mastodon or a short-faced bear, and this was where we would look. All of this would be sunk behind a boulder that I had been trying to split with a sledgehammer and chisel for days. It was the largest boulder in the room, and I flew at it until I was exhausted.

The children were the most serious of workers in the cave. Even more serious than the adults, who had waited all year, who had planned and studied for this. Nothing slipped by the children. Their parents worked here, researchers from the Denver Museum of Nature and Science and the Western Interior Paleontological Society. Following their parents, they grew up with dust and darkness and the small bits of fragile discoveries. Some preferred the romance of dinosaurs to these dead mammals. One boy, fond of geology, handled bones with mild interest as long as he could get to the rocks.

Kate Johnson was twelve years old. She was tall and thin, a basketball player at her school in Denver. She worked in the back room, in one hole, with such studious intensity that by the second day she was put in charge of the dig in a room she discovered, one that would be named after her. She did not blink. "I will need three people at least," she said. "One down in the hole with me, two up top."

Lunch, we sat in the sun outside the cave entrance. Kate appeared last, distractedly signed out as she pulled off her hard hat. She came straight to me. Into my open lunch pail she poured a mound of dust and small bones. "This was what I found this morning," she told me. She fingered through each piece, explaining how it was uncovered. Rabbit vertebrae and hollow long bones. There was a short claw to a bird and half a beak belonging to a raptor; a small hawk or falcon. When she took the bones back and secured them in a metal canister, she told me that I would need to clean my lunch box before I used it again. Hygiene reasons.

Her prize find was the canine tooth of a young bobcat. It had the smoothness of porcelain. Because it came from a young animal, there was hardly any wear. A third of a million years old. She carried it as if it were a gem and unwrapped it over and over to show it to me. She was frustrated because it had to go to the museum, because it could be years before it was ever displayed. "I don't think they should have it," she brooded. "I should have it. I'd take care of it, you know I would."

I told her how important it was, that each bone had been a clue, and this, a carnivore tooth, was one of the most important. I stuttered, looking for something that made sense so she wouldn't feel so bad. But I believed her. The museum had so many teeth by now. The tooth would go to a woman named Elaine Anderson, a research associate and occasional curator at the museum in Denver. She was a good enough reason for Kate to hand it over.

"Elaine will take care of it for you," I said.

Kate looked at the tooth, her lips pursed.

Elaine and Kate were hardly different, only Elaine was forty-four years older and the years made her the softer, more round woman. Her body was slightly bent starting midspine, the way a person will crook during a life of digging in holes and meticulously picking through small bones. Elaine and I sat together at the field camp, just outside of a canvas canopy. It was dusk. Lightning laced the dark clouds to the north. She opened a metal canister she had marked "wrapped goodies." Contents were to be taken to her home, bypassing the museum. She would wash them in her kitchen, letting them dry on the table. Her cat, she said, watched over them. From the canister she withdrew an object wrapped in white tissue, and she unraveled it slowly. It was the jaw of a ferret, excellent condition. When she handed it to me, she smiled deeply. The carnassial teeth were still sharp to the touch, lined up in the fashion of a mountain ridge, jags and valleys.

"They are so different from the rodents," she said. "Carnivores are such distinct animals. You can see it so clearly."

She was the carnivore woman. Among specialists in the world, she was one of the top minds in carnivore paleontology. A Fulbright Scholar, she took a PhD in Helsinki, Finland, with a dissertation on the Quaternary evolution of the genus of martens, *Martes*. She co-authored *Pleistocene Mammals of North America* with the late Dr. Björn Kurtén, probably the most knowledgeable person ever to have studied the topic. When she talked about other caves, ones producing few carnivore remains, she said, "It was awful, all of those rodents," and she nearly pouted. She taught bear and wolf classes in Yellowstone each summer and mammalian osteology in Colorado.

Elaine had a gentle voice that would quiet you from a mad panic. Everything was handled with care. Give her a tooth, a rodent tooth, and although she had no strong interest in rodents, and although she had seen more of these teeth than anyone can count, she would lift it with two fingers and place it the proper distance from her eyes. In time she would smile as if she had found something new. "Yes. A marmot incisor. The upper one," she would say. I would have expected a woman of this experience to have done it by feel, not taking attention from work at hand, making a quick pinch and flatly identifying it. But Elaine had time for everything, even rodent teeth. She was not a busy, painful scientist. She would lift the smallest fragment, an eighth of an inch long, and identify it perfectly. It would be, perhaps, the broken ulna of a juvenile porcupine. She would know. Each of this cave's seven thousand cataloged specimens, with a single number sometimes given to a hundred limb bones, passed through her hands.

Here she was treated with powerful admiration. All unknown objects were brought to her. Among geologists and paleontologists working the cave, she was a celebrity, yet she had the simple air of a grandmother. She brought several bags of homemade sugar cookies and she shared them at every lunch break. Working outside at the sifting screens, she wore a broad-brimmed hat and a light plaid shirt, cuffs buttoned. When we talked, when we shared bones, we sat on the ground. She told me about a site in southwest Mexico where a human tooth was excavated recently. A colleague dated the enamel and it turned out to be eighteen thousand years old. When I shot her a questioning glance, she only nodded with that faint, clandestine smile of hers, one that told me she had her head packed with surprises of this kind. This new date, when it comes out officially, is going to throw North American anthropology for a spin.

Many people brought folding chairs for casual evenings of conversation and dinner. They walked by, offering their chairs. "How can you sit that way for so long?" someone asked her. "Please, please take my chair," someone else begged. Elaine looked at me from the corner of her eye and grinned secretly. "People should learn to sit on the ground more often," she whispered. Her early childhood was spent on Tennessee Pass, outside of Leadville, Colorado, where her father ran a logging camp. She learned well enough how to sit on the ground. She said that paleontologists were turning soft.

This was when Kate came with her bobcat tooth, after holding it all day. She kept it in her fist as long as she could. When the tooth, painstakingly wrapped in tissue, went from Kate's hand to Elaine's, Kate's eyes were on the ground. Elaine nodded slowly, understanding the girl's sacrifice. "Thank you," she said, not to anyone else, not to the bobcat, the cave, or any of us within earshot, but to Kate alone.

At the campfire behind us, a man boiled the head of a possum in a steel soup can. He tended to it with a stick, bobbing it in the water. He found the creature alongside the road on his way out from the

East Coast, and to the dismay of his two boys, he tied it to the top of the car. After the steamy, curdling smell of death settled, he would have a clean skull. Scientists.

The next afternoon I was outside, awash in the blowing dust of the screens and the sifting. I came out of the cave for sunlight, to help with the tedious work of sorting through excavated debris. The material passed through screens of different sizes, shaken down to the details. Bones were picked out, hundreds of bones in an hour. The leftovers were bagged and labeled—1/16" SCREEN, VELVET ROOM—to be sorted again at the field camp a mile or so down the mountain. I found in one screen a wad of bone, almost thrown out for being a rock. I passed it to Elaine. We wore dust masks, bandannas tightened over them, and goggles. Elaine took the bone and pulled down her goggles. A bandit stripe of dirt covered her face. She smiled and leaned across the screen, hugging me tightly. This meant to everyone that there was a discovery, and they looked up from their work. The bone was the toe of a musk ox.

Down in the cave I came to believe that the boulder was more important than the camel. I put all of my energy into splitting the boulder. The more I worked, the more of it there was. It was now eight feet long, angling down slightly where it disappeared into the ground. Three days ago it was not even exposed, and when I dug its peak away, I thought I might be able to get it out with my hands. That was when it was a rock. Today it was a boulder.

It had crashed down with the ceiling of another room, a big collapse thousands of years ago that rolled through the passage, over the buried camel and all other beasts, and came to rest here. The stratigraphy was excellent. You could count the changes in the cave by digging through compact dirt, down to the boulder and its clutter of large stones, to the loose fill where the camel rested atop another level of stone breakdown. That was where I found the teeth and leg bones of a marmot. I traced the stratum back to the camel and found them to be on the same level. The marmot and the camel arrived together. More marmots came out, their arched incisors dug from the floor like jewelry. Four marmots, then six.

We held a meeting at the boulder to discuss the teeth. The person rotating marmot teeth in his hand was Don Rasmussen, one of the excavation organizers. His son found the first bones here in 1981, almost a century after the cave had been opened. Don wiped fine dust from his face and gently shook the teeth as if they were dice, as if they told him something. He hulked in his overalls with an air of wisdom watered down by his excitement. Whenever he found something, he grew anxious, telling the story of the animal as he examined its remains and the rockfall around it. "The camel was here during a cold climate," he said, shifting to find a seat in the debris pile. Headlamp beams drifted through the room, coming to rest on his hands, which held the teeth. "Marmots were strictly high-elevation, cold mountain animals. So it was an Ice Age camel, a woolly camel. There was an opening up there, and it had to have been open for at least, say, ten thousand years. The camel probably slipped down on the ice, which led it to here, where it died. It was without a doubt Ice Age."

"Which one?" I asked.

"Seventeen ice ages ago. One of those."

Most of the animals that were here at the time of the cave are still somewhere in North America, shuffled among changing climates. And if they are no longer living, they probably metamorphosed over time into other species, leaving the original husks in this cave as evidence. Camels in North America went extinct here. During the two-million-year time frame of this cave, about ninety species became extinct in North America along with the camel. Most of them vanished between twenty-five thousand and eleven thousand years ago.

Camel remains first appeared in California, then in Alberta, Arizona, Wyoming, Idaho, Mexico, Nevada, Oregon, Saskatchewan, Utah, Texas, and the Yukon Territory. It was an animal well heeled to the West, and now the species belonged to Colorado. Its legs were 20 percent longer than those of today's camels, making for tall animals. Its upper lip was large and mobile, acting as a hand for the grasping of food. It survived in this area into the past ten or eleven thousand years.

The Camel Room was too small for everyone. Most people worked in the Velvet Room and Mark's Sink, another twenty-five feet beyond the camel, up a chimney and down to another vault. The bones coming from Mark's Sink turned the place into an assembly line. To keep the dust down they installed a vacuum pump that ran to a generator outside. A full-time sifting operation. Wood posts were erected to hold up the new rooms. Here at the camel, it was quiet. Even twenty-five feet away, sound was beaten to nothing as it traveled between rooms. Around the boulder was room for two people, Dennis Hopkins and me. We spent half the time working from an angle in which we pressed against each other, with enough space to lie on our stomachs but not to lift our heads above our shoulder blades. The other half we spent down with the boulder. My nemesis. We had a tool we called Big Mamma. It was a seven-foot steel bar with a head at one end for a sledgehammer and a blade at the other. Dennis could not get between the rocks. "Bring in the Big Mamma," he said.

Dennis is a genius. There is no doubt. He was seventeen years old at the time. At a Western Association of Vertebrate Paleontologists conference two years earlier, he gave a talk on a fossil fish, a talk that amazed most scientists in the room. At the field camp he kept a bulging folder of research on a fossil plant from near Castle Rock, Colorado. He pored through it after dinner, into the half-light, when he finally had to put it away. He had not come with a parent or with friends. He was here as an employee and volunteer with the Denver Museum of Nature and Science. I tried to remember what I was doing at seventeen. High school. Making out on the bench seat of a Ford pickup in the desert. Little else.

Dennis was tall with broad shoulders, and he laughed well. In fact, he laughed easily enough that it did not matter how intelligent he really was. We both volunteered to cook at the field camp and we hiked back together each day, leaving early, walking down the long, narrow drainages. We made stew and gave each other tastes. It was agreed that the stew was good and nothing else was needed. We posted torn cardboard signs at the big pots: SPICY and NOT SO SPICY. Each morning Dennis and I walked to the cave together. He asked me about my life and I went off with rambling stories about rivers and deserts; compared with him I felt like a fool in the wilderness, but I didn't tell him this. Some people are bright and some are brilliant and there is nothing that can be done.

We followed each other into the cave, and sometimes we did not stop at the excavation. We climbed into back passages. Down through holes into rooms filled with crystals and a domed chamber with stalactites melting from its ceiling. We inched our way into smaller and smaller causeways until someone had to back out, wedged headfirst against the end of the cave. In one room we stopped and shut off our lights. We did not talk then. It was darker than sleep. There were passages from there like wormholes. They crossed into one another, honeycombing the walls, and dropped forty feet into jagged pits that opened again to tunnels leading in opposite directions. We took fetal poses to bend around corners, jerking our knees to our chins before popping out a hole.

Eventually Dennis and I returned to the task at the camel. We pried rocks apart with Big Mamma and dug out the small bones of marmots. When the bones left our hands, they were worked through several times, later cleaned and sorted, identified by species, labeled with tiny, exact writing in India ink. They each had a specific destiny at the museum, most of them going to the Small Bone Room, a vault packed tight with cabinets, part of the thirty-three thousand bone specimens gathering in back rooms where men and women do silent, intricate work. The bones are occasionally removed from the hold, examined, and compared. Doctoral students come and rearrange clues until the cave releases another bit of knowledge.

Elaine Anderson's desk was wedged between wooden cabinets at the museum. It was at the end of a long room that, from every crack, sprouted elk antlers, bighorn sheep horns, and massive femurs. Near her desk rested a majestically huge Kodiak brown bear skull taken from southeast Alaska. It was the size of a milk crate.

I went there on a Wednesday, gathering information. On her desk were stacks of papers and canisters and jaws in plastic bags and books and skulls. The only wood visible was a small space where her right hand rested when she wrote.

These were oddly quiet places, the off-limits rooms of the museum. They smelled of beetles and cotton rags. Drawers were filled with Guatemalan quetzal birds with iridescent feathers, an entire elephant skeleton in a locker, anteater skulls, saw-whet owls, walrus tusks, an African lion skull as big as a grizzly's head, the skins of tiger cubs, whale vertebrae, and the heavy-browed skulls of gorillas. Cabinets, fifteen feet high, continued row after row until hundreds of specimens became thousands. When I was there, two older women sat at a table, tying paper labels to the legs of stuffed sparrows, hundreds of sparrows, drawerfuls of them. Like in the cave, the sounds from the outside—the talking of a thousand visitors, crying babies, and the shuffle of feet—did not leak through. There were, in a few quarters, the tinkering sounds of tweezers sorting through vertebrae and the scratch of pencils on paper.

Elaine took me to a far corner and unlocked a small metal door. From inside she withdrew a pallet and gestured toward a skull. I lifted it gingerly. It was a moderate-sized grizzly, older. It was female, the cranial ridge not as pronounced as a male's. I glanced at the identification card beneath it, its words struck with a manual typewriter.

Ursus arctos Grizzly Bear
6840 F SN SEP 1979 CO: Conejos; Headwaters of
Navajo River
Missing one scapula

Farther down the index card was handwriting in pencil:

Last grizzly bear shot in Colorado

I looked at these words for a moment, skull in hand. Then I looked to Elaine. She nodded softly. It was taken in 1979 by a bow-hunting party, by a man who said he was charged, that he would have died had he not shot the bear. The bear was old. An upper canine tooth had rooted itself right out of the jaw, piercing her skull. Advanced stages of arthritis had taken her body, so much so that it was painful to see. Her spine had developed calcium cobs and spurs common to chronic arthritis. Her entire skeleton had begun to reshape.

"This bear did not charge anyone," Elaine said, and her voice sounded delicate, sad. "She was slow and old."

The bow-hunter's story may not have been good enough. He claimed a fierce attack, and Elaine told me that years later someone admitted that the hunting party had come upon the grizzly as it foraged in the tall grass of a meadow. She had been killed without warning. Her teeth had been worn to smooth bulbs. Her claws were flat.

I held the skull as long as I could. I pitied for a moment the man who killed this bear. Pity for the weight of his sin regardless of which story was true, for being the one person to make the single, critical move that rid the southern Rocky Mountains of another species.

It was a wolf skull, however, that I came to see. The skull was in the Small Bone Room. It was the best wolf specimen from the cave; *Canis edwardii*, extinct. As I had been told, behind the eye sockets were two small holes, evenly sized, about enough to take two sewing needles. Holding it in my palm, I could now see that the holes were unmistakable. Measured out, they revealed the width between two canine teeth of a cheetah. A few hundred thousand years ago, this wolf and a cheetah had a conflict and the wolf survived, evidenced by the healing that began to close the holes. Two specimens in one. The tale ended there. Everything else would be guessing and good storytelling.

All that is left alive of this wolf is its genus. The successor is *Canis rufus,* the modern red wolf, an animal that in the last several decades has toyed with extinction, dropping to as few as seventeen individuals. The red wolf is still dangerously close to vanishing, barely reaching a population of three hundred. *Canis edwardii* probably evolved to become the red wolf, but if the red wolf ends here, a half-million-year evolutionary line ends.

The lineage of the cheetah that put the bite on this wolf is now scattered across the globe. This brand of cat, so much a part of the African savanna, has proved itself to be native to the region around the cave, native to Colorado.

The oldest known cheetah in the New World came from Texas, two and a half million years old, barely outdating our cave cheetahs. This cheetah was built like a feather with teeth and muscles: long and thin limb bones, a light body, and a small head. It was of a slightly different build than the modern African cheetah, with a more powerful rear. Its claws were fully retractile, a trait lost in modern cheetahs. It was a combination pouncing-and-sprinting cat, somewhere between mountain lions and African cheetahs.

Originally the extinct American cheetah was thought to be related solely to the mountain lion, an animal whose fossil records show it has never been out of the western hemisphere. In the late 1970s a Berkeley paleontologist, Daniel Adams, sat down with all the bones involved and had a closer look. He discovered that the similarity between African and American cheetahs was no coincidence of parallel evolution on different continents. In fact, they were veritably the same animal. The New World cheetah and the living mountain lion were merely primitive makings for the modern cheetah. When all the bones and studies and bags of cave dirt were shaken down, he concluded that mountain lions, American cheetahs, and African cheetahs were all from the same place. The ancestral genetic blueprint of the African cheetah is in North America.

As I walked to the cave each morning with Dennis, it seemed that I should be looking for cheetahs. When I did, when I imagined the lanky form of an American cheetah sprinting after four-horned antelope, when I shook loose the vision of an African cheetah with black spots and replaced it with an invented coat, perhaps darker and more uniform like that of a coyote or mountain lion, all I saw was a procession of glaciers and a fast-forward migration of herds and forests. Climates have been running through here as unwieldy as the weather they created. At the time of the cave's natural closure three hundred thousand years ago, climates were caught middance. Grasslands in Alaska were being overrun by forests and muskeg. The Great Lakes region became dry, causing a spread of pine and hardwood forests, driving off the existing spruce thickets. Summers in Colorado became dryer, winters colder. It was the next line in a lengthy song.

We got back to the dolomite boulder, a rock of ancient ocean floors that settled here long before mammals, long before dinosaurs. Nautiloid fossils and pieces of horn coral dangled from the ceiling. The Pleistocene was not long ago in comparison. Two other people began work above the camel, coming in from another angle. They too found marmot teeth. Below the teeth they unearthed a portion of the camel's spine, and we all crowded into the small chamber, beaming our lights against the bone. The room was two and a half feet high and there were four of us, squatting, pressed, and contorted. Each breath could be heard, each shift of weight. It was still very quiet. The bone had been here for one million years.

I left early for the day, back to camp to start dinner, stacking my gear at the cave entrance and slapping dust from my clothes. Dennis got in with a group of geologists and walked with them southeast along a ridgeline, following the boundaries between formations. I walked down alone, through the small groves of aspens. Long, barren hills shouldered off the mountains. I hunted for cheetahs and watched for the long-legged gaits of camels across the glaciers.

I walked along a creek toward the field camp. It was a mumbling, small loop of water. It meandered beneath a worm-pole fence, working east, eventually to the Arkansas River. My hand went down only six inches before reaching the gravel bottom, hardly deep enough to lie in. This was the creek that was once a river. Now it was an easy step from one side to the next. Giant river otters once swam here, bigger than anything we have in any of our rivers today, here in a creek that is now hardly large enough to receive a name.

When I imagined the lives here, I imagined them like wind coming upon me, shivering the grass twenty feet ahead, taking my hair back and moving behind me without pause. It is all wrong to think with teleology and consider this point in time a destination. The wind will not stop here. The ground sloths will become red-tailed hawks, the humans will become wolves, the glaciers will melt into arid bushes with intricate yellow flowers. A sparrow fluttered out of the grass when I came too close and it startled me. The bird banked north no more than a foot off the ground, through cinquefoil shrubs, and landed out of sight.

Camelops hesternus

DEER

October's hunters have gone into the mountains. Smoke from their campfires rises from wild green canyons. This time of year the deer descend into low country for the coming winter, setting out with the first frost, the first light snow, the first booming echoes of rifles. They come down to drift and mingle in fields below the mountains, touching damp noses to one another, neighbors from distant valleys meeting in cool evening light.

Younger bucks stay together, stepping like teenagers abreast of one another, their parades of antlers nearly touching, but not. They cannot hide their lives in the open country of their autumn range. Everything they do is visible. When I spy older bucks alone, I think them senile, perhaps, dominance gotten to them so they can hardly look at anything but the spread of their own territory. They seem paranoid and irritable, nipping at the hinds of does to get them out of the way, while young bucks watch with anticipation.

Autumn is the season of rut. Fights break out. One at a time young males with four fresh points on their antlers break away to challenge old ones who wear six or even eight points. They provoke each other over fields of females. They posture and snort. They wrestle each other to the ground with their antlers. I saw them do this one moonless October night. I was driving south when two bucks swung into my headlights. With heads butted nearly to the ground, they locked antlers, dragging and shoving each other into the middle of the road. Hooves coughed up dust. They did not even glance at my sudden headlights as I stepped on the brakes. My little boy was in the backseat and I told him to look, that buck deer were fighting. He leaned his body as far as he could out of his buckled car seat and asked why they were doing this. I told him it is a season called autumn, or fall. Deer fight this time of year to see who is stronger. Sons try to topple their fathers. My boy stared over my shoulder, astonished.

The two animals moved swiftly, throwing each other this way and that, catapulting across the road and out of my headlights. They continued into the black of night, where they went on in my imagination, tearing and scrapping like gods through the rest of time.

Near winter, on crisp evenings, you see events like this. The deer, having made their lives public, sleep, eat, fight, and copulate below wrinkled folds of mountains. They come in such numbers that many are killed by cars, their carcasses leaving streaks of blood and muscle across the road. Some lie in ditches, bundles of legs. Others are left cocked in the middle of the road, hit by a truck, the driver getting out to inspect a broken, bloodied headlight, then getting back in to drive away, steering around the warm, dead animal. The eyes of these killed deer look like tarnished glass, and in the morning their milky, curved surfaces are touched with frost.

In twenty years of driving back roads, I've never hit a deer. There were close scrapes, of course, clipping off a bit of tail hair with my door handle or nicking a dewclaw, but I never hit a deer deadon. My mother hit one, as did my wife. Everyone I knew had hit a deer, and some had done it more than once. I thought maybe I was blessed. Deer medicine. Ungulate fortune. I talked to them through my windshield when I saw them approaching the side of the road, telling them to stop, directing them left or right with a hand raised off the steering wheel. Each time, these unseen gestures worked, the deer avoided me, and I began thinking myself invincible, a deer whisperer.

My luck ended with a young buck. It jumped a fence in the face of a radiant harvest-light sunset. I pumped the brakes hard and urgently muttered, "*Stop.*"

The buck did not stop. I was going too fast to avoid it. I jammed the brakes all the way down and my truck skidded, fishtailing across gravel. The animal was square in the grill plate when I saw it shoot into the air. It was making its escape, all of its life given to a single fleeing bound, muscles coiled into flight. It was so close I thought its hooves would clatter across my hood. In that half second I felt a gust of relief, thinking we were going to barely graze past each other, another near hit.

Then came a dark thud. Four slender black hooves spun in the air and my truck came to a halt. Copper-colored dust welled up around the road. My hands were gripped tight to the steering wheel. I looked over the hood, where the deer snapped back to its feet. Then it dove from the road, sailing over barbed wire fence into another field. Again, I felt relief and let out a nerve-racked sigh. I thought, *The deer will be fine.*

But once the deer reached the other side of the fence, it fell into a weakened hobble. I closed my mouth and drew my lips tightly together. About forty feet from the road, it dropped into grass up to its shoulders. My heart sank. From the way it fell to the ground, I could see how its body was wrecked, internal organs skewered by broken bones. Adrenaline had been its last defense, just enough to get itself out of the road.

From the truck I could see that the buck's breathing was labored, almost convulsive. I opened the door and stepped out. In a week, I thought, that place in the grass will be occupied by ravens. Magpies will land on the carcass, looking like jesters, with their black-and-white feathers, their long tails. The buck will become bones by winter, ribs splintered by coyotes, antlers sticking out of snow.

I felt awkward, not sure if I should get back in and drive away or if a formal apology was needed. Should I hop the fence and slowly walk across the field, where I would plant my hands on the buck's heaving heart, where I would explain that I had been in a hurry to get to town, and the sunset was so bright in my eyes? The buck looked back toward me. The way he held up his head, alert, seemed to tell me not to bring my apologies across the field. He would simply have to rally again, taking his last bit of life to reach another place where he could die in peace.

I did not cross the fence. I stood and watched the buck work his breath in and out.

A small herd of does passed nearby. One separated from the others. She walked over and stood beside the fallen buck. She lowered her snout and nearly touched her black nose to his side. Then she lifted her head and stood still for a long time, the buck's antlers raised beside her. Both of them were preserved by sunset light, everything about their living and dying naked in this autumn field. It was too private to watch. I got back in the truck and drove away.

Odocoileus hemionus

Et Cetera

SMELT

G ary calls early in the morning and asks if I want to go smelting
with him. I tell him yes. He says the tide will go out around
noon and then asks for my shoe size. When I say size ten, he says
he has a pair of waders that might fit and he'll pick me up at eleven
o'clock.

Eleven thirty, I am at Gary's house. He hurls a bucket of food
scraps into the hog pen, then rifles through a garage for smelting
gear. "These will fit," he says, and flops rubber waders over my
shoulder. He runs the dip net through the open windows of his car.
It sticks out three feet from either side. When we drive we have to
swerve so we don't hit other cars, road signs, or the guardrails.

We drive to a beach along the Strait of Juan de Fuca, where the
ocean squeezes between Vancouver Island and the state of Washington. Smelting is never as good in the strait as it is on the open
ocean. But that doesn't matter. We sit in the car, facing the strait, a

white pail between my knees, waders in the backseat smelling like something dead. We drink beer and gesture at the water. You always have to say something about the sea when you are there, even if it is only "Damn..."

Gary's got a deep, roving voice. He is in his midthirties and has a dark, clever stare. He wears suspenders. Always wears suspenders. When his children are around they hug him and push their cheeks against him as if he were a mother bear. Gary is a man who is a relief to speak with, like finally getting a gulp of oxygen. I was on the phone with him once, hadn't spoken to him in months. What was said was mostly about his new four-hundred-fifty-pound sow and how it gave birth to six good pigs. Well, seven. The seventh, the only one Gary named (I can't remember the name), was crushed or smothered or both by its own mother. He said it was resting in her favorite sleeping spot. "I suppose when you're four hundred fifty pounds, a tiny piglet is inconsequential when you sit on it," he said.

He looks at me, his beer propped on the steering wheel, and says resolutely, "Well..."

That is when we have to put down our beers, open the doors, get out the net, and go to work smelting. The tide makes a slow turnaround where the East Twin River meets the strait. Water leaks from the Olympic Mountains, comes eight thousand feet down, and here is where the smelt will come to spawn. Here, where the river has feathered sand into a long plain, where the smelt will roll in their milt-and-egg dance until we nab them. We move to the beach with big rubber waders hanging on us like pajama bottoms.

The tide is patient at the turnaround. We wait for it, walk out a few feet, and are battered back by a big wave. We stand on shore then, wet, drinking beer, watching a belted kingfisher. The bird hovers over the water. It is up twenty feet, scanning for fish. It has to make calculations from there, subtracting fifteen visual degrees for the refraction of light underwater, measuring the distance between the flash of a fish and where the prey actually lies. When it dives, there is a hole cut in the water and no other evidence. In two seconds the bird flutters from the water and flies into the forest, fish skewered in its beak. The fish is a smelt.

"There we go!" Gary shouts, hauling the dip net over his shoulder. He marches through the water to where the kingfisher plummeted. I waddle behind him to catch up. He turns and grins through the spray of the waves. "They're out here. The tide's going back, they'll be coming in anytime now."

We stand side by side and drop the net into the water. It is a hand-carved cedar pole with a rectangular net at one end. The pole is for our hands. The net is for the fish. His grandfather made the thing a quarter century ago, tied the knots out of monofilament line so that smelt would wedge themselves when they came to spawn.

"It's not like the ocean," Gary says, and spits. "They come like mad in the ocean. You get the right day, and the smelting is just crazy. Seagulls everywhere, coming after you and the smelt. Not like the ocean at all here."

I have never gone smelting in the open ocean, so I believe him. He is the father of two sons. He is a carpenter and a logger and a descendant of French colonists, of Irish, German, and English immigrants, and of Skokomish natives. He knows much more about smelt and seagulls and the Strait of Juan de Fuca than I.

Two hours. No smelt. The kingfisher drops north of us and south of us, each time coming up with smelt, and each time we follow with our sloppy rubber waders. "Forget the kingfisher," Gary finally says, and we leave the net where it is.

While we stand, a sea otter bobs through the surface and rolls to its back. From a stone's throw away it watches us, stiff whiskers arcing from its face. Its slick tail curls and brushes its belly. I point at it, and Gary reaches his arm into the water, down near his feet. He comes out with a round river stone and hurls it at the otter. This surprises me, but I say nothing. He knows more about this place than I do.

"Suppose I shouldn't do that." Gary eyes me, knowing that I am startled.

Hesitant, I almost say, *I wouldn't have thrown a rock at an otter,* but I don't.

Gary knows what I am thinking. "We're competing for the same food," he says. "He'll scare the smelt off. They see an otter, and they won't come near us. It's how it works here." He looks at me from the corner of his eye to see how I respond.

Gary is right. Or he is wrong. We are animals. We, like the otter, can digest the flesh of smelt in our gut and can roll to our backs, hands clutched over our chests. We, like the smelt, come to the edge of the sea to live and we scatter when there is fear. We lick our fingers clean, sleep when we must, and dream when we sleep, like any animal. We are also animals who are taking up an incredible amount of space for our size, throwing more rocks than anyone can afford. For a moment I think Gary has stopped thinking about it. Then he shrugs, throttles his hands farther down the cedar pole for a good grip, and says, "Well, I don't know. It's hard to say."

We both watch the sea, waiting for smelt.

There is one wave. It is like every other, and I have become fluent enough to tell one wave from the next by standing out here, having cold water sloshed down my waders. The net jerks and in the water I see a spasm of fish. The net comes out of the water in Gary's fists. "Here we go!" he shouts over the wave and we haul the net to shore.

Six smelt are lost on the walk and, with a big hole in the net, ten were probably lost to begin with. We end up with five. They are thin like rulers jabbed into the net, no more than seven inches long. Thin and silver fish like Christmas tree ornaments. They struggle, fluttering with an electrical anguish. Just getting your hand on one is like holding down a live, convulsive wire. They are not trying to get out of the net to survive but to hit the sand and reproduce. In the sand, the milt and the eggs combine to make a rich, fecund soup. Milt from the smelt is milky and viscous, and it fertilizes the glittering eggs as waves come up.

Females drop thirty thousand eggs at a time. Unlike the eggs of most marine fish, which are buoyant, smelt eggs sink to the bottom. Within ten days they hatch, and the larvae float instantly. They race to the open water. A continuous wave of nearly invisible smelt larvae is heading to sea while a continuous wave of adult smelt is heading to the beach. It is a numbers game. Most animals this far down the food chain play it. A scant number will survive, perhaps no more than a few tenths of those hatched, which are perhaps a tenth of those fertilized. The smelt are shotgunning themselves into the world, beating evolutionary odds with sheer volume.

The maddening instinct to reproduce is riveted into their bodies. When they fall back to the water from the net, there is no pause. They continue, shooting straight to the beach. The memory of Gary and me and Gary's grandfather's dip net is gone. There is only sex. I catch a few of the escapees in my hands. Their bodies are mostly transparent. You can see inside, to the working parts. Straight into the brain casing, and down to the fine rib bones and to the connecting muscles of the head and jaw. Embedded in their crystalline backs is an incandescence of green dust. This adds to the offsetting refraction in the water, scattering light even farther so that the kingfisher must think twice before diving after a smelt.

We shuttle them into the white pail. They are to be smoked over alder chips and fried with cornmeal and lemon. Fish tacos with cabbage, habanero sauce, and squeezed lime. Served alongside strong, meaty Pacific oysters and mussels pried from the rocks, geoducks hauled from the sand with a posthole digger.

Now that we've had a catch, now that the taste is in my mouth, I am willing to go farther out and I will take the cold seawater down my waders. Even if it soaks my jeans and fills the waders to my knees. I lay the net into the surge. When I pull in another crop of smelt, I strip them into the pail the way Gary first showed me and then walk even farther into the strait. Water comes high, tossing me back, and I lean into it, my legs sideways to the waves. Gary is a larger man than I, and when a strong wave comes, he steps in front of me to block it. The water smacks off his body and he steps back.

At the break of the wave on sand, the mating is rough-and-tumble. It is mostly luck. Fish roll against one another, dropping whatever loads they have in a matter of seconds, and race to sea before they are stranded. It is some of the quickest sex known. Whose eggs are fertilized by whose milt is rarely clear, and sometimes males out-number females to such a degree that it is all milt and no eggs. The milt is let free to mix with any eggs that have stuck themselves to the sand. The more a male impales himself against the land, the better chance he has of reproducing. And the better chance he has of getting caught in the dip net. Females are larger than males by almost a centimeter, which is enough to matter in Gary's net. Many females won't fit through the mesh, so they bounce off while the males following close behind become suddenly ensnared.

End of the day, five thirty. We have a pail with twenty-five fish, mostly males. Enough for a few dinners, and Gary says again that it is nothing like the ocean. So the next day we go to the ocean, ten miles down a muddy road. He has a family house, a ramshackle place strewn with fishing nets and colored glass balls that floated from Japan. It lies between Cape Alava and Point of the Arches on the Pacific Ocean where a creek runs to the sea. A good place for smelting.

This time my then girlfriend has come. Gary invites his brother, and we are accompanied by all of the children. A picnic is brought to the beach from the end of the road. We have two nets, one on his grandfather's cedar pole and the other on a yew pole that Gary carved twenty years ago. As Gary had said, smelting at the ocean is different. The fish dive at the nets and tangle at my legs. Seagulls litter the beaches and swoop to the water. As we pull the smelt in, I have to stop, getting down on my knees to rework his grandfather's knots, resetting the mesh where fish have torn through.

Just before the wave breaks I can see into it, and in the moment of glass, there are a hundred dancing fish. The wave takes me, digs my legs into the sand, and the dip net is quaking with smelt. Smelt like birds. Silver flashes and the lunging.

When I walk back with a full net, there are those that wiggle loose. They fall to the water and race past my legs. They charge to the shore like knives. When I dig them from the net, I am painted with sperm and eggs. Thousands of eggs, pearl white and small as pinheads. Eggs in my beard. Sperm to my elbows.

Fourth-grade boys wait at the bucket. Sons of loggers. They go at the fish with authority, grabbing them by their heads, plucking them out of the net. The ones that will not come are snapped in half. These boys are the pit-stop crew, working with the seriousness of professionals. As if plucking fish changes the world, as if it is bypass surgery, the cutting of an ancient tree. Important work. Some fish hit the sand, and the boys flounder to get them back to the bucket.

When the net is cleared of smelt, the boys slap my leg and say with ardent, impatient voices, *Go.* They say it quickly, with certainty, and push me toward the ocean. I turn, loft the net over my shoulder, and lumber into the waves. Smelt batter my legs, striking and flipping as they race to shore.

Then it is said, and it is said in a painful, hesitant way, almost under the breath. It does not matter who says it.

"We're going to have to clean all these fish."

Peering into the bucket, you do not want any more smelt. You want the net to be empty and you just want to stand in the ocean with the force of tides at your waist.

The bucket is two-thirds full. Two hundred smelt. Very different from the twenty-five smelt from the Strait of Juan de Fuca. Once you think about cleaning two hundred smelt, it is time to stop. You think of cutting heads off and getting blood down your arm, past the roll of your sleeve. You think about the whetstone and having to sharpen your small knife several times just to work through all these fish. You think of the gutting, the bucketful of heads and intestines, something so foul that you must joke about it for the hours of cutting, jokes that prevent gagging. The remains will go to the hogs and they will gobble it like cake.

A few more good catches, maybe. Wait until the net is completely full before dragging it from the sea. Still, smelting is over with those words. Even the boys at the bucket, even they are tired and have pulled enough smelt from the nets.

Gary keeps telling me that he has to stop, but he walks out in the water again. I find him just standing there. His net has been flushed to rags by smelt and it will no longer hold the fish. He doesn't want to come in. He stands in the waves and stares at the sea, working his hands on the cedar pole. Around his legs is a race, the incoming and the outgoing, a flux of evolution and procreation. With smelt whipping our calves, we are standing in the middle of creation. It is an irreducible flood, perfect and ultimate.

"Every day is good for something," Gary shouts over to me. "This is a good day for smelt."

Hypomesus pretiosus

PORCUPINE

My hands are down the dog's mouth, holding it open. Its teeth are on my knuckles. My knee is in its side, holding it to the ground.

The dog is a puppy, only a few months old, but it has grown large already and it has a bite and it has good muscles. The man, the dog's owner, has his hands all the way inside, digging with his fingers behind the dog's tongue.

"Damn, there it is," he groans. "I can feel it."

The dog yelps. The best it can with four hands in its mouth. It whines and growls and cries, and I keep it down with my knee.

"Got it, got it," he says. "Got it, just about..." He yanks and out it comes, the porcupine quill, dislodged from the roof of the dog's mouth like a fishing hook from the palm of your hand. The dog spasms and yelps.

When we let go, when I get my fingers out from between its teeth, the dog goes belly-up. It opens its legs and whines and licks. A submissive posture, looking for comfort. We rub its stomach and scratch its ears. The last quill of seven is out. The dog doesn't know what has happened.

It's not just the puppies. They all want porcupines, even the old ones, especially if they've never seen one before. Porcupines are perfect targets, slow and obvious, except for all the quills. If dogs have seen one, then they have taken a bite out of its quills and they are different animals about porcupines. Thirty thousand quills on the back of a porcupine. Each barbed so well that with every contraction of the victim's muscles, the quills work deeper. Another half inch, another inch. Then the offending animal dies with swords in its heart and in its lungs.

Quills are modified guard hairs, filled with a webbed sponge that makes them rigid but light, and incidentally no good whatsoever for insulation. White shafts, black tips. In one case a porcupine researcher took a single quill into his elbow while trying to capture a porcupine. It embedded and disappeared into his arm. Two days later the quill emerged through his forearm far from its original entrance, and he found the object loose in his jacket sleeve.

Porcupines have indeed killed more than forest animals. In 1934 a man ate a meal of porcupine. Twelve days later he died in a hospital from a single quill that had stabbed through his stomach from the inside out.

Touching the quill, you find it is smooth in one direction, coarse in the other. Under an electron microscope it displays overlapping, downward-pointed sheets with slightly upturned tips, just enough to turn itself into a powerful nuisance.

And the porcupine itself, soft eyes and a stubby nose. Complacent and calm, as if it does not have so much fierceness and violence riding its back. It is a contradiction of personalities. I have rarely seen a porcupine agitated enough to alter its pace. It turns and strolls, quills lifted. Simply enough, leave the porcupine alone, and there will be no qualms.

I live here in the forest and chase porcupines around just for the satisfaction of watching them run. It's hard to get them to pick up the pace, but when they finally do, they move with a direct gait, giving them the appearance of very short, very fat men trying to jog. When they climb the nearest tree, their needles rattle and scratch against the bark like venetian blinds on an open, breezy window. They are exceptional climbers for all their waddling and brooding. They lock their tabular, beaverlike tails against trees, using the friction of stunted, blunt tail needles to support themselves while they reach up for the next step. Their foot pads have the texture of patterned rubber soles.

The porcupine living by my tipi in the spring stays at the aspen grove, where bluebells have taken so well each year. It chews the soft aspen bark and fumbles with twigs in its sharp, curved claws. Whenever I come to it, on my hands and knees, nosing up until we almost touch, it remains calm.

It looks like a mop, a bundle of ponderosa pine needles, a mobile hairstyle. It takes a while to find the front end, the side with the two dark eyes. Teddy bear eyes and a short snout. Doesn't give a damn, just stays there and watches me as I crawl closer. They cannot throw their quills, as some people fear. The quills will become loose during a confrontation and readily fasten into the skin of the attacker, but they won't be hurled in your face from across the forest. I inch closer and rest my chin on my hands, looking at the porcupine. If I could ever be this calm, I think, if I could ever lay myself down on a fallen aspen and be so quiet, then I would know something. Peter Blue Cloud wrote, "When porcupine goes night walking, he doesn't look behind himself and say, 'Ah, yes, I got my quills with me,' he knows what he's got."

A predator had already gotten to this one, had taken the only attack possible. There are no quills around a porcupine's face, and someone had taken a bite from this one's snout. Not long ago, maybe only a week. A gash runs from the side of its nose almost to its eye, healing slowly, with crumbs of necrotic skin hanging loose. Usually it is a smaller predator, maybe a coyote, with the ability to attack between the quills and hit the porcupine's face. The big ones, the mountain lions and bears, must contend with quills, being too large to strike so small a region.

Whatever it was got a good bite, but there are bare patches on the porcupine's back. Maybe a hundred quills are missing. The predator may be dead already or may be in the forest now, chewing mercilessly at its own flesh.

The porcupine keeps its head low, resting on its paws. I have been tempted to give it a name. Scar Face, or something like that. But my presence has probably been troubling enough, so I won't add to it with a silly name. It must be uncertain of me. People out here shoot porcupines because porcupines eat things. They eat everything you leave out. Car tires, plywood, canvas covers, the front door. Their unconventionally lengthy digestive tracts can pass nearly anything. I come to see it each day, sometimes just to walk through the aspen grove and watch for its shape.

The wind has been hard out of the west. Spring wind. It has been knocking down aspen trees, and I had to drag one off the county road so that I could drive to town. Every day the wind makes the aspen grove fluster like a field of bulrushes. Bending, swaying, and coming back. I come to the grove in the afternoon, when the wind rises to a climax. The porcupine is not here. It has gone, maybe to the next grove. I think it might be tired of my daily visits. Or it is off looking for a mate.

I've always considered the mating of porcupines to be a messy scenario, fraught with danger and pain. It is, instead, delicate. Porcupines can easily take all day in their sexual matters, unlike most animals, who complete long-awaited copulation in seconds. There is a nuzzling and a courtship process as they stand on hind legs to rub noses. The male then comes around, leans against the soft underside of the female's upturned tail, and there is whining and gentle whistling. This may continue off and on for an entire day. Everything they do takes time. Even the gestation, over two hundred days, is very long, considering its size. This prolonged pregnancy turns out a single porcupette. The infant's quills stiffen by the second day, and the next four months, another unusually long period, are spent nursing.

Walking back, trying to imagine a pair of pincushions having sex, I look up and see the porcupine suspended over my head. Thirty feet up in an aspen tree, it is wedged between branches. The tree is flying, taking to the wind like a kite. Aspens are built to bend. Their long, nimble trunks have the consistency of hard rubber and the bark is as flexible as skin. Again, the porcupine is unfazed. It lies against the branches so well that even in the wind its legs dangle apathetically. Claws are unhinged like baby fingers. It regards me as it swings above. It blinks.

I call up to the porcupine, say hello, ask how its day has been. The porcupine sways and weaves with the tree. It gives no response. A porcupine spends most of its life in trees. Once, I was skiing in the backcountry and came across a tree girdled with debris. I spent a minute thumbing through the chewed branches and bits of scat a foot and a half deep. Then I looked up to see a porcupine who was spending its winter in one place.

Two things a porcupine body does well: climbs trees and digests them. Nearly a third of its body weight is relegated to digestive organs capable of breaking down the complex ingredients of leaves and bark. A great deal of time is spent resting and processing the leaves that it crawled to the branch's end to eat, which explains the apparent lack of motivation. The porcupine is always, at least in the summer, working on a full stomach.

I want to get up to the porcupine's level, see what it is like at the top of an aspen. The aspens of this grove have many branches and are not too bad for climbing. As the tree bends in the wind, my body goes with it.

I reach the porcupine's level, fifteen feet away. I call over to it, asking it about fear of heights. By God, it's windy, isn't it? The porcupine does not move, so I keep talking. I have to yell because the wind has each leaf in full flutter and it sounds like a waterfall up here.

The wind comes in long pushes and the entire grove leans eastward. Then it lets off and the trees recoil. I have to hold tightly as the tree and I describe long, smooth arcs over the ground. For all this motion and these bursts of air, it is fluid up here. The tree never makes any sudden starts. It pivots above the earth and we swerve back and forth, the porcupine and I. Now the animal is lying there, perfectly cupped in a crotch of branches. Its right foreleg hangs lazily and drifts in tandem with the tree. I relax my grip and let my fingers loose, thinking like a porcupine. No meditation, no trances. Just keep still and quiet. For an hour I stay there. It is hard to hold my grip and I have to keep shifting.

Don't be misled by their casual manner of hanging from trees far overhead. They are no daredevils. Porcupines do fall. Some falls result in death, others in quill heaps at the bases of trees. Autopsies of porcupines have revealed common falling-related injuries, including that of one porcupine that had a four-inch pine branch permanently lodged inside its body long before it died. The truth about porcupines is that they fall more often than you would think. This painful habit was uncovered by Uldis Roze, a man who probably knows more than anyone about porcupines.

Roze was the researcher with the quill stabbed through his elbow, and he could not help wondering why the grisly trauma of a quill passing through one's flesh leaves no infection. In fact, while it was under his skin, he forgot about the quill until it popped out on the other side. He then took a close look at porcupine quills and found that they are coated with a greasy layer of fatty acid. Putting the acid through a gas chromatograph, he then discovered that porcupine quills are blanketed in mostly palmitic acid, which is a strong antibiotic as effective as penicillin. This led him, by way of typically scientific and hypothetical logic, to the conclusion that porcupines regularly fall from trees.

Why antibiotic quills? If you are going to stab your enemy, it makes little sense to clean your knife first. The purpose lies elsewhere than in the well-being of a quill-infested coyote muzzle. Knowing that porcupines are adept at removing self-impaled quills, Roze set out to find whether accidental self-mutilation is common among porcupines. He went to museums and studied their skeletons.

Roze found healed skeletal injuries on about 35 percent of porcupine skeletons. Just to make sure, he checked other animals. Ten percent of raccoons had similar injuries, and 7 percent of woodchucks. Porcupines, it appears, are good at hurting themselves. Being famous tree climbers, but equally famous dullards, they must be cracking their skeletons by falling out of trees. Thus, antibiotic quills. You have enough problems if you fall thirty feet out of a tree. If you survive that, you don't want to die of infected stab wounds from your own quills.

The trees are flexing like cello strings. The porcupine moves now and then, scratches its left eye. It almost stretches, but not quite. The porcupine leans its chin around the other side of its branch. Birds come through, a pair of mountain bluebirds, one flicker, one Lewis's woodpecker, and one red-winged blackbird.

Sunset comes. The wind is cold now and I've been watching an essentially immobile porcupine for too long. I almost shout something, but I don't. The porcupine continues to hang on. Not for dear life. It just hangs on, trusting that the tree won't drop it.

I walk back to the tipi. Red-winged blackbirds clack at me and dodge through the wind. Grass turns against my calves. My footsteps are now so slow that it will take until dark to get home, just inside the next grove. But that does not matter. I keep walking slowly in the wind, exactly as I learned from the porcupine.

Erethizon dorsatum

PRAYING MANTIS

F riends and neighbors gathered around a table for dinner, set in a purple-flowered alfalfa field. It was an epic picnic, with white linens and bottles of wine in summer light at the foot of the Rocky Mountains. We ate and laughed and talked, passing back and forth dishes of chanterelle mushrooms, goat cheese with mint leaves, and tender lamb. Blackbirds flew by in revolving formation. A great blue heron sailed overhead, while below on earth we drank chardonnay followed by Riesling, then by cabernet. Never in my life had I felt such prosperity, such delightful company, when suddenly I saw a scuttling movement up my shirtsleeve.

A praying mantis paused on my elbow, green grim reaper with hooks extended toward me. It tipped its head up to face mine as if rapidly assessing me, mechanical insect body floating on four slight legs. The sound of silverware and laughter stopped in my head as I peered back at a predaceous insect the length of a finger, a dispatch sent from death itself.

Its green goggle-eyed head swiveled as if mounted with a gyroscope, tracking me no matter how I moved my arm, keeping its gaze even with mine. All mantid species have this uncanny ability for motion. They can rotate their heads 180 degrees, and tilt them from side to side, lending them an almost disturbing illusion of cognition, of acquaintance. They seem eerily familiar.

"Hello," I said to the insect on my sleeve.

The mantis's head bowed, its thousand-pointed eyes regarding me, whatever me it saw, a creature a hundred times its size. With its two compound eyes, and a third simple eye positioned in a triangle between its antennae, it was able to discern shape and color. It picked out my form, my electricity, my pheromones, against a backdrop of blue sky and uncut alfalfa. At least in flies, it has been found that the insect brain can actually focus its "attention" on one point or another. A form of perceptual concentration allows one narrow band of information to be processed by the brain, so that researchers can determine exactly what a fly is looking at.

The bisymmetrical brain of an insect looks and functions like a miniature version of the hippocampus, the center of a human brain that processes spatial navigation and memory. A human brain contains about a hundred thousand times more cells than an insect brain, but size may not matter. Insect brain cells are designed differently than those of humans, able to compress information in such a way that many more kinds of data can be transferred at once. Researchers looking into the function of these bug brains have recently found indications of higher cognitive functions. Complex neural systems are engaged in massive feedback loops previously unexpected in the class Insecta, the most diverse group of animals on the planet. Upon discovering this, one researcher commented that he has stopped indiscriminately killing insects.

A praying mantis has no such qualms. Denizen of the invertebrate underworld, wearing its skeleton on the outside, the mantis is a purely anatomical killer. It relies on speed, hooks, and rippers rather than poisons or sticky webs to subdue and devour its prey. It consumes mostly insects, but mantids have been known to take down bats or small rodents. In one documented case a garden-variety praying mantis struck from a flower and buried one of its hooks deep in the chest of a hummingbird, instantly killing the animal. It held the hummingbird with one hook as it reached out and disemboweled its victim with scissoring mandibles.

I have never taken a praying mantis's geometric efficiency for granted, never brushed one aside like a fly or an ant. This one had me locked in a stare. The sheen of its paired eyes said nothing, like a mask. Seeing its barbed forelegs drawn in the air, I felt somehow that I had the under hand, a twinge in an ancient part of my brain telling me to keep absolutely still. I do not know if I was so taken because I was fascinated by its mechanical parts or because somewhere inside I was actually afraid. I simply stared back, spellbound by its pitiless gaze, its air of recognition.

In Greek, "*mantes*"—from which mantids are named—means "prophet," or "soothsayer," which is particularly revealing, considering that a handful of researchers believe that insect brains lie at the root of what we know as consciousness. Its grasping forelegs are generally kept upright and folded as if in prayer, making it a holy mercenary, a predatory oracle. There are more than two thousand different kinds of mantids, all of them slender predators, the largest as long as a human hand, the smallest no longer than an office staple. A *Choeradodis* mantid is hooded like a cobra, its mantle green, veined, and shiny like a leaf so it will not be distinguishable by those who might prey on it—the mantle also prevents a bird or reptile from being attracted by suspicious movements as this mantid consumes its prey. Central American *Acanthops* looks like roughened bark and dry leaves, the macelike head sharply pointed, the eyes formed into spikes. They kill whatever they can. Females are well known for twisting around and devouring males in the middle of copulation. A male missing its head and eaten down to the abdomen will continue insemination unfazed, its nerve trunk still delivering the last message sent by its lost speck of a brain. I am reminded of a tenet written in the *Hagakure: The Book of the Samurai*—"Even if a samurai's head were to be suddenly cut off, he should still be able to perform one more action with certainty. If one becomes like a revengeful ghost and shows great determination, though his head is cut off, he should not die."

Little warrior, green as grass and leaves from head to toe, this mantis tracked my every move. I gave it my hand to crawl on. It did, rapidly, its body poised strategically. It sped across my finger, traversing my palm onto my upheld wrist so it was even nearer to my face. Its motions were as assured as swift chess play, each step precisely weighted. It was so close to my eyes I had to hold my breath, fearing it might suddenly lunge and topple me from my chair with a crash of flatware, my wineglass flying.

My wife, sitting across the table, reached out her hand and asked to see. I passed the mantis across. It raced up her arm, over her shoulder, and into her hair. People sitting beside her recoiled as if she had a rat on her.

She smiled. "It's just a bug."

Mantodea

RATTLESNAKE

It could have been any of us bitten by a rattlesnake. We were all likely targets, working as guides and field instructors on the lower Colorado River, a place well populated by rattlesnakes. Wearing river shorts and sandals, we picked up gear boxes and snapped out tarps, constantly exposing our bare flesh. In some ways I wished it had been me, just to get it out of the way and to answer my curiosity.

It was not me, though. Instead it was a friend working a few miles upstream. He stepped on a rattlesnake in the night, when the desert was warm and the only light came from an ambient bluish glow among the stars. He was wearing his river sandals, and for an alarming half second, a snake, some *Crotalus* species, thrust its knuckle-length fangs and forty milligrams of venom into the arch of his foot. The venom moved quickly into his cells and began at once digesting his foot and leg from the inside out. Within minutes vascular breakdown began as his heartbeat carried poisons through his system. I did not hear from him at the time. All I heard was the sound of a boat passing alone in the night. News was shuttled up to my camp around tents and kitchen gear that a rescue was in progress, my friend being hurried downstream to the takeout. Five hours from the nearest hospital, I stood and listened to the silent, meandering river. I looked across the dome of the night, wondering what was happening on that departing boat.

Like the rest of these guides, I was out all the time. I took my days off in the desert, where I carried water and food left over from the last river trip, and set camps under towering cacti. I had nearly stepped on several rattlesnakes out there, my body literally taking flight at the sound of a sudden buzz beneath my stride. A few I nearly sat on. I urinated on one on a cool morning, noticing too late its camouflaged body coiled in the dust at my feet. None of these snakes even struck the air to ward me off. It seemed *Crotalus* and I had developed a tenuous truce around each other. I did not smash their heads with a rock and, thus far, they did not bite me from out of nowhere. At times they seemed even courteous, rattling loudly as each slid out of my path and poured its long, mosaic-scaled body into the nearest hole or rock crack. In return, I backed away without following them, without trying to touch their buzzing tails as they departed—though at times it was tempting to dodge in and feel a rattle snapping between my fingers. I never did. It was best to leave them alone.

However respectful I was, I still felt as if I were pacing in the desert's waiting room, listening for my name to be called. I expected a sudden bolt of an arrow-shaped head from out of a pant leg I was putting on in the morning, a jolt of pain in the skin between thumb and forefinger, or at the back of my knee, or on the side of my neck as I leaned down to drink from a spring without noticing a serpent resting beside me. It is not like the fear of being torn apart by a grizzly or dragged into a tree by a jaguar. This is fear of a sniper, a bullet from nowhere, the sound of a rattle coming too late.

My friend who was bitten did not die. There was not enough venom to stop his heart or plunge him into a coma, so he remained conscious, gritting his teeth as he lay in the bottom of a boat heading for the takeout. Without a precise antivenin on hand, there was little to do but tie a loose strip of cloth above the bite and hope he did not die en route. After being carried off the river, and after a jostling ride across the desert to the town of Yuma, Arizona, he lay in a hospital bed, waiting for the poison to subside. Using antivenin is a dangerous procedure that can be fatal in itself, so the doctors decided just to watch him, making sure his throat did not seize. He had to wait it out.

There is more than death in a rattlesnake's bite. Its venom is a pharmacological menagerie of highly evolved proteins. These proteins have numerous restorative powers. Rattlesnake venom is known to cure some cancers. Its method of breaking down cell walls—using an atom of zinc to cut through membrane like a sharp tooth—is the same process by which cancers travel through the body. A drug made from such venom reduces blood clotting and has been successfully administered to stroke victims, allowing them to regain physical and mental abilities within a matter of hours. A number of people who have intentionally injected doses of rattlesnake venom like daily vitamins have lived to an old age with few physical complaints, no colds or flus to speak of. But it is not something to trifle with. Dosage is a treacherous balance. Death is always waiting.

When I saw my friend a few days later, of course I wanted to hear every detail. He told me the bite itself had felt like a glowing-hot ice pick stabbed all the way to the bone. He described a burning sensation of poison entering his veins, how layers of pain seemed to unfold his very being. He said I could pull away the sheet covering him, and when I did I saw a foot and leg hideously swollen and black as coal. His skin, which looked like it should have exploded from such swelling, was grotesquely fireworked with burst blood vessels. I saw deflection in his eyes as he hid the constant wince he was feeling.

I smiled at him as I re-covered his disfigured leg. I thought he was a better man for this. I said, in reverence, "Snake medicine."

Knowing what I meant, knowing that he now had the physical presence of a rattlesnake inside of him, he nodded uncomfortably and repeated, "Snake medicine."

———

Over the years we all left the river and took different jobs, but some of us came back to this desert. We returned and met for long reunions in the wilderness. A decade after we had worked together, three of us headed into Sonora, Mexico. We got a ride one night from a herpetologist, forty miles down a sandy two-track into a black and moonless void. The plan was for the herpetologist to drop us off in the desert with enough water to walk our way out, something done purely for recreation. It would take almost two weeks for us to reach a town on the other side.

As we drove, a coiled rattlesnake appeared in the headlights, and the herpetologist slammed on his brakes. He flew out his door, wielding a long pole with a net on the end. I do not know where the net came from. It simply sprang out of his arm. Without pause he swept the net across the ground and, in one fluid motion, dove a single hand inside. He had a cord of muscle writhing in his grip. Like pulling a rabbit out of a hat, he lifted a Colorado Desert sidewinder, *Crotalus cerastes laterorepens*, into the headlights. His thumb pressed behind the snake's skull, his forefinger shoveled under its jaw. The snake's body flipped back and coiled around his arm. It was not a long snake, less than three feet. But it was animated.

I was not ready to see this. I had climbed out of the truck to observe a snake on the ground, to squat down in front of it maybe, watch its tongue snap at the air from a safe distance. But suddenly this man had a rattlesnake in his grasp and was looking into its eyes from a couple of inches away. It was like looking straight into the steely gaze of Shiva, the destroyer god, something you just don't do. I stepped back, almost stumbling on my own feet.

"Oh," I said breathlessly, all I could say.

The snake was really pissed now. On the tip of its tail, an amber-colored shaker moved so fast it whined. The rattle appeared to shimmer, a stack of dried, segmented scales vibrating at about sixty flicks a second. It sent a single loud message: *Touch Me Not.*

As if in a trance, with a fascinated smile on his face, the herpetologist muttered, "Ah, it's beautiful."

After a moment of reluctance and disbelief, I stepped closer. I was fixated, my heart thrumming under my shirt.

The herpetologist excitedly turned the snake's spear-pointed face and pushed it at mine. "Look at it," he said.

I backed my head into my shoulders.

"No thanks," I whispered.

"But look at it," he insisted.

My whole body leaned away from the snake, yet I stared at it just like he said. "It's okay," the herpetologist said. "I got it."

It's too much to hold, I thought. *What does that mean, "I got it"?* I slowly lifted my face so that I passed for one second across the sidewinder's irate gaze. Its eyes burned intensely. They were like glass marbles, their interiors decorated with dusty colors and patterns matching the rest of its body, the entire animal the color and texture of barren country. Its expression was infinite, no ability to blink or to smile with its fixed stare.

The sidewinder wrestled its head an eighth of an inch out of the herpetologist's grip, enough that it could stretch open its mouth. I was looking into a pink, pillowy, fleshy interior, hardly even a pinprick for a throat, down which it can pass bird eggs, lizards, and rodents. As a reflex, the rattlesnake's paired fangs hinged outward, both thin and translucent as glass needles. They looked like small surgical weapons. I stared at them, unable to speak or move.

We were about to set off on a long walk in a country of rattle-snakes, and I felt uneasy about what was happening here. A rattle-snake bite in Mexican wilderness would be dire. Helicopters would not come to our rescue. As scientifically minded as I wish to be, I felt as if we were broadcasting ill will to all sidewinders in the vicinity, adding to our risk. I thought to tell the herpetologist to put the snake down, but I could not. I was spellbound. The snake closed its mouth, and I looked as closely as I could into its sand-colored eyes. Its body thrashed, tail buzzing, unable to free itself. After a minute, the her-petologist stepped back from me, finding a clear space between us, where he released the sidewinder onto the ground with a thrust of his hands, not throwing it but setting it down very swiftly. The snake flew away. It barely touched ground as it glided off to my side, its movements elegant and quick. Such locomotion is why the species is called sidewinder, its body sliding broadside across the ground like a rope of water racing away.

Other than having a single lung, rattlesnakes are more or less the same as all vertebrates, including humans, only they are stretched long, the red bead of the heart resting above a cigar-shaped liver, followed by a ravel of intestines and a pair of lengthy kidneys. The snake has a few hundred sets of rib bones compared to a human's twelve. Ribs are connected to an equal number of vertebrae, which are hinged off of one another with ball-and-socket joints, allowing the snake to freely articulate its entire body.

Drawing across the sand, the snake aimed at one of my compan-ions — inadvertently, I was sure. It was simply trying to get away from its holder. My companion, wearing sandals, did not move, though he was aware that such a species smells heat through facial apertures and is not tricked by still animals. A desert traveler, he knew rattlesnakes well enough that he thought better of making a sudden leap out of the way, bare-ankled as he was. He stood like stone, and the snake passed across his foot, brushing his toes with quick scales. With every increment of motion under its control, this sidewinder blew past him, moving out of our white headlights and into the dark desert.

Everyone visibly relaxed, shoulders let down, hands loosened. Someone laughed out of wonder.

Half joking, half not, I said, "I hope it doesn't come back to haunt us."

———————

From there the herpetologist left us. We three who remained began navigating by stars as his taillights paled in the distance. No one used a flashlight. Instead we kept our eyes adjusted to the dark. The desert rolled out in front of us as we focused our eyes on the skim of earth and sky in the distance, counting stars as they set.

Black wind-sharpened boulders lay across undulating beds of sand. I trudged ahead, my mind fogging from the weight of water on my back. We each moved into our own heads, shoulders leading us forward, breath riding in and out, eyes moving through stars. A rattle erupted from the ground between us, and suddenly we all woke, bodies snapped into action. We could not see the snake, but we knew exactly where it was as we circled in. It sounded like a small one, a young sidewinder. We looked down at nothing, an emptiness on the ground that was making a buzzing fury.

Someone said to it, "We're just out walking, nothing to get excited over. We know you're there."

The snake's rattling subsided and then stopped. Maybe it was tired or thirsty, not willing to expend any more energy. Or it simply had done its job and was safe now, having quelled the large, lumbering beasts that had come upon it.

I looked down at the dark place that was now silent, and I thought it indistinguishable from every other dark, quiet place around me. It looked like the entire desert. *Who knows how many rattlesnakes are out here?* No sense stewing over it, though. We turned and kept walking into the stars.

In the last hour of dawn, I woke from a long nap in the sand. I crawled from my sleeping bag, which I had pulled out when we all dropped our water weight sometime in the night. Our camp looked like abandoned debris in the middle of a rippled, tawny-colored dune field. A void encircled me, occupying every horizon. There was no wind, only a still and pale sky. I got up and stepped barefoot across sand as fine as table salt. Not three feet away, I stopped at a fresh track left by a sidewinder. I followed it with my eyes back toward my gear, finding that while I slept a snake had passed beside my head. It had left a graceful, rhythmic print, something written in script. The sand was so smooth it revealed each slick, broad scale on the snake's belly. I stepped over the track without scuffing it. I came upon a second sidewinder track, and then a third beyond that, and a fourth crisscrossing a fifth.

At first light, rattlesnakes had sought shelter in holes and hard-pans between dunes, where they could wait out the heat of day. It looked as if they had been up all night, painting the world into exis-tence, smoothing the earth into shapes that would soon receive the sun. I thought the tracks beautiful, but was quietly disconcerted, knowing how many sidewinders had been busy in my sleep. I had to be careful.

Well before sunrise, we gathered our things and kept going, each bringing a hundred pounds of water. It was easiest to go bare-foot. Without boots we glided better across the dunes, but mostly we did not glide at all, rather we shuffled and dragged under the weight of our packs. Frequently we doubled over to rest, holding ourselves with palms on our knees. Daylight came. The sun broke the horizon.

We continued until heat drove us into the shade of a single scrub brush. There we lay quietly, and I thought us clumsy, slogging animals, while rattlesnakes moved around us unseen, able to travel with only a whisper of friction, vertebrae rolling against one another like marbles in a bowl. Sidewinders eat lizards and kangaroo rats, taking as much water from them as can be salvaged, while we haul every precious drop with Sisyphean effort.

A wind started up. It began scouring our cheeks, and we lifted hands, blocking our faces from a gauze of blowing sand. So much wind came that it was hard to breathe without covering our noses and mouths. We stood and shouldered our packs to keep going. Sidewinder tracks lifted off the dunes and flew around us.

Different species of *Crotalus* deliver different kinds of venom. I know someone who was bitten while on a desert island. Rather than experiencing lucid pain, he said he was racked with twenty-four hours of wild, nightmarish hallucinations. For those seemingly endless hours, inside his mind he watched his body being torn apart, as if he were trapped in a psychosomatic cell. Barely able to communicate with the companions who were helping him to safety, he heard only echoes of voices until the venom faded.

Victims of rattlesnake bites tell of dreams like these even long after recovery. Those who survive especially severe bites say that, like drug flashbacks, mystical and terrifying visions continue for years, decades, even their entire lives. It depends, really, on the species and the dosage.

Some rattlesnakes deliver mostly blood poisons, or hemotoxins, that lead to rapid cellular breakdown, causing internal hemorrhaging. Some specialize in nerve poisons, or neurotoxins, that infiltrate the body's neural network and turn off vital organs switch by switch. Most rattlesnakes contain a cocktail of both hemotoxins and neurotoxins. It takes a hundred milligrams of western diamondback venom to kill a person, and a mere ten milligrams from a Mojave rattler. Sidewinders are an in-between species, not always deadly on the first bite, but quite dangerous and potentially fatal, especially if the bite occurs many miles into untrailed desert.

I thought about venom as we walked, keeping odd hours, bare feet trekking across sand. Moving at dusk, I contemplated the possible feel of venom in my system, wondering if it would cause my throat to close, and I asked myself—as I had countless times before—if I would panic or would be able to still my terrified mind with some handy mantra. At dawn on another day, I played scenes through my head, imagining myself sitting out a snakebite, twisting and retching in the sand for a couple of days. I thought I would come out a better man for it. But I wanted to be a better man without actually having to take the bite.

At midnight, when I could see nothing but stars and the faint outlines of my companions walking in the distance, I felt myself unraveling across miles of sand. My apprehension about rattlesnakes became a song, a drumbeat. It turned into everything around me, indistinguishable from indigo sky, from wash of sand, from pulse of breath. Half awake, half dreaming, I listened to the mantra of my own hushed footsteps. I was no longer afraid of rattlesnakes because fear required contemplation, a chore well out of my range at this hour. Slowly, I felt as if I were starting to fly. My feet floated off the sand. Even though my pack felt like a boulder strapped on to me, I spread my arms. Its weight gradually glided off of me. I no longer counted stars for bearings. My feet touched sand like touching a balloon in the air, sending my body ahead. I almost laughed at the feeling, amazed that in all these years I never learned to fly the way I do in my dreams, effortlessly sailing with every step, walking on the moon.

I have found that mild, dreamlike hallucinations are to be expected from time to time when I am traveling in the deep desert.

Given an oppressive weight to carry, and an endlessness to a terrain, a person discovers that his waking mind quietly loosens its grip. The only problem with such episodes is that later I cannot recall whether the hallucination was the fact that I was flying or the logic that I was not.

So much like in the dreams of those bitten by rattlesnakes, we climbed a steep dune, three of us sailing up its side, jabbing our hands into a mountain of sand, pawing with our feet. Breathing bile, our lungs heaving with strain, we flew all the way to the top, where we fell onto a crest jutted into the stars. We unbuckled our packs and let them roll to the side. For a long time we lay panting, better men for what we were doing, I was sure.

———

Eventually we walked into a Mexican town beyond the dunes. Bedraggled nomads, we appeared from the desert, and a few spectators came to their doorways to watch us pass down the street. The town's sole policeman stepped out from a veranda and urgently summonsed us out of sheer morning sunlight. He took whatever ID we had. We didn't much care, our hair wild with sand. He asked in Spanish where we had come from, and in Spanish we told him. He did not believe us, and asked again. We pointed at a beige washed-out horizon, explaining that we were just fools, travelers who walk in desolate places. He said there is no water out there. There are rattlesnakes. No one comes from out there. We did not argue. We waited as he got on his radio in his cinder-block shack, slowly repeating our names into a black microphone.

The policeman came back out, asked more questions. We told him our dates and places of birth, and he went back in to his radio. He seemed certain we had a ruse, but there was nothing he could prove. He came out once more and handed back our identification. He figured we were telling the truth. We were, really, just fools.

We carried our packs into the dusty street, and when the first vehicle came, audible for some distance, we held out our thumbs. A truck stopped for us, and we climbed into its bed with our gear, packs light now, nearly empty of water. The truck took a long, singular road out of town, and we sat against wheel wells, hot wind blowing through our teeth. As I watched the desert pass, I thought that the policeman was right to suspect us. Yes, there was a ruse. It was a simple trick: surrender. We traveled barefoot across a sea of snakes the way mystics walk on hot beds of coals, unfolding layers of ourselves as we went, becoming nothing, weightless. We weren't fools. That part was the lie. We knew exactly what we were doing, taking snake medicine in long, measured doses.

But I won't lie to you. I am still pacing the waiting room, bracing for the day when I might be bit. The idea has only sharpened my eyes, leaving me on the edge of my seat, the tips of my toes. I am no less fearful now than I ever have been, down on my knees, forever begging the snake for just one more day.

Crotalus

SEA LION

O sea goddess Nuliajuk
When you were a little unwanted orphan girl
We let you drown.
You fell in the water
And when you hung onto the kayaks crying
We cut off your fingers.
So you sank into the sea and your fingers
Turned into the innumerable seals.

You sweet orphan Nuliajuk,
I beg you now bring me a gift....

— *Netsilik magic words for hunting seal*

On a night of surprising coolness, I walked to the tip of a small uninhabited island in a desert sea off the coast of Baja. A full moon perched in the center of the sky, a light over a table illuminating everything below, bright enough to read by. Waves heaved against the island, exploding on hard gray rock. Plumes of seawater cascaded upward into the light before falling back. I timed my approach, stepping between waves on wet, bubbling rock, waiting for the next wave, and the next, before darting ahead. This way I kept dry. I walked to a rock pedestal at the very end of the island, as far out as one could stand. I took my place like a conductor looking across an orchestra of big-tent waves, the moon lighting every frothing roll beyond me.

This small island — all twenty square miles of it — lay unseen at my back. From my vantage point, it seemed as if I were lost at sea. I could have fallen out of the back of a boat or lost my kayak and paddle to high, wind-driven waves. I envisioned my desperate gasps, arms and legs stroking to keep me afloat. What song, I wondered, would be going through my mind as I drowned?

As I looked across the sea, I saw a glint of moonlight in the water. Something was out there. Waves rose and fell, and I saw it again. It was a small face. It popped underwater and was gone. The waves parted once more, and I glimpsed a slick black head. It was closer now, fifty feet out, and its gaze was fixed on me. For a moment it looked, impossibly, like a person. I figured it must be a sea lion. It vanished and then poked its head up again even nearer. A wave lifted it to eye level, its two shining eyes returning my gaze. It stayed longer this time, and watching it, I again became lost at sea, landless. A sea lion would come to me just this way, I thought. Would it then nose up beneath my belly and carry me to safety or would it curiously circle me at a distance, watching me drown?

The sea lion slipped out of sight. I looked for it again, but it was gone. I stepped back from the edge.

I returned to the island along a fractured peninsula of rock. Waves cymbal-crashed on both sides as I carefully timed my moves, not willing to get wet. A cloudless cold front had moved in, and I, along with three companions, had become stranded far from our camp. A day hike across the island had left us here with little water to drink and insufficient clothing. We had been dropped off on the island by a Mexican fishing boat, with a promise the boat would return for us in a couple of weeks. The desert had lulled us. We had made ourselves at home, rolling up our sleeves on pleasant autumn nights. We did not plan on the desert's winter coming so suddenly, a cool wash of air and a brisk wind on a night without sleeping bags or warm hats. We had a long night before us, mild, dreamy hypothermia, more uncomfortable than dangerous. I was biding time, taking a walk to look at the sea.

I turned back to our makeshift camp, a flickering eye of fire in a cave just above the water. The cave sat in a cove of cliffs around a bay, which softened the waves and cut some of the wind. Everyone huddled close to the driftwood fire, coals shoveled into a heap. I moved in and crouched among them, two women and a man. Around the fire were piles of crab shells, little rock crabs we had cooked and eaten hours earlier.

"It's spectacular out at the point," I said.

The others looked up at me, eyes weary after a long day of walking, prepared tonight for little sleep. I flicked a coal back in with my fingers.

"I saw a sea lion," I said. "It came in close. It seemed curious."

After a spell of quiet, one of the three stood up. He said he was going to the point, and he walked off. An hour later he returned to our hovel of stones stacked against the cold. He said he saw it too, a black head slicked by moonlight. It made no sound, only stared at him the way it had stared at me, with the intent of a person.

Our fire burned down, and I went for more fuel, picking up sticks, snapping them in my hands. I walked waterlines terraced above a rising tide. The sea was not so rough in the cove, but still it had strong waves washing onto a hard-cobble beach. As I combed for flammable debris, I watched water sloshing around rocky headlands at the mouth of the cove. There, I saw the sea lion again. The instant I spotted it, it dropped from view, dashed underwater. Several seconds later it nipped its head up even closer. The animal rode the waves for a little while, then dove, leaving only a dimple in the water where it had been. When the sea lion appeared next, it was hardly more than a stone's throw away, its attention focused on me. I stood still with my handful of sticks, looking into its eyes looking back at mine.

It was the same sea lion, or at least I thought it had to be. A head the size of a crystal ball rode up and down atop the waves. It seemed wistful, the way it propelled itself just enough to look out of the sea and observe this other world above. Its inquisitive manner struck me. We seemed to be mirrors of each other, one with feet, one with fins.

Considering the array of cleverly designed, outrageous, spiny, gelatinous, and brittle-bodied species the earth has produced, the physical difference between sea lions and humans is not so remarkable. We are both mammals who give live, placental birth on land and raise our young on mother's milk. We both have hair covering our bodies, even if it is short and goes more toward a sheen than a mane. Neither of us can breathe underwater, and we must hold our breath to dive for any length. We have the same basic kinds of finger bones and toe bones, be they in feet, hands, or flippers. When you look at the skull of a sea lion, you will notice it has the snouted, crushing-tooth appearance of a land animal, a dog or a bear.

Bear is the right answer. Back in the twenty-five-million-year-old lineage of sea lions is a singular ancestor, an arctoid, bearlike animal. This ancient coastal carnivore, which in one form or another had been living on land since the earliest mammals, took a turn for the water. It became a fishing bear, a diving bear, perhaps working tidal pools for its meals. Land became secondary as it went deeper, developing webbed paws, its appendages shortened, needed now to reduce drag and propel the body through water, head and neck thrust straight forward to snap up fish. It kept an association with the land, able to haul itself onto a beach and rest in the sun, and there give birth, but for the most part it became a marine animal.

In evolutionary mythology we tend to think of animals only rising from the sea, crawling out on stubby fins to better themselves on land. Rarely do we imagine evolution working the other way. We like to think left to right, east to west, but in fact species move wherever they can, splintering into classes and kingdoms to fit the environment. An isolated population of pigs, for instance, has recently started down an aquatic path. About three hundred pigs living in the Tokelau Islands in the South Pacific have been observed foraging along shallow coral reefs. Though these pigs have not developed any apparent physical adaptations for their tasks, they appear to be excellent swimmers. With heads submerged, searching for mollusks, sea slugs, and fish the way farm pigs root through trash piles, they spend much of their time wading in tide pools.

Another modern example of land mammals' turning to the water is so-called marine sheep, which graze in kelp beds off the coast of Scotland. For centuries these long-necked, long-legged sheep have been plying cold lagoons and bays, their bodies well endowed with scraggly wool that makes them look like floating debris as they swim from one kelp bed to another. They even beach themselves to rest in the company of gray seals.

All mammals that now live in the sea came first from the land. Whales likely started off as hoofed, artiodactyl land mammals in the Paleocene, and sirenians such as manatees share ancestral, terrestrial roots with elephants and aardvarks dating back some fifty million years. Sea otters made the most recent jump, turning away from their weasel-like cousins about five million years ago to hunt and mate solely in the water. What spurs such a leap? In the case of pinnipeds—a term meaning "feather feet" that applies to sea lions, seals, and walrus—it was probably a climate change thirty-six million years ago that cooled the oceans and altered their flows. Cold, nutrient-rich waters began welling up along the coasts of Europe and

North America, where pinnipeds first appear in the fossil record. Their common bearlike ancestor must have started swimming to take advantage of new resources, and there it stayed.

Now the pinniped was looking back, and I wondered if this lone sea lion in the waves remembered what it was like many millions of years ago when it stood with me, at least an early version of me, on a cobbled shore. It remained in front of me for a couple of minutes, staring into my eyes. We had made two different decisions, seeking two different lives. Again, I thought it looked like a person, someone who could just as easily be over here with me.

Do I know you? I thought. *You're one of us, aren't you? You're one of us gone to sea.*

I stepped forward, and the sea lion slipped beneath the surface. Not even a ripple or splash showed its departure.

In a late-night stacking game, my companions and I kept ourselves awake, coaxing flames with the last of our wood. It was too cold to sleep anyway. Waves dashed up to within a few feet of us before rolling back, clubbing rock cobbles against one another as they went. We had not counted on the tide coming so high, even on a full moon.

"There it is again," someone said.

I looked up from the fire and spied the same head and face, a sea lion in the moonlight. It was close enough that I could make out whiskers, and drops of water sparkling on their tips. Its nostrils flared open and closed. It had been studying us off and on for well over an hour, appearing and disappearing in a blink.

I remained cramped at the fire, looking over at a sea lion that was quick and capable in the water, washing back and forth, closer and farther away. I could see its ears, two small rolls of leather laid to the sides of its head. I saw no zoological necessity for it to remain so long in front of our fire. It had to be curious. I thought it must be like us in some way, driven by longing.

My mind became flexible in the cottony space between sleeping and waking. Whenever I looked up, I saw the sea lion. I was lost at sea again, a castaway on a rocky uninhabited island, and this pinniped came to me like a mermaid, a selkie wearing the slick black skin of a seal. Waves carried her closer to me, and then back, and then even closer, until she reached shore. Water fell off her back, revealing a long beached body. For a moment she was on land, standing upon her chest, flippers out like palms on the ground. This was no gentle hypothermic hallucination. What I was seeing was real. No wonder we have stories of fin-folk living in the sea. They are, indeed, true. The sea lion's snout pointed at me beneath two glistening moons of eyes.

No farther than a few arm's lengths away, she seemed transfixed by the small rack of flame between us. I thought the animal might shimmy up to us, might nudge us aside to see burning twigs, bright pirouettes of fire, an inexplicable phenomenon on an island dark every night but this. I imagine if the animal had been a beetle or a lizard, it would have categorized us long ago and gotten on with its business. This sea lion, on the other hand, had unanswered questions. Willing to expose herself on a stony beach, she lingered, teetering on the edge of her own amazement. A wave broke over her body, and she spun like an eel into a retreating skim of water.

I fell asleep, my head nodding until the tide finally pushed down our wind shelter of rocks. Foam rushed into our glowing coal bed, turning it to spurts of steam and hissing ash. A second wave buried the coals, leaving them black. We took up what little gear we had and ran along the beach before the tide completely pinched us into cliffs surrounding the cove. In a barren gloaming before dawn, we scurried like wild mammals back to the desert and its dry, hard rocks. Before leaving sight of the cove, I turned and looked for a black head and searching eyes. The sea lion was not there, and I wondered whether I was truly the one who was better off, remaining on my beloved ground while this animal glided into the vault of the ocean with a breath of air clasped in its lungs.

Pinnipedia

RED-SPOTTED TOAD

The night was refuge. I was naked, the only way to sleep in this kind of heat. I sprawled on the belly of a sandstone mound in the resonant dark of a moonless night. A powdering of stars was above, and the red of Utah rock, a single rock five thousand feet thick, continued beneath my back and into the earth. My gear was around me, eight days of supplies. There was no wind in the dark. I was sweating. It was three in the morning. Maybe four. Feverish, fitful dreams came. Then I woke and moved, carrying my pack farther into the desert. The sky breathed in the northeast and turned light.

In the dark I had gone by hand, groping into places where the scorpions live, into frail handholds that burst in my fist. I left at night to avoid the triple-digit temperatures of the day. Up through tight black chimneys in the sandstone, pulling my pack from above, pulling until my muscles shivered, until sweat braided my face to the tip of my nose. I had skirted the outside ledges of towers, making moves that would be impossible during the day, when I could see the plummet. I followed the scrambling of a porcupine on its nocturnal trek. It showed the way up a small canyon until it wedged itself into a crack.

Now I moved into dawn, trying to walk as far as possible before the sun hinged off the horizon. I squeezed between stone fins four hundred feet high. I climbed out of them, across the open spaces between pillars of Navajo sandstone, the fermented dunes of a two-hundred-million-year-old desert. Past Anasazi petroglyphs on the walls, a thousand years old. Past ragged five-hundred-year-old junipers and coyote tracks left during the night.

The sun came and I was in the open. It was one hundred degrees already. I sat with my pack against my spine and used its shade to rest. There was no sweat. It evaporated before it could gather on my skin.

A single young cottonwood tree grew in a canyon. Its leaves were a punctuating green. The tree marked water. Of anywhere out here, this was the one hole that could answer prayers. I had it on the map, a mark at 4,500 feet. It was a deep hole in which rain from a month ago had accumulated. I remembered that rain, how it got the big canyons running, how mud flushed into the streets of Moab. The wind had been cool like witch hazel, and I stood out in the desert with my arms open, taking drops in my mouth. This was all that was left. Eight feet long, three feet wide, elbow-deep. I dipped my clothes into it, then wrung them over my head. I filled water bottles. It was dark water, its surface thronged with water striders. This part of the desert has few locatable reservoirs. There are no long drainages to transport water when it rains. There is so much sand in the canyon floors that rainwater will sink before it can gather. Only here, only in this fissure, was there water.

The sun came to the water too. I walked away, to the east, looking for a place to wait until night, looking for shade. My clothes were dry already.

I walked the rims and benches, beginning to hate myself. Beginning to see things that were not there. My joints were nervous from heat and fatigue. I glanced over edges, into the canyon floors. The desert was bright, embedding shards of straight white sunlight into my eyes. There were no turkey vultures in the sky; coyotes were asleep in concealed, shaded holes. The two most prominent animals, scavengers of the dead and dying, were in hiding. At the back of one canyon, I saw a strip of darkness where the walls narrowed before touching. I came to the edge, which sloped through alcoves and walls to the shade. I pulled out the climbing rope and rigged a harness around my waist. My fingers fumbled through the straps. I rubbed my eyes. They stung from salt.

A solitary juniper would be the anchor, and I circled its leather trunk with webbing. The water knot securing the webbing took a long time to make. I had to follow through inch by inch, laughing at the irony. A water knot. My fingers were swollen from the heat. They barely held a bight of the webbing. The pack went down first, with the rope run through its straps. I rappelled behind it, spinning into the canyon. When I clipped off the rope, I was too hot to work out of the harness. I walked along the canyon floor, gear clanking from my waist. One wall leaned over the next. It was dark in the bottom. My eyes did not burn any longer from the summer light. Cool air gathered in the pit. I leaned my head back so that my jaw dropped and air cooled my lungs. It was a trick learned from ravens, keeping my mouth open to move heat out of my body. The sun would not come here, not ever. I collapsed in the bottom, in the sand. My arms pressed against the fresh temperature of the rock.

When my eyes were closed and I breathed steadily, there was a rustling. I turned my head against the sand. In the dry mountain mahogany leaves ten feet away was a small toad, working its way through. There was no water in here, I knew this. I glanced several hundred feet above the toad and myself to the hot walls in the sun. The toad had to have fallen in. Or it spontaneously grew from the rock. Otherwise, it made no sense that this animal found its way into this shade.

The toad shuffled toward me. It was a red-spotted toad, the size of my thumb. With my eyes turned hard in my head, I watched its progress. The toad, like a crawling infant, made cumbersome, groping moves through the debris. Designed half for water, half for land, the amphibian was not an adept land traveler.

I was tired, too tired to wait. The toad would not reach me for another hour. My eyes closed and I listened to the sharp, sporadic turning of leaves, the only sound for fifty miles. I should have gotten myself up and crawled over to the animal, had a closer look. It seemed to be an impossible thing to find here. But I could not move. I thought of the map. I thought of how far this desert stretches, and of how little water exists here in any form. The chances of finding a toad were not good. Toads need water, and not in the way a bighorn sheep needs water, or a raven needs water. A roving toad must have water on hand. Distances between water sources holding no more than a half quart each can be three or four miles over a landscape of cliffs and stone swales. If a toad was to be seen here, it would be a red-spotted toad, *Bufo punctatus,* common to more parched reaches of the Southwest. The word *"Bufo"* itself sounds like a toad, like a fat little squat thing in your hand. This was what I was looking at, a first-class bufo, loafing around in the desert.

When I say "common in the Southwest," I am referring to a statistical average of perhaps one half-ounce toad occupying each unit of ten square miles. That is twenty miles with no toads, then twenty miles with two of them. Unlike other water-dependent creatures such as clam shrimp, water boatmen, or mosquitoes, the toad cannot fly or be carried in the wind between distant water sources. Dehydration is rapid, and a toad caught out, away from water, will become a dead, leathery pouch by early afternoon.

If they can do it in time, they will dig themselves into the ground before shriveling. There they estivate in a state of dry dormancy, waiting for the next water, into which they will emerge and reproduce before digging again. After a year in the hole, patience runs out, the body winds down, and the toad dies. If they do not receive water soon enough, they mummify and are preserved in the sand until exposed. A Northern Arizona University archaeologist said he has excavated several dead toads tunneled just beneath the surface around ruins.

That last rain two weeks ago brought small floods down the canyons and filled familiar holes. They probably lured this toad out of the ground. The water had since dried from everywhere but isolated refuges. I had the map in my head, the miles upon miles of fins and sand dunes and waterless canyons. On the map was a single red-spotted toad. I fell asleep thinking of this, thumbing through the possibilities and odds. My last thought was spent wondering how a toad found its way into the only reliable shade for miles.

At dusk I sorted through my gear, set a camp, and walked along the corridor. I could not find the toad. There were enough turned and stacked rocks that it was well hidden. I wandered through for a sign of water. There was a film of dry moss in some cracks. Maidenhair ferns and diminutive lip ferns extended from the overhangs where moisture eked out of the rock's bedding plain. From beneath one boulder grew an outlandishly luxuriant brand of wood fern. It was the greenest item for miles in any direction. It was an alien here.

Even at protected desert springs you shouldn't see a fern like this. Its arms, green as peas, draped flagrantly over the rocks. There was no trace of physical water here. There was not even a dampness to the sand. Of course water was down here, tapped out by the ferns from deep in the sandstone heart. The particular fern was a *Dryopteris filix-mas* (the common name is "male fern"), a plant associated with cool, wet forests and even swamps, thriving in half-lit or entirely shaded areas. Its range extends into Utah only along boreal, mountainous fingers, not into the desert. You are as likely to find a pompous amanita mushroom squatting in the back of the canyon. But here was *D. filix-mas.*

The maidenhairs, hanging above from the cracks like women waving to the crowds, are built for dry regions. They were *Adiantum capillus-veneris* and *A. modestum,* their skin waxed to hold moisture, their gametophytes fertilizing and developing without water, a skill out of reach for sexual species. The wood fern does not have this kind of protection. To cultivate the wood fern, you need moist garden mulch and partial sunlight. A maidenhair is difficult to grow at home, its rocky habitat with drop-an-hour liquid far more complex than a dark, swampy bowl of potting soil. I allowed the fronds of the wood fern to pour through my fingers. They brushed like feathers, dropping out leaf by leaf until the fern was again resting on the base of the canyon wall. Its roots were anchored into fine blow sand. It should not have been here. The toad was a shot in the dark, but the fern was a breach in protocol. Put a million monkeys at a million typewriters, and they may type a toad into this canyon. Their keys would cross if they tried for a wood fern.

Science, three hundred years ago, would explain the emergence of a toad and a wood fern as spontaneous generation. It was the method by which sudden or unlikely appearances were explained, such as how maggots magically wriggled from exposed meat, how animals showed up on remote islands. It was the hand of God. When details of genetics, evolution, reproduction, and basic scientific methods came about, spontaneous generation was abandoned as a theory. The toad's presence would have then been attributed to atmospheric dispersal. Lightweight toad eggs fall with rain. Prospects of this, although fanciful, have been flatly disproved. The most likely reason remaining, which is the hinge of modern science, was that the toad and the fern came here by accident. They came as if this canyon were an incognito terrarium.

I climbed out of the canyon, inching my way up the rock. A blanket of heat hung in the desert, even with the sun down. The rock was still too hot for bare feet. It clutched the sun inside its greedy sandstone chambers. Most of the canyon floors were black with the first of night. Other than three ravens flying down-canyon, there was nothing alive, plant or animal. I walked along the spine of a fin, high over camp. From my vantage point on the fin, I could see maybe three miles in all directions. Above the stone horizons in the last blue light, other fins broke a skyline of sandstone temples. It gave the sense of the infinite contained within a finite space. In the deepening shadows, you could find anything in there. I came here to wander across the place. With the rope and gear and full water bottles, I would need all of my strength. The red-spotted toad had already crossed the distance. It did this with a pace fumbled by a ground litter of leaves and pebbles. With a topographic map and a knowledge of how certain formations wear against time, I found my way to the same destination as the toad. This was where I would stay.

A few hours into sunrise I was in the shelter, sleeping in the back, my shoulders tight between walls. I turned to my side and felt movement in my hair. When I shook loose and opened my eyes, a red-spotted toad fell to the sand. It landed on its back and squirmed to right itself. It was hopping away. It was small. Smaller than I remembered, and I saw another toad a few feet farther.

Two toads now. I turned to my stomach and crawled behind them. They were both a dull grayish brown, with pale red jewels scattered on their backs. It made sense that there was more than one. Otherwise, the toad population for this canyon would end in solitude and with abruptness. When I was no longer looming over them, they stopped and situated themselves, rotating their bodies until they were pressed flat to the sand.

The toad, being an amphibian, was the first critter to swim out of the primordial sea 250 million years ago and waddle its way across the land, forever marrying the two elements. "Amphibian," in fact, means "double life" in Greek. In the case of the red-spotted toad, the species left the water and kept going, leaving its wetter half far behind.

A toad will not drink water. Not with its mouth, at least. Toss a thirst-starved toad into a pool, and it will appear to do nothing, which is exactly how it gets water. It is the folds and furrows and wrinkled channels of toad skin that draw liquid. Epidermal sculpturing, it is called. The surface area of the toad is like a wadded rag: a lot of rag and not a lot of toad. The more skin it can expose to water, the more it can "drink," as water osmotically seeps over the skin, around the outside of the toad, meandering over the corrugated lines of its tissues as far up as the spine, then moving into the body. Transported through neither muscle movement nor chemical rearrangements, a toad's water supply is moved by capillary functions, cohesion, adhesion, and surface tension. One researcher took his finger and drew a circle of grease around the back of a toad. He noted that the water stopped at the grease mark, unable to get past it because it was the water, not the toad, that was doing the work.

Water here, in the canyon floor, exists in an amount that would hardly volunteer its presence to the most sensitive of equipment. The only animal that can actually put these traces to use is the red-spotted toad. It takes water through a "seat patch," a flat underside along its belly and between its hind legs that the toad snugs against the ground. The seat patch brings moisture to the wrinkled skin, and the body acts like a sponge. Red-spotted toads were set on water-saturated tissues in one experiment. Without moving, the toads sat, bellies pressed to their soaked blotters. When next checked, the tissues were completely dry. It is feasible then that a red-spotted toad can settle itself into sand where there are trace amounts of moisture and patiently draw water from stone.

Occasionally, the experiment's toads would rise, rub their seat patches with hind legs, then return to the tissue surface. The function of this move is to sweep off sand particles that have been sucked dry. When the toad resettles, it has worked down to the next layer of ground, sometimes one sand grain deeper, where there is again moisture.

Another group of researchers tossed their lab toads into bowls of salt water. Salt water accelerates dehydration and is dangerous to a freshwater, skin-drinking amphibian. What they found was that before the salt could physically enter the toads' bodies, the toads made hormonal realignments for the saline imbalance to come. So the skin turns out to be more than a drinking tool. It is a chemical-sensitive receptor that warns the body of coming events.

Researchers have never scattered toads in the desert, miles from water, to study their divining instincts. Even though red-spotted toads can withstand a 30 percent drop in weight from water loss and can store up to half their body weight in reserved water, I have met no one who has encountered a toad on a long, open-desert trek from one shady spot to the next. Saltwater bowls and grease-covered toads have yet to explain how this small population of red-spotted toads found its way here into the wood fern canyon.

I followed the toads on routes between pieces of fallen wood and small stones. Their maladroit gaits led me up the canyon to where there was another toad. And then a fourth toad. Then I could not remember the exact difference between the toads, and there may have been five. Or more.

When the toads calmed from my intrusion, I took a quick nap. The heat was getting into the canyon and I could not sleep well. I hauled up my day pack and walked into the desert. The desert, mid-day, was a clean slate of absolute heat. By the end of the day, it would be like melting brass. Then, at least you knew the sun was setting. Morning came and you still remembered what it was like to be a breathing, thinking human being. But midday was a fiery baptism. It would be better if I were here for a reason. If I were here to find red-spotted toads, to map water holes, to seek heat-induced, maddening, hair-pulling, salt-encrusted visions, or to find some Holy Grail of Anasazi petroglyphs. But I was not. I was here to be here, to carry my gear across the back of this desert. It was hard to willfully do this to myself. So I was now here for the toads.

At night I clung desperately to the lukewarm air puddled to the canyon floor. And I thought of toads. Or I tried to think of them, but when I walked outside the canyon, it was hot again and I could not think. I forced contemplation of how they survived here, of how an animal tied directly to water through evolution ended up here. But all I realized was that this was hell and let the toads have it if they were so damned smart that they could scramble twenty miles with their fat little feet to find shade in the perfect, absolute middle of nowhere. Then I stumbled behind a boulder in the scalding shade of midday and slumped my skull over as if my spine had melted.

I clambered back to my nest, slipping down the rope and burning my right palm. When I hit the sand in the back, I was asleep in seconds. I woke and it was dusk.

The toads were out. Clinging to the walls. Wandering in the detritus. Toads waiting for water. Water means sex because eggs require water. Otherwise, there would be no sex. So the toads regarded one another with casual disinterest until the next water. All the croaking and gripping hormones were latent. When it does happen, when it rains, these little toads can be startlingly loud. They croak and grope and cling to one another with incomparable zeal. One unromantic researcher sawed off the hind legs of a male clutched to a female, and even then, it would not let go.

Bufo punctatus is one of only two toad species to lay eggs one at a time rather than in mats (both species occupy analogous habitats and are genetically similar). The adaptation, these single eggs with sticky sheaths, spreads out the possibilities for survival in the last drop of water—say, in a sandstone bowl or an animal paw print—outlasting flash floods or enduring a dry summer. Common toads merely lay a patch or a string of eggs in a body of water where there is little concern for drought. If a red-spotted toad were to put all its eggs in one basket, so to speak, the chances are high of that basket's shriveling in the capricious and hazardous climate of the Southwest.

It was not long ago that this desert was not even here. It rained here at one time and winter snows were deep and the summers were paradisiacal. The last Ice Age came out from under the lounging plants and animals ten thousand years ago. It is painfully abstract, this notion that the American deserts are new, fresh as sticky paint. I liked the fantasy, lying here, waiting for my body to cool. The scene of toads piled layer upon layer among thick ferns, tiny legs trying to get out from under one another like lobsters in a tank.

This was, in fact, a somewhat boreal environment at the time. Thickets of piñon and juniper thrived a thousand feet below here, and this was the home of a deep ponderosa forest. The more I speculated, the more it made sense. The Southwest is now littered with populations left over from the Ice Age like orphaned children. A snake specialist I knew called the Southwest a herpetological Galápagos. With all of its ridges, mountains, and canyons, the Southwest is a checkerboard of isolated climates. This herpetologist suggested that if Charles Darwin had come to the American desert rather than sailing around all those islands, he would have been equally as convinced of the validity of evolution. The only thing that would have stopped Darwin is that ten thousand years is simply not enough time to alter genetics and turn an old species into a radically new one.

As the planet warmed, the continent split into biological islands now teetering in the middle of adverse climates. Plants and animals withdrew to the nearest mountain ranges. Some, like milk snakes, adapted regionally into different colors and sizes. Rock rattlesnakes, designed for cool regions, were stranded in secluded mountains above the deserts of New Mexico and Arizona. Douglas firs were left clustered to a single shaded north face of a desert cliff on the Colorado Plateau, where there isn't another relative for a couple hundred miles. In the deeper canyons of the Sonoran Desert are leftover palm trees, and desert pupfish still exist in the last year-round water holes. The Southwestern deserts hold forty-two independent mountain ranges. They are geologically considered to be an archipelago. They are islands.

A canyon, one boxed off and dark, could also be considered an island. Like this one, a bare spit of sand in the ocean. Toads do not change quickly on their islands. Their genetic alterations are as slow as their metabolisms, so the toads alive today are virtually the same as those of the Pleistocene. There have been no extinctions and no new arrivals. They are tanks, these toads, perfect mechanisms for survival in limited niches. If this was indeed a relict population of red-spotted toads abandoned by a retreating Ice Age, the genetic adaptations would be too slight to be visible.

The key was in the back of the canyon. It was the wood fern. You don't find a wood fern discarded in the desert without a long story behind it. I will make a bet, put all my pocket change on it, that the ferns were dropped off during the birth of the North American deserts. They would have thrived here about fifteen thousand years ago, stretching out of wet canyons into the surrounding land of ponderosa pines, where now there is only sand and blackbrush. Like clothing stripped on a hot day, they were left in the trail as the Ice Age returned to the high mountains. And maybe it was a package deal, ferns and toads.

It was a good idea, a story at least. The proof was in the fact that I had nowhere to go but here, licking salt off my skin, huddling with a fat, delicious fern and a bunch of toads. It was easy enough to believe anything, to cool myself with the sweet images of everything working just so. I could drag herpetologists and botanists out here, and maybe someday I will, and they will answer all of my questions with perfect answers. I may rig them to the juniper and belay them into the canyon. More likely I will leave the toads alone and come back only when I am desperate or crazy.

It had not been eight days as I had planned, and I didn't know how many days it had really been. I could hardly walk anymore. I shuffled through the desert in the morning. I was no good here. The heat was too much, so I pulled my equipment together for the walk out. It was not that the desert lacked vitality at a time like this. Rather, it was I who was lacking, who was stumbling to get out of the heat. The desert is a momentum, not a moment. It is not merely one blinding-hot day, but days of thunderstorms sweeping the canyons, days of February blizzards. The things that are alive here would not be so if there were not days like this. A bird of paradise cannot live here. A cutthroat trout cannot live here. A marmot cannot live here. Yet a red-spotted toad can live here, and it is the vitality of this kind of day that allows it. Anyplace that has a toad is dynamic and rich. A place that receives only a handful of rain each year, a place that is composed of bare stone, most of it vertical, and has a toad to boot, that is a place of miracles.

Bufo punctatus

RAINBOW TROUT

I was born into a time when the fishing was no good. It was the end of the sixties, during the last of those square, grainy color photos with unimaginable numbers of fish strung between gangly, smiling boys in drab, baggy outfits. I will never have a catch like those. There will never be so many that I will give up remembering the number exactly. It is always *two*. I have caught *two* fish.

The numbers slowly dwindled through history until I was old enough to fish. That is when I was hearing all of the stories about fish, as someone older than I riffled through a drawer to produce one of the photos as proof. These old men always point themselves out as the ones holding the stringers, but all of the faces look the same. I think it is just one photo used over and over.

Because I come from a line of master fly fishermen, I learned to fish. It was not with squirming bait and all of their smells and excretions, or with metallic artificial lures like silver spoons with red race-car paint. It was with the hackle, the calves' tails, and the elk hair of flies.

With this approach, it is a very pure sport, and I see why it is held in such high esteem by the philosophically inclined. The only industrial material in these flies is the steel of the hook, but that is certainly outweighed by the peacock feathers and horse tail hairs. The act of fly-fishing is not necessarily a meditation. I would reserve that appellation for the motionless waiting on catfish with hook and bait. Fly-fishing, on the other hand, is always in motion. How the line and fly land speaks truthfully of what you are. Every thought has an influence. Perhaps it has gained such insightful notoriety because very few events allow a person to focus for so long on something as small and intricate as a fly.

It is all good for philosophy. But it always seemed more like fishing to me.

I learned how to fish, I will qualify, not how to *catch* fish. The few I actually catch seem so distinct from the act of fishing itself that fish are some other event entirely. I spend my time perfecting the technique, studying the living creatures under the round, slick creek stones and meticulously working knots out of my two-pound leaders on the creek bank. Not catching fish.

I fish the small, rare creeks of the Arizona high country and have done so since I was young. And only with dry flies because the wet ones reminded me of dead worms. I couldn't see them in the water, so what use were they? I have become like an endangered species clinging to a tiny niche. That niche, of course, has hardly any fish in it. It is a creek that runs off the Mogollon Rim. The creek upon which I presented my first fly. It rides down from the old, round mountains. It runs toward the Salt River, through the Apache and San Carlos reservations.

My mother brought me to one of these creeks when I was six weeks old, following my father and his fly line. She tells me that she had me in a carrier, up to her waist in the swift water of Oak Creek, trying to cross. She was lifting the carrier so that it would not be swept off. Had she dropped me, I could have become the Moses of Arizona, found in the reeds somewhere around the town of Sedona.

A few years ago the Department of Wildlife stopped stocking rainbow trout at the headwaters of my creek. So the crafty, spooky brown trout introduced from Europe in the last century ate the remaining rainbow trout fries and either died because they grew too huge for the water or were caught by my father and eaten by both of us.

The end result is a creek with only a few massive browns, which refuse to be caught, and a number of very skittish rainbows. The creek is only about ten feet wide and has barely hollowed out a course in the river willows and ponderosas. Getting a fly around in here is difficult. Every metaphor of frustration can be held taut on a line caught twenty feet up in an oak tree.

Catching a brown trout is the supreme principle when I fish with my father. I always check his catch and am not impressed until I find the browns. Even if the rainbows are big. They are dark, German browns, like spotted chocolate. They can survive in warmer, less oxygenated water. Meanwhile the native trout are driven to the higher watersheds, where the water is cold and fresh. The browns are hard to catch. They are at the peak of this art. Strike a brown once without catching it on this creek, and it will not strike again. The brown is a skeptical fish.

Since I rarely catch browns, leaving that higher accomplishment to my father, I have cultivated a solidarity with the rainbows. The rainbow is native to this side of the continent. Because of the nature of Rocky Mountain and Pacific Coast drainages, creeks become isolated from one another, and the trout living near the cold, oxygenated headwaters have scattered into subspecies specific to each drainage. The rainbow has a penchant for hybridizing. The Gila, Apache, and Mexican golden trout have been born from these branching waters.

My first catch ever on this creek had been a rainbow. I was young and dazzled by its color, so dazzled that there was line all over the place and my father's rod was abandoned, floating downstream. I was holding the leader in my hand, giving the trout enough slack so that it could swim at my feet. I did not yet want to force it into this alien world of air and light. I wanted to watch it before I was to eat it. I crawled down into the water, knees on the brown stones.

Tiny motions that followed the length of its body caused great momentum. It moved as if it were solid energy prepared to erupt but satisfied with remaining in place for a short time. It was as if water had taken a concrete form and speckled itself with lavenders and reds. What would happen if I were to pull it out? I had seen my father's full creel before, the browns all stacked in wet watercress. But they were not trout. Their guts were split open, their substance had been pulled out and tossed far away from the stream. Their eyes had dulled and did not move. They were rigid. They were table fish, ready for corn-bread batter, onions, and potatoes on an oiled cast-iron skillet at camp. Ready for us to eat while my father talked to me about stars and things wild.

This was a live, animated trout on my line. It was the most beautiful creature. A trout is not a fish. It looks nothing like any other fish. It is a sleek river animal, melded into a fluid shape by spending its life braced into strong currents. When my shadow crossed it, the rainbow flashed out. The fish raced upstream and I saw the streak where water cut away. It caught the line, cinched it on my hand, and I was nearly pulled over. I was small then.

I heeled back on the leader and discovered that there was an amazingly tangible force at the other end, invisible in the creek. Rainbow trout fight harder than browns. They leap in the air. They are colored with rainbows, I imagine, because all that leaping in sunlight and water has left their sides painted with prismatic brilliance. The source of their fame is in strength. In places like British Columbia they grow to fifty pounds and more, but in these high

Southwest creeks, I will know only the strong tug of the four- and five-pounders.

I hauled in the trout and it zagged the width of the creek. I pulled it toward me so that I could see the Royal Wulff fly attached to the outside of the fine jawbone. I reached into the water and slid my fingers around the trout, afraid to lift it from the water. Not wanting to touch it for fear that this wild energy would lash upon me, that I would be crossing boundaries that should not be crossed. For fear that I would get sticky stuff all over my hands and end up with a hook jabbed into my thumb. We touched and it bolted. Then I saw the detached fly, floating alone, drifting. I looked upstream and did not see the rainbow again.

On this day, on the creek to which I belong, I have caught nothing. It is a perfect day, although I lose an unprecedented number of flies in the willows. My casting is doing well. No fish, though. I am content to sit and pull knots out of my leader, or watch a tan water snake cruise the streambed, or create a forty-foot arc of line in order to set a pale Elk Wing Caddis into the sweeping froth beneath a rock. The fish do not respond.

My father joins me after a day of no catches and an empty creel, driving up from Phoenix. We carry no two-ounce graphite rods unmarred by lack of use, we have no official training. We have been fishing here as fishermen only, maybe not for the fish, maybe not even for the sport. As he gets older, he keeps fewer fish, and his language in describing the fish becomes more involved. When he was a child, he gave up hunting large game with his family. Later he stopped bird and rabbit hunting. Now it is the trout that are tapering from his diet, and I have seen him cry when speaking about them. He admires the trout more than he does any person. There are no flaws in the trout. They do not question, harm, or betray their instincts. Soon he will take no trout, when his thoughts have come back so many times that trout fill his dreams and he must let them free. Until then, he will catch enough to make up for me so that trout can be eaten by both of us on the day they are caught.

I do not consider myself a fly fisherman, compared with my father. He is a person whom people meet along the stream, and they will talk about this stranger and his fishing for years afterward. He does not appear to strive toward anything when he casts. It all simply unfurls around him. He has achieved grace. I have watched his fly line above the river willow, drifting back and forth, and in the sweeping back-cast I have mistaken it for a spiderweb floating into the sun. Anyone else he encounters along the creek he refers to as "that asshole." He brusquely criticizes their styles. "The bastard was casting downstream," he says.

He fished here first in 1970, not far from the family's ancestral fishing waters of New Mexico, catching twenty fish on his first day. Twenty-four years later, throwing out our best lines, we are jointly catching nothing. To him it is a slap from the gods. To me it is typical. I know he will catch his trout regardless. He speaks to them. They hear him.

I am really no expert on what is hatching and what to present to the trout. It rarely occurs to me that if I switch to another fly, my fishing will improve. And if it does occur to me, that switch will be random. From something big and feathery to something not so big and not so feathery. Meanwhile my father is a mile away on the creek, smelling the air, looking under rocks to see what aquatics are ready to metamorphose, and popping open his fly case to select what will work at this time of the day. When I was fairly young my father told me that the Royal Wulff had a good attractor pattern on this creek. The humpies work well too, he said. So I use a caddis only when I grow bored with those two, or when it's late and I need bright hackle to show me where I am fishing.

I can get my line damn near anywhere I want, bounce it off a rock or land it two inches under a snag, but my mind is not on the fish themselves, and we rarely commune. I like watching the fly. It seems to be the apex of the mountains, the forest, and the river, all meeting at a single point where white feather wings drift on clear water.

I am not like my father. I am not sending out the right message from fingers to line, to leader, to fly, to water, to trout. Or perhaps it is that I am sending out a message and he is not. He is the hatched caddis itself, riding the creek. I am the watcher of the caddis.

Today he gives me a House-and-Lot fly. There is a rumor that Dwight Eisenhower invented this fly. My father dispels the rumor, saying that it was only one of Eisenhower's favorites. He tells me the name of the man who invented it. He dispels a number of rumors about Ike's fly-fishing.

The sun is about to set, and mist ascends from water in spectral filaments. I present the House-and-Lot to the smooth dark water that swells below a rock. There it floats, before the leader is captured by the current. I do not like the big rivers. There is too much water, not enough cottonwood roots and ponderosas fallen from one shore to the next, not enough tiny holes and hanging brush. The big rivers do not make the same ornate, subtle sounds as these waters. The creeks of Arizona are idiosyncrasies in motion. There will be no two similar currents. Some watercourses here were named by Spanish explorers in the early 1600s, others took whatever came to mind first: Buckskin, Clear, Canyon, Black, and Cibique. They all drop off the alpine mountains into deep gorges, rapidly merging with the Sonoran Desert below.

Fishing this creek is like walking a childhood path to school. Each bend is familiar. It holds certain channels for years, then a particular spring runoff will jump it into a dry bed. It will run there, jump after a few years, and eventually I will be fishing the original course again. I have watched it fill every channel here. I cross the same barbed wire fences that are pushed over by floods. My fly catches on the same rusty barb each season. There are exposed rocks I have cast from many times, and I do not recognize them until I have been casting off their backs for ten minutes.

The House-and-Lot is moving out of the slow current, and I begin to draw it off the water. I see a shape for an instant and I strike the line. A rainbow flashes from the creek. I keep tension to set the hook. The rainbow is struggling up the river, and I can feel individual trout muscles transmitted through the line like shock waves. I can feel the particular rocks it is streaking around.

I've got line dangling all over from drawing it in, and I have to unravel it from my ankles, stepping out of nooses that are coiling around me in the current. My feet are studying the creek bottom, hunting, without the use of my preoccupied brain, for something stable. When I work the trout into the shallow cobbles, I can see the fly holding to its jaw with barely enough purchase. I trail it out of the water and land it on the dry rocks around the creek. As it hits, the fly pops off.

I pounce on it. I clasp my hands around it, but in a streak of iridescent colors, it dives away. Trout always know which direction the water is. It hits the shallow. I am on it. I sprawl, lurching my body out. My hands hit it again; they get all the way around it and I am trying to hurl it back to land. But the slick skin slips away. I jump again. Rocks bang my knees and chest. My face is in the water.

This is the other sport. The fish part of fishing. For me it is more frantic, more accelerated. I know we need the trout for dinner tonight. I will not let it escape. Debris is churning, mayfly larvae crawling to safety as spent larval casings soup the water. The rainbow squirms into the open. I kick off with my feet, trying to baffle it with motion, and I can again feel it on my hands. The form dissolves.

It darts into a deep pool, free and clear. I actually stand and lumber after it. It is floating, turning with flicks of the tail fin. I am strategizing about how I will corner it, dive in, and grab it by the gills.

I am not going to catch this trout in four feet of water without the aid of rod or fly. I tell myself this. I tell myself to stop. I am up to my waist in the creek, and I am very wet and cold in the autumn dusk. My fly rod is floating downstream without me.

The rainbow hovers, regaining its senses. It is a shape in the dim transparency, drifting forward and away. Its tail snaps and it is gone. Kingfishers are flying in the purple light, chattering at me, laughing. I wring water from my clothes, find my rod, and walk upstream to return to that other, quieter sport of fishing.

We usually fish until the tip of dusk, when the only difference between earth and water is sound. During autumn evenings, the forest of bugling elk sounds like an ocean full of mourning whales. The calls rise out of the valleys, rebutting continually with fierce, ghostly insistence. A bull elk comes to the creek above me. Six points on his antlers. The gathering mist webs him into the background. He turns to look northwest, where a competitor is bugling, and his monumental rack follows him like a warrior's headdress. He sinks his thick brown neck, lifts his head, and releases a sound like a French horn in a cave. He waits for the response. When he hears it, he moves on.

I reel in the fly and leave the water. I find a toppled cottonwood, old and silver-gray like a fallen elephant. I sit on its back and watch the creek. There is not enough light to even see movement. I am not fishing at this perfect moment because I know my father has caught the fish that can be caught. He is in his ritual now, somewhere in the dark with a sharp knife, turning them from brown trout to table trout. Tonight we will talk about stars and things wild, and we will eat the sweet flesh.

Salmo gairdneri

MOSQUITO

He stumbled as if he'd been shot. His plate and food spilled on the ground. I ran to him and grabbed his shoulders. He was in pain. His face was obscured by mosquitoes. They were all somehow inside of his head net.

"Oh my God," I whispered.

He sputtered, his eyes wet from frustration. "I can't do this any-more," he said, then madly pawed at his face, crushing the insects against his skin.

We had pushed our canoe onto the Yukon River not long after the ice breakup several weeks ago. That was at the town of White-horse, in the Yukon Territory of Canada, where we had great aspirations for this expedition. Todd Robertson and I were now traveling north to the Arctic Circle, planning to cover a thousand miles in forty-six days. We had just got the bad news yesterday at the town of Carmacks, where we stopped after two hundred miles to restock a few things. People there said the mosquitoes never had been worse. It's the flood, they said. And the early warmth this year and then no cold snap in May to kill the first wave of the creatures. Couldn't be a worse year to be out in the wilderness.

Well, they added, there was that one time, back in the fifties. Then nobody said anything else because either they were too young to remember or they remembered the mosquitoes back in the fifties and didn't want to talk about it.

Ignorance had been bliss until Carmacks. We knew that there were those before us who had floated the river, and the knowledge gave us comfort. People had been coming down the Yukon for thousands of years and somehow they had dealt with the mosquitoes. We were good, strong people then. Certainly we could endure as well as anyone. We pulled head nets tight, wore gloves, kidded each other, and tried to live as best we could.

It was all over now. We knew the truth, the truth that we had every reason in the world to lose our minds. A record flood swallowed the forest, and great mats of trees surged down the river. Long spruce poles javelined into the river bottom and breached the surface, vaulting against the sky. There were times that the flood stole all of the shoreline. We paddled into the dark timber, looking for land, for camp. Weaving between drowned trees, we found our camp as far back as we could get. Unfortunately it was in the musty thickness where mosquitoes thrive like backstreet thugs. Tie the canoe to a tree and deal with it. Todd was teetering on the brink of insanity, just about to go. I let loose of his shoulders and stepped back as he wrestled with his head. Eight hundred miles remained.

What we were dealing with was a genius of sensory organs, a nightmare insect that will find you anywhere you hide. Of any creature this size, the mosquito has the most complex mechanical wiring known. Fifteen thousand sensory neurons reside in the antennae region alone. The sensory organs of the head are arranged like clockwork. Electron-microscope examination reveals interconnected rods and chambers, pleated dishes and prongs and plates. It looks like a science-fiction world of satellite dishes and receiver towers. These take the mechanical and chemical environment and translate it into a tactical array of electrical impulses to the mosquito's brain, a brain the size of a pinprick on a piece of paper.

If a mosquito is released in still air, it will come directly to you even if you are standing one hundred feet away. Through the air, the mosquito senses the carbon dioxide of your breath, lactic acid from your skin, traces of acids emitted by skin bacteria, and the humidity and heat of your body. If there is a slight breeze, a mosquito may be able to locate you from across the length of a football field. If there is a strong wind, your signals are broken and scattered, and the mosquito can rarely find the source from a distance.

It was windy on a shoreline evening. A strong wind, twenty miles per hour, came down the Yukon and pounded our camp. We were both working on dinner in the midnight sun, coaxing the stove to light. The mosquitoes were excited by the weather, coming in fast, piercing skin, and becoming gravid with our blood in a matter of seconds. They were able to fight the wind by clustering on the leeward side of our bodies. There, they rode the turbulence, hundreds of them massed just within reach. I flailed and dropped the stove. I drove them from my body. It was an outrage that they were using me as a windbreak. The mosquitoes flocked back into position before I could gather pieces of the stove again. I screamed at them, muscles tightening at my neck.

Margaret Murie, who came down this river into the Yukon Flats in 1927, wrote in her book *Two in the Far North*, "And there is no escaping the mosquitoes." We are about to enter the flats. There, the Yukon sweeps over the Arctic Circle and expands to a width of about twenty miles, riddled with tens of thousands of islands, lakes, and sloughs. This is the center of the world for mosquitoes.

A fisherman came to our island on a motorized skiff. He unloaded a pile of gear and introduced himself. He lived downriver, but he had to come up here to build an elaborate salmon net. The mosquitoes were making it impossible at home; he needed a bare island with a decent breeze so that he could at least concentrate. "I've been living here since 1976," he said, "and haven't had to use bug dope until now." A few hundred miles ago I talked to a Dawson historian named Dick North, who told me that it was definitely the worst since 1965 or 1966, but he put the real date back to some horrible, indefinable year in the fifties. I told him that I'd heard of that year.

In the name of science, two Canadian researchers once walked into this Arctic frenzy wearing only shorts. They stumbled back to shelter and counted swollen welts on each other's body. Nine thousand bites per minute, they figured. With each bite taking five microliters of blood, half of a human's blood supply would be lost within two hours. You were dead long before then. If not from volume-loss shock, then from insanity.

Human blood is not high quality. Isoleucine, an amino acid required for egg production, is deficient in humans, so for maximum egg-making, a mosquito is far better off seeking a moose. But with the number of mosquitoes versus the number of animals in the Arctic, it has become a feeding frenzy, and whatever blood one can get will have to do. And the Arctic has the greatest concentration of mosquitoes in the world.

Blood is strictly for eggs, so the bloodsucking habit belongs to females alone. It is the males who avoid death-by-slapping and all associated risks of attacking a host. It is the males who must merely join in a buzzing column and wait for a female gravid with stolen blood to pass.

A tuning fork vibrating at about four hundred to six hundred cycles per second will instantly send male mosquitoes into a mating posture. This is the pitch of a female's flight noise, the pitch that will echo in the bowl of your ear when one slips in while you are trying to sleep. It is about eighty-five decibels from a couple of centimeters away, nearly equivalent to the back-up warning signal on an industrial bulldozer. The frequency of this buzz mounts as a female becomes engorged with blood, trying to hover with the increased weight. Higher frequencies propel males into delirium, so they flock to a blood-filled female with enthusiasm. The sound is not as meaty as the drone of a bee or a fly, but far more sinister.

We did have our own last-ditch defense on this river. It was in the dry box, down in the corner, triple-wrapped in plastic. If we ever needed it, we knew where it was. It was 100 percent *N,N-diethyl-m-toluamide*, a toxic chemical concocted by the U.S. Department of Agriculture in the forties. Commonly, it is called "deet." When slathered on skin, it keeps mosquitoes away. The bottle tipped over during a run down a rapid several weeks ago, and deet oozed from under the lid. It melted through all layers of plastic and began to corrode a hole into the industrial-strength, hard-plastic dry box. Since then, we hesitated to use it.

Deet works. It turns skin so toxic that mosquitoes have no wish to poison themselves on it. They hover in maddened droves but fail to land. The problem is that this stuff that melted our dry box quickly enters the bloodstream from the skin. The first published report of brain damage from deet came in 1961. Following several weeks of deet use, six young girls developed toxic encephalopathy and suffered convulsions. One girl died. Mostly, the effects were neurological: headaches, dizziness, slurred speech, and confusion. You could also get a good dose of nausea and abdominal pains. In the Arctic on a year like this, the trade-offs between deet and mosquitoes were nearly equal. Agony versus agony.

Otherwise, it was head nets and gloves. At the town of Eagle, Alaska, I met a biological technician for Yukon-Charley Rivers National Preserve. His name was Ira Saiger, from Maryland. He had stopped smashing hundreds of mosquitoes with single slaps and instead took a more ethical approach. He killed them one at a time by crushing them in his hand as they flew by. His record was then 151 in a row without a single miss. He complained that in the field mosquitoes were violating the space between his gloves and sleeves, leaving a swollen wristband of bites. He wrapped duct tape around his forearm and found that, although mosquitoes could pierce canvas and neoprene, they could not pierce tape. After weeks of this, his skin reacted allergically to the tape and broke out in boils. It was a difficult decision, he told me, but he finally opted to halt the use of duct tape, and the mosquitoes feasted on his wounds.

They excel at finding tight places in clothing. Knees and shoulders pushed against clothes as I moved, and that was where they congregated. Usually, they all broke through at the same time, and the stabbing heat more than once caused me to flail and scream like a madman.

Blood, for a mosquito, is a delicacy. They otherwise feed on the nectar of flowers. Lewis Nielsen, a scientist who has worked extensively with mosquitoes, found pollen grains of more than thirty flowering plant species clinging to a mosquito. Flowers such as the bog orchid that grow in the tundra are dependent on mosquitoes for pollination. Nielsen has suggested that these bloodsucking vermin are much more necessary for the prosperity of wildflowers than we would like to admit.

Flowers aside, I have little love for mosquitoes. Blood was streaked along the inner wall of my tent. To get to bed I had to take a running start. A hundred yards would do, and in that final crash, flinging the zipper, then slamming it closed, about thirty mosquitoes adhered to my body and entered with me. I spent the next hour killing them, smashing their bodies against the nylon wall.

I took pleasure in loitering at the mosquito screen on the front of my tent. I rubbed a place with my finger and instantly a mound of mosquitoes accumulated on the spot. They jabbed their tiny proboscis mouths through the mesh and I grabbed them. With a silent pluck, I removed the organs and grinned. They died, of course, losing the working ends of their heads. They clung to the mesh for a moment and fell. Never had I felt such brutal joy. Never had I wished such an end to any creature. But I did it, over and over, gathering a handful of proboscis threads, mumbling to myself with satisfaction. Todd shouted at me from his tent and I stifled my laughter.

If you have ever noticed that you are being eaten alive by mosquitoes while the person next to you is unaffected, there is a reason. In an experiment in Tanzania, three volunteers slept in open tents with mosquito traps. It quickly became apparent that one of the people did not attract nearly the number of mosquitoes that the others had. The researchers concluded that it was a difference in odors causing the imbalance. Sweat, especially from below the waist, mainly from the groin area, attracts mosquitoes, as do volatile substances produced by skin bacteria. Some people stink more than others. The degree of the stink, subtleties we may never comprehend with our noses, is like a field of wildflowers to a mosquito. Different types of smells, or at least stimulants, emitted from a body either tell the mosquito what type of blood you have or enhance the mosquito's ability to track you down.

Host selection also comes down to size, coloration, age, and sex. Mosquitoes are more likely to go for a man than a woman, an adult than a child, a person wearing black rather than white, and someone who is physically large. Jay Keystone, writing for the Tropical Disease Unit at the University of Toronto, concluded that "a large person with an irresistible odor, especially a man huffing and puffing while jogging in dark-colored shorts through a mosquito-infested area, is likely to be invited for dinner—unfortunately, to be the main course."

On a warm day, when my body does not stand out so sharply against the background temperature, if I keep my breathing slow and keep movements to a minimum, I have my best luck with mosquitoes. When they come in numbers, though, it takes Herculean will, which I do not have, in order to breathe slowly and keep movements to a minimum. The more mosquitoes come, the faster I move and the harder I breathe. This attracts even more mosquitoes, which makes me slap and jump and breathe rapidly. More mosquitoes come. The circle grows ever tighter.

When a mosquito's array of sensors has found you, there are only two things that will stop it: death or satiation. Stretch muscles encircle its gut, and until they are pushed to the limit by blood, the host-seeking receptors will not be disabled. Meaning, until it has your blood, a mosquito is unable to stay away from you, even if it wants to. The insect is compulsive in the worst of ways. In cases where stretch muscles have been surgically severed, mosquitoes have inhaled blood until their bodies popped open. Flicking a half-filled mosquito off your arm will not rid you of her. Nor will it work to brush her away from your ear. Nor will it help to kill her companions in hopes that she will fear you. Once she has you imprinted into her brain, she will not stop until those muscles are tightened like a belt around the waist of a sumo wrestler.

When she has your blood and is clear of your swatting hand, she will lumber with her load to a landing space and process the goods. Eggs are bathed in the pilfered blood for several days. Water, nitrogen, and hemoglobin are separated and eliminated. The remaining pulp of proteins is broken into amino acids by digestive enzymes, and what remains is pure energy for the growth of eggs. Up to one hundred thirty eggs in one mosquito. Without blood, on nectar alone, a mosquito may be able to produce a mere two or three eggs.

I have a theory. If you kill more than one hundred thirty or so mosquitoes for every one that makes off with your blood, it is no longer feasible for the species to seek you as a host. Swatting only ten or fifteen will not be enough. You must kill them all. Do this for the rest of your life, never let down your guard. Teach your children, friends, and neighbors to do it. Pass the word on, and after one hundred thousand years, about thirty thousand human generations, evolutionary adaptation should kick in and mosquitoes should stop biting humans. The numbers are tough — you will have to be vigilant.

It was late at night when we arrived at the village of Beaver. Perhaps it was one or two in the morning, and we dragged our canoe up the dirt ramp. Red strips of salmon hung from wooden drying racks. Chained sled dogs barked and licked as we came by and ran our fingers through their coarse hair. Beaver was a metropolis of mosquitoes. All twelve Arctic species were here at once.

There was an old man at the ramp. His eyes were moist and sunken. He was an Athabascan Indian, and although I once believed the natives had found a way to deal with mosquitoes, I have since found that we are no different. Under his arm he carried a spray can of Raid. Raid is not a repellent but a full-blown insecticide. Cockroach and ant killer. He shook it and sprayed his face. Then, noting that I was being tormented by mosquitoes, he offered it to me. I politely turned him down with a shake of my tired head.

He showed Todd and me through the village, around the poles upon which great moose antlers were mounted. We laughed with him and talked about life in the North as the three of us swiped and swung at the air. He pointed to a building, a wooden shack.

"You want to stay here tonight?" he asked. "Feel at home, please."

We all looked at the cabin from there. A darkness of mosquitoes hung over it. They swarmed out of holes in the walls. I could hear them. Todd and I glanced at each other.

"We should be heading downriver," Todd said to him. "But thank you, it's a kind offer."

"Where downriver?" the man asked as he shook the can again and sprayed the back of his neck.

"I don't know." I shrugged. "Just somewhere away from these damned mosquitoes."

The old man chuckled at my delusion and walked away.

Aedes

....

SQUID

A long the Sonoran coast of Mexico, high tide encroaches into parts of the desert, forming remote *esteros*. Warm water fills in around sandy islands bristled with cactus. In one of these *esteros* I moved through knee-deep channels with a homemade spear lifted over my shoulder, ready to hurl it at the first thing that moved. I was hungry. I needed to eat, and there were plenty of fish. For a desert traveler accustomed to sun-shot desolation, the abundance of life here was astonishing: oysters gripped to mangrove roots, and small octopuses hid in abandoned clam shells beneath glittering schools of fish. I had skewered two fish already in the past half hour — long silver animals whose name I did not know — and kept them on a stringer made of wire and mangrove branches. I needed a few more for a meal, and I moved very slowly, careful where I cast my shadow in clear turquoise water.

With my arm cocked, I stepped into a raceway of fish that shot past my legs. I waited for the right moment, gauging distances in tide-rippled water, the sun reflecting up at me, almost blinding. Just before throwing the spear, I noticed an aberration of light, a very small rainbow beneath the water's surface. It was pulsing, an unaccountable bit of brilliance, and it had no apparent form other than light itself. Transfixed, I lowered the spear and slowly stepped forward.

Now on one knee, seawater nearly up to my shoulders, I inched closer but still could not tell what I was studying. It looked like a floating prism no more than a few inches long. Moving little by little, I planted the spear tip in the sandy bottom and reached out with my hands cupped together underwater. As I lifted my palms around this glimmering, lucid object, I began to see an outline. It was a translucent squid, its tiny arms and tentacles stretched out before it. It floated as if still in the sea, secure in the bowl of my hands.

Light scattered through the squid's body, amplified, broken into colors. This is a phenomenon — known among nearly all squid species — in which the skin's surface is densely freckled with pigment cells known as chromatophores. These cells allow squids to rapidly, almost instantly, change color or pattern. Each chromatophore is an elastic pouch colored on the inside, opened and closed by a ring of threadlike muscles so that the skin appears either colored or bare. The squid in my hand pulsed gently. Its chromatophores opened and closed like breath rippling up and down its body, as if the squid were languidly dreaming.

I had never before seen a squid other than those piled on a plate of fried calamari. It was illuminating to encounter a food animal in the wild, seeing its sheer, organic form without breading, without a fork in my hand. I tipped my head down and looked into one of its silvery eyes, a kind of eye proven to observe even more detail than a human eye. The squid did not seem troubled or alarmed in the least. It merely floated within the confines of my hands, a pair of gossamer wings undulating at its side. I saw ghost shapes inside its body, elongated, transparent organs leading from head to tail. An invertebrate, the squid has no bones, no spine, in fact no hard part but a single sharp beak used to crush prey, located at the nexus of its arms and tentacles. Unlike mammals or birds, which have explored countless evolutionary branches and environments to get where they are now, the squid still lives where it began several hundred million years ago, never once leaving the sea. It is one of the original forms, creature of an ancient world.

One thing we do not know about squids is whether they are intelligent. This may seem like a ridiculous notion, seeing as how squids are cousins to simpleton clams and snails, but it is a legitimate scientific inquiry. Researchers have long been sending cephalopods—squids and octopuses—through mazes, giving them colored balls and food rewards, and wiring their brains to find out what they are thinking. One problem is that it is difficult to determine where a squid brain begins and ends. There is an actual brain inside what might be called the head—the term "cephalopod" means "head-foot," as if to highlight the lack of physical distinction in such animals. This brain is remarkably developed for an invertebrate, oversized and highly differentiated, bulbed with a pair of optic lobes, and textured, somewhat like the brains of higher animals. A squid brain connects to a column of axons running the length of its body, and these axons perform as much mental assessment as the brain itself. They consist of the largest and most finely tuned neural cells known in the animal kingdom, able to detect infinitesimal changes and respond with unparalleled speed. In essence, the entire squid is a brain, a single live wire that "thinks" faster, or at least reacts more quickly, than any other known species.

Coloration has a great deal to do with this complex nerve structure. The opening and closing of chromatophores is a voluntary act, meaning the squid must reasonably decide how to distribute color across its body from moment to moment. One researcher off the coast of Hawaii recorded an individual octopus—which uses the same kinds of chromatophores as squids—changing its colors and patterns nearly a thousand times in seven hours as it passed through changing lighting, encountered others of its kind and others not of its kind, and even replicated ripple patterns on the floor beneath it. A complex processing system is required for this level of calibration. A squid can go from a solid color to tiger stripes in less than a second, changing its appearance both for camouflage and to communicate with other squids. For instance, the Caribbean reef squid, *Sepioteuthis sepioidea*, has been observed presenting different messages on opposite sides of its body. To a prospective mate it shows a solid gray color, and at the same time flashes an intense zebralike display for a rival male on the other side.

The late Martin Moynihan, a behavioral evolutionary biologist who studied reef squids, believed these shifting patterns and colors represented a visual language. Observing colorful, communicative schooling behavior, Moynihan recognized component signals squids use interchangeably with one another like rapid-fire conversations. He found signals so numerous and tactical that he thought they might specifically warn of predators, convey sexual readiness, or indicate the presence of prey. In general, the scientific community resists the notion that squids have an actual language, arguing that even flexible combinations of signals do not prove a language. Of course, none of these people have logged Moynihan's hours with live squids. There is much to be said for field intuition.

Moynihan was among the first to seriously consider whether squids might be intelligent in a way we can recognize. He is followed by William Gilly, a researcher at Stanford University who has been looking closely at squid brains and squid behavior. From his laboratory work, Gilly discovered that squids actually learn by trial and error. He found that they start out somewhat like human infants, unable to control their muscles, and over time move with more refinement. As a rule, juvenile squids have a hard time holding on to prey. When one attacks its first spiny crustacean, it startles itself, and its four axons kick in, sending the squid shooting backward without having captured a meal. Over time, however, squids appear to learn how to control their highly sensitive nerves. Curious where he could go with this, Gilly set up control groups of captive squids, giving one group meals of swift, spiny copepods, while the other was fed slow brine shrimp. The two groups manufactured their own hunting strategies, which actually altered the way their brains developed. Gilly stuck wires into their axons and discovered that the shrimp-fed group had little control over large axons and tended to shoot away with false starts, while those who grew up using quicker, more subtle movements to capture prey developed sophisticated control over their muscles. One group became more graceful and skilled than the other, and this difference physically changed the squids' neural patterning. In other words, squids permanently learn from their environment at an early age, a trait also seen in higher mammals, particularly in humans.

Cupping this small, glowing animal in my hands, I looked into its unblinking eye and did not wonder whether it was intelligent or not. We were not the same kind of creature. I come from a lineage of vertebrates who once grew a single neural cord, swollen at one end, to make a brain. The squid took a different path long ago and developed axons and ladders of ganglia with no bones to hold itself in place, only the pressing ocean. What fraction of a spectrum I see as intelligence has little bearing on how a squid might or might not think. I was not going to begin talking in colors to this squid, my skin erupting into stripes and dots. I merely let it down unhurriedly, returning it to the open water. As I slowly tilted away, I must have startled the squid because suddenly it was gone, an arrow shot through the water. I lifted myself on my spear and stared into the crystalline vault, wishing I had held this strange creature for just a bit longer.

———

The white coast of Sonora passed under my feet as I walked south, carrying my camp on my back. I was now far from the *estero*, and the hunting was poor along a dry coast. I ate clams and silver-dollar-sized crabs, cooking them on fires of driftwood and lost, broken boat parts. During the day I walked a shoreline made of nothing but creatures, dead and washed up. Mostly they were shells; clams and periwinkles and conchs rolled from unknown depths, stacked by the high tide. All were bleached by the sun; whalebones and bird skeletons, little whorls of opercula and tumbled cowries. So rich is the sea that it shovels its coins onto shore.

Uninhabited desert extended to my left. To my right lay a sea blinding under a clear and arid sky. Miles trudged past. My pace was thoughtless, a cadence of shells crushing beneath me. My only encounters on this desert coast were with dead and rotting animals. I arrived at a blistering porpoise, its skin peeling off, toothy jaw stuck out like a neolithic war club. A few miles after that I reached a drowned cormorant, its wings spread open in coarse sand, angelic. More miles passed. The day's heat shouldered onto the beach. I began smelling foulness in the air, shifting in the breeze, flesh decomposing. As I came closer it became stronger and I closed my mouth, breathing only through my nose. I thought, *It must be a beached whale, many weeks old.*

I saw something sprawled in the distance, driven up by the tide and abandoned. It had no form or girth I could discern, like a bundle of dark fabric tangled by waves. Its smell became overwhelming. As I walked to it I found a great squid strewn across the beach, its body mostly collapsed under its own weight and decomposition. The sun had melted its flaccid form, turning its skin a boiled red. It had to be the Humboldt squid, *Dosidicus gigas,* the only species this size in the area; fifty pounds, six feet long, and known locally as *diablo rojo,* the red devil, for its aggressiveness and its ability to change color. The species comes up at dusk from two-thousand-foot depths to feed nearer the surface. This one must have perished from age or disease during one of these rises, and waves had washed it to shore.

No slim animal to fit in my palm, this was a monster. I crouched at its side, where ravens had pecked oozing, briny holes. Wincing from the odor, I crept a bit closer and crooked my elbow around my nose to breathe. I reached out three fingers and touched it. The skin felt like hard rubber, sticky, but no more so than a raisin. I picked up a nearby pelican bone, part of a wing, and used it to poke at the squid's ventral fin, one of two it had used to glide in the water. The fin was the size of a dinner plate. The whole squid, in fact, was about the same size as I. If we met in the water, we would appear roughly equal, other than our wildly different shapes. One visible eye swelled in the sunlight, its surface baked black. It was bigger than my fist, the largest eyeball I had ever seen.

It seemed almost like this was a dead centaur, some mythical beast, proof of an unseen world. The largest animal on the planet is a squid, a rubbery predator that lurks in deep sea trenches. There are some that reach lengths of sixty feet, known only by their rare, gelatinous remains. One species has an eyeball a foot across, almost twice the size of my own head.

The order of the squid, Teuthida, occupies impressive heft in our imagination, yet it is one of the least understood creatures on the planet. Encounters with the largest squids are extremely rare, as they hunt in the deepest parts of the sea. A team of Japanese research-ers caught the first images of a live giant squid, *Architeuthis dux,* in 2004. They dropped a camera on a three-thousand-foot cable in a region where sperm whales were diving in search of squid. In the black depths of the sea, a giant squid rose to take a sack of chopped bait hanging below the camera. The images from this encounter are a monochromatic blue, the only color found at that depth of water, and they portray a single eerie creature emerging from blackness, its twenty-six-foot-long form coming into view as it wraps tentacles as thick as a man's thigh around the bait. In some of the photographs white suction cups are visibly studded along every arm, and in each fleshy cup is a bony hook as sharp as a cat's claw. When I first saw this footage, I was deeply alarmed, as if seeing live proof of a nightmare. To know I share this planet with such a creature is disquieting.

This midsized *Architeuthis* was filmed for four hours as it struggled to disentangle one of its arms from the cable apparatus in which it had become caught. Finally, the squid shot away, tearing off an arm and leaving a radiant picture of its remaining arms spread outward, suction cups strung brightly like Christmas lights. Then it vanished into the folds of the sea.

In one camp of researchers, *Architeuthis* is seen as a gentle cruiser of the deep, no more malicious or ill-intended than a jellyfish. Another camp of cephalopod scientists counters that the giant squid is a fearsome beast, the most dreadful creature on earth. In 2003 the first so-called colossal squid, *Mesonychoteuthis hamiltoni*, was picked up by fishermen off the coast of Antarctica and transported to the Auckland University of Technology in New Zealand. Up to his elbows in rotting, blubbery flesh, one researcher there exclaimed, "This animal, armed as it is with the hooks and beak that it has, not only is colossal in size but is going to be a phenomenal predator and something you aren't going to want to meet in person."

It is well known that squid cannibalize one another, and some researchers on the peaceful side of the argument are quick to defend them, saying this is merely a case of mistaken identity. Squid, they say, would not knowingly eat one another, as if such an act were a social taboo. When parts of one giant squid were found in the stomach of another, a flurry of wild speculation erupted, Jules Verne–like visions of gigantic cephalopods wrestling each other to the death in a pitch-black sea. In a response verging on cephalopod erotica, Steve O'Shea, a researcher in New Zealand, explained that this was probably accidental cannibalism that occurred during copulation. "The male giant squid has to use a puny 15-gram brain to coordinate 150 kilograms of weight, 10 meters of length, and a 1.5-meter-long penis," he said. "He physically plunges this penis into the female's arms, which are rather unfortunately right next to her beak. Because he is coordinating so much with so little, I think occasionally bits get chewed off when they inadvertently get too close to the beak."

A little of what we know about squid is science. The rest is imagination. As we sink cameras deeper into the sea and for longer periods, we find the darkness populated by previously unknown shapes and sizes of squid. They sail through the water like science-fiction contraptions, some as small as a finger, some as large as a bus.

One member of these large-brained predatory mollusks lay dead before me, its body spread across the beach on a desert coast where no one else would ever see it. I turned and looked at the water to my right. I had been walking beside its dazzling blue mirror for days. Now it seemed even more limitless. My imagination continued below its surface, where squids move like submarines, all heading in the same direction, waiting for night to fall in the world above so they can rise and hunt. It was a marriage of strange creatures, this squid and I meeting on this boneyard beach. Fleshy and decorated with soft appendages, we were both rare creatures here. Fascinated with the corpse, I remained crouched until I could no longer bear its odor. I finally stood and walked on, resuming my cadence, crunching through shells as I returned to the sky and the sun, my own familiar world blazing around me.

Teuthida

WASP

Over the course of eighteen days, I watched a lone wasp build a peerless gray-paper nest beneath a rock overhang. It was an immaculate job, a small geometric chandelier of brood chambers tended by a fiercely armored creature of yellow and black. There was promise in this spot. A much older wasp nest was nearby, abandoned the year before, perhaps the place where this very wasp cut its way out of its own white-silk cap. It may have returned hoping more of its kind would come. As I watched the wasp construct its nest day after day, I wondered what kind of hope this single insect might have, if there is a chemical signature for longing.

No other wasps came. Eight days into the construction, this lone wasp stopped working, perhaps sensing the other chemical: futility. It was most likely a female, but no eggs were laid in her chambers. The work stopped but the wasp did not abandon the place, wings tucked as she clung upside down to the perfection she had built, her eyes immovably stern. At night I would go to her with a light just to see if she was still there. Spiders were hemming her in with their webs as if the wasp had merely become part of the geography, no longer one of the swift creatures that slices through the air.

I have my opinions about wasps. They are warlords. A kind of evolutionary evil, wasps are one of the earth's most numerous creatures, ranging from tiny, dot-sized stinging insects to ones hovering loudly like toy helicopters. Nearly all of them are parasites exploding from the guts or skin of caterpillars and still-breathing spiders. They pack squirming, twitching insects into their brood chambers and seal the entrance with a single, ominous egg inside. A tarantula turned upside down, paralyzed, legs folded inward, is forced to witness its own soft body ravaged by a hungry grub. It is the nest upon which larval wasps feed and grow.

This kind of transaction is typical of wasps. It is believed that the inability to reproduce independently is a derived characteristic, something evolved over time (compared to viruses, which have always required a host for reproduction). Wasps evolved from a common ancestor shared by ants and bees, hive builders and queen-led societies. These are all, indeed, considered *social* insects. Wasps took their own, unique turn when they became parasites and began using host oak leaves or animal skin or cockroaches as breeding grounds — in essence, making unwitting creatures around them part of their own society. At its most basic level, parasitism is a form of symbiosis. A symbiosis in which all parties benefit is called a "mutualism." If only one party benefits and the other is indifferent, it is called "commensalism." If one party benefits at the expense of the other, it is called "parasitism." Wasps have mastered their parasitoid kingdom, honing themselves to whatever host suits each species best, even to the point that some hosts are unaware of the offense until they feel their organs consumed from the inside out.

The emerald cockroach wasp, *Ampulex compressa*, uses a cockroach as a host by essentially taking over its mind. A first sting is precisely delivered to a ganglion in the thorax, causing the roach's front legs to collapse, which gives the female time to position an even more accurate sting to the head. Her stinger pierces the roach's exoskeleton and maneuvers into the brain, specifically to the region controlling the roach's escape response. There she delivers a different kind of venom, one that works solely on the nervous system. The roach, which is much larger than the wasp, drops into a state of suspended animation, its metabolism lowered by a third, its brain reworked so that it lacks any self-motivation. It will now do whatever the female wasp commands. She leads it to her burrow, where she buries the live, perfectly healthy but senseless roach with one of her eggs glued to its underside. A wasp larva soon hatches, tunnels into the roach's body, eats all the soft part, then cocoons itself within the host's exoskeleton. In four weeks an adult *Ampulex* wasp breaks out of the hull that was once a living cockroach.

Wasps are the indelible nightmare the earth has given us, sharp as knives, heartless as generals, so clean in their killing and strafing attacks that they lie beyond cruelty. I have been cramped by the unexpected sting, my body suddenly doubled over as I swipe like a madman to get it off, not knowing what transgression I made but knowing the sting was a wasp's.

I watched this one as she crept behind her own nest, no others coming to complete the circle, to make a society of wasps under a rock overhang. Left alone, this wasp fell into forgetfulness, no longer sailing out for water with which to build more hexagonal chambers. Her last season of living was wasted. When I could no longer bear her loneliness, I touched her with my fingertip and was enlivened to see her rise like an electric wire, body cocked, willing to kill the entire world if she had to.

Vespidae

BLUE SHARK

The northern tip of the Queen Charlotte Islands points from British Columbia to Alaska. It is raked from the ocean just far enough to decorate its back with a rain forest. Where the forest and the ocean rub shoulders is a line of light sand. This is a marginal land, the remnants of a continent left out in the weather. The waves wear it down, turning one island into two and three and four, into peninsulas and estuaries, even as these waves slip quietly on the sand like lace veils.

On the beach, just in sight of camp, I have brought an armload of dishes. Everyone in camp shifts duties as we hike along the coast. Today I am the dishwasher. I chase water back and forth, scooping sand and ocean into dirty hiking pots, then retreat with the ocean lapping up the back sides of my boots. I am at my haunches, scouring burn marks from the steel. A wad of seaweed tumbles against a wave crest, rolling on itself as if it were a dead body. I walk over to look at it while scrubbing out the pot, grinding at the corners for the small, caked pieces. As I look closer at the seaweed, I see a form within it. The seaweed must be hung on a log. As each wave approaches, it seems to bend. I dump sand and reach down to scoop more, keeping an eye on the object.

When the largest wave comes, promising to soak my boots, I peer intently into the water. With an abrupt surge, the water opens. The bludgeoning nose of a shark breaks through, pounding into the shore.

I drop the pot and stumble backward, nearly falling over myself. The tail swishes, and a five-foot shark heaves its entire body out of the wave and onto the beach. It slides to the edge of the water like a wet sack of flour. With the next wave it pushes even farther and I have to scramble out of its way, landing on my hands. Instantly it gyrates. Its body flexes so that head and tail curl upward, nearly touching like a blue crescent moon. The pot is pushed aside by the shark and is drawn into the ocean.

For a time I am on my knees in the sand. There is no chance of this happening, and yet we are here.

The shark wrestles as if fighting something, an invisible opponent. The body moves like a mass of flexible cordage. At first I think it is here for me. Why else would it have charged out of the ocean an arm's length from my dishwashing perch? It could be following the lead of local killer whales, who rush to shore and clamp on to a basking seal. But this is not the behavior of a shark. Lifting myself slowly, I do not think it sees me. Something else must be happening here.

I come near and it lunges. I leap back. I approach again, with the caution of a person trying to handle a cobra. When it bends to the sky, the mouth gapes and I can see the caving gills leading to a sealed point above its gut that looks like a deformed navel. It is like putting your eye to the barrel of a shotgun. I can look through half the shark from right here. Teeth come in barbed rows, grotesquely arranged with such a lack of order and size, they seem barbaric. They unfold from the interior of the jaw, constantly in rotation, replacing each tooth every eight days. They lie almost flat in the back, pointing into the abyss, offering to release nothing. The waves form light gowns that dress the shark, then slip back.

It is a blue shark, *Prionace glauca*. There are angles to its head, sharp lines absent in the bodies of any other fish. Not like any animal. It is something of architecture, made with T squares and clay. The eyes are blunt. They are eyes of a different world, focused on things I cannot see. The tail is an instrument, not an appendage. It smacks the ground, and sand quivers to liquid all the way to my feet. The thing has the constitution of a single sprung muscle hammering on the beach. It digs itself deeper, gaining a hold on the island.

The shark has got to be blinded out here. In the water it has a spatially concrete view of the world, beginning with a radius of more than one mile, increasing with detail toward the center until it is not a three-dimensional setting but four- and five-dimensional. From a mile away, it can hear you whisper in the water. Sounds not only enter through the shark's ears but are amplified within the body through fluid-filled sensory canals that read the pressure of your voice. Its entire body vibrates with every message. At a closer range, within hundreds of yards, it detects electricity. Fifteen hundred sensory pores on the head gather information from the electrical discharge of a flexing muscle, perceiving surroundings in terms of fields and fluctuations and amplitudes, rather than light or sound or touch. The pores sense directional changes as small as five-billionths of a volt moving one centimeter. That is the twitch of a hand, half a turn of the head. That is the electricity of fear.

The shark is able to smell one part of blood in one million parts of seawater. It has color vision and can see even when it is ten times too dark for a human eye. Its prey-finding bioelectrical system responds to the alignments of the earth's magnetic field, giving it a reference to north and south. The world understood by sharks goes farther than that whisper one mile away. They know where they are on the planet.

The world at my feet must be sheer white noise, an electrical storm over the shark's head: the deafening sound of my boots in sand and of my heartbeat when I come this close. I inch to the side, to a region in the middle of the shark. In a moment when it is not jerking so fiercely, I reach out and place my spread fingers on its back. The skin is like sandpaper and I can hardly slide my hand across it. If you were brushed by a shark in the water, it would abrade your flesh. The skin itself is made of toothlike scales, small enough to be hardly visible, sharp enough to cut. I touch the thick dorsal fin. It is barely pliable.

I know damn well I should not be so close. If I lose a hand, an arm, or the left side of my torso to a sudden veer of jaws, then the water will be filled with blood and there will be instant fury. Documented attacks come to nearly a hundred each year. For the few that are fatal, a person's demise is often blood loss after the shark has left, meal unfinished. If they bite humans it is usually for a taste, a sampling before spitting us out, but from time to time a person will be eaten inside and out.

I keep to its tail, although the shark can flip around as quickly as I can get half a thought through my head. I have heard people tell me that at times they wish to get in touch with the animal spirit. I will tell you this about the animal spirit: it will tear you in two as quickly as it will bring you wholeness. It is not a thing of value or judgment. It is a thing of purity, and it will not take issue with either death or ecstasy.

I talked to a man who was taken from behind by a great white shark. The thing was eighteen feet long and he never saw it coming. It was like getting hit by a bus with teeth. Don Joslin was his name, and he thumbed out five photos for me. They were of his right leg, taken before the meat could be stuffed back in and skin sewed together. When he showed me these color prints, he was seventy-nine years old, and he watched carefully to see my response.

"Gruesome pictures," he said.

"Hmm," I said, reaching up and lightly touching my throat.

Shark pictures are always like this, surgical openings around a sausage-grinder melee of blood and muscle. They are not like bear pictures or mountain lion pictures, not random gashes and hunks of twisted tissue as if the victim had been in a car crash, but precise incisions of medical quality. Don's were along his right leg, a single eighteen-inch bite from knee to ankle. One fractured long bone and a severed festoon of tendons. It was painfully clean. Grisly and red with flesh, blood, and exposed pieces of organic mechanisms, but still classically tidy and straight as if it had been carved with a scalpel. I turned from one photo to the next. He mentioned that he felt very little other than the weight of the shark behind him. He did not realize the extent of the damage until later. It was the trademark of a good surgeon: you won't feel a thing.

Don was fifty-three when the shark sampled his leg. He was coming up from an abalone dive in California's Tomales Bay, thirty miles from where he would later live. The bay is a prime breeding ground for great whites, part of a region studied over and over because there is no other place in the world as frequented by these sharks. As he cleared a kelp bed to the surface, the great white came from below, took his leg, and threw him clear out of the water. He landed on his back, his leg dissected and puffing blood.

"You never knew it was there?" I asked, and he shook his head, looking through the photos.

"Had no idea."

By the time he straightened his mask to look down, the shark was beneath him, swiftly rising for a second attack. In one hand Don held an abalone iron, similar to a tire iron, and he jabbed it toward the shark so that it deflected off the animal's snout. The shark swerved and erupted from the surface beside him. With all of his force he pounded the shark with a right hook. The only thing left to do. *He hit the thing in the face.*

Its rough skin tore his glove and scraped flesh off his knuckles. His shoulder nearly dislocated from the blow. It was enough, though, to give the shark pause. The shark sank into the water and vanished through the kelp bed. Don swam to the boat and was dragged in by his partners, bleeding all over the deck as if he had been rolling in razor blades.

He said to me, "I should have been frightened when it happened, but you know, I wasn't. How can you be afraid that fast? It was just there and I only did what I could think of doing."

"I don't know," I kept saying, looking at the photos, skimming over the account in a shark attack book and in a deck of yellow 1969 newspaper articles. "I don't think I could punch an eighteen-foot great white shark in the face."

"I think it was sixteen-foot," he corrected. "They just put 'eighteen-foot' down when they documented it."

Sixteen-foot, eighteen-foot, the size of a large truck. I don't like the thought of anything that big coming up from below or the thought of punching it. Don saw only two great white sharks in his diving career. The second attacked him. The first, five years earlier, attacked his partner, LeRoy French, in the Farallon Islands, not far south of Tomales Bay. Although he pulled in French's body, streaming with blood from bites to his shoulder, leg, buttocks, and arm, and although he had his own leg nearly removed at Tomales Bay, he put his faith in the idiom that lightning does not strike twice in the same place. As soon as his cast was removed, he was back in the water. Never again was he troubled by a shark.

A particularly fierce shark bite comes to nearly forty-three thousand pounds of pressure per square inch, about one hundred thirty-two pounds of direct force from each tooth. It is an impressive number, but abstract. So bite your hand. Get it back in the molars and go at it. Bite until you tear your flesh and crush your bones. It is possible.

We have not atrophied so far that we are no longer animals. If you have bitten well, if your teeth have met through the skin and muscle of your hand, then you have done a fair thirty thousand pounds per square inch, your molars putting down two hundred pounds, seventy from your incisors. Some human bites even exceed the force of maximum shark bites. Be proud.

If only we had the teeth.

This blue shark is holding its energy for another bout of writhing. There must be a mistake. Maybe this shark's sense of direction has momentarily failed. Maybe this is a suicide. A shark may have many reasons to fling itself onto a beach. I place both hands against its side and push toward the ocean. I am pressing my full weight against it, like trying to propel an old American-made car to a gas station by hand, and the thing barely budges. After enough shoving I have got the shark out of its rut and am sliding it into the waves that rise around my boots. I grab the pot while I am out and toss it to shore. We are both in good water. I back away carefully. It can fully swim here. It bursts into motion. Water comes off its back so all I see are the dorsal fin and the spray and the shape of a shark under the surface. It spins toward me, then toward shore, and again pitches itself onto the sand.

There it digs itself a hole, and the pale, soft skin on its underside is rubbed raw, bleeding in places. I roll it back out and it lurches to shore again. The five people in camp have spotted the shark and me. They are running toward us.

I have seen a shark in deep water, when it carries with it the speed and control that have been sacrificed to this beach. I saw the shark in the islands and reefs along the east side of Central America. I held the line of my kayak, swimming down to gather conchs. Later the shells would be broken open to reach the flesh that would be pounded with a knife butt and softened for soup. I had been down long enough to forget about things, long enough to store my breath and wander the coral floor. I tugged the kayak line and swam into the darker coral crevices, turning my shoulders so they wouldn't scrape.

Things come from behind so quickly when I am snorkeling that they are suddenly there. I forget that I am not a fish, that I can see no farther than the angle of my mask. I turned and a seven-foot tiger shark slid through the coral behind me. It was a sliver of glass, its back decorated with articulated sunlight. Its snout was blunt, nostrils large. It switched course without warning, as if it had used the refracting light to trick me, to play its image in whatever direction it wished. I saw no wish in the shark, though. I saw no intention. I saw only a shark. It was a length of perfectly honed cartilage and fin. The distance between the shark and me could be closed in about two seconds.

That is when I remembered I was human, that I might as well be navigating through lead. I held tight to my line and drew toward the kayak. The shark turned once more, describing an arc that sent it behind a mushrooming head of coral. A surge of small fish flashed in another direction, their bodies dark purple with fluorescent yellow specks like a sampler of night skies. I could not see the shark for that moment. I had to hover and watch until I saw it again.

I thought to make no sudden moves, not to appear desperate or injured. Move smoothly. My feet fluttered, lack of oxygen driving me upward, my urge to remain calm holding me down. I had the moves of a struggling animal, broadcasting panicked electrical impulses through the ocean. I caught images of the shark sweeping between coral heads. When I thought it was moving one way, it appeared elsewhere, moving another. Tiger shark stomachs have produced, according to one researcher, "boat cushions, tin cans, turtles, the head of a crocodile, driftwood, seals, the hind leg of a sheep, conch shells, a tom-tom, horseshoe crabs, an unopened can of salmon, a wallet, a two-pound coil of copper wire, small sharks and other fish, nuts and bolts, lobsters and lumps of coal." I could be no less edible than these items.

I reached the surface and inhaled a powerful breath of air. Coming into the kayak, my body behaved like a beanbag, legs entering last after an urgent struggle not to leave them in the sea. Water boiled with my kicking. Then I sat, looking into the cataract of shapes and colors in the water.

On the beach in British Columbia, compared with that time in Central America, I have swapped places with the shark. Its swift skill has fallen prey to gravity. When it moves, it struggles. There is now a small gathering of people around the shark as we watch it die. It gasps by thrusting its mouth into the air. No one knows what to say, or if something should be done. The tide is falling out behind it. The shark had hit shore just at high tide, where it got a hold at the farthest point. It has been abandoned by the sea. I think it is sick, that it is dying already, and rather than face the brutal death of an injured animal in the sea, it has come to land, for the quick death.

It is unusual even to see a blue shark this close to shore, much less *on shore*. I have talked to shark researchers and no one has heard of an incident like this. One Northern California scientist has been researching the effects of electromagnetism on decision making in sharks, trying to make them choose different courses by altering surrounding electronic signals. His suggestion is that the shark may have been disoriented. He said that bands of strong and weak electromagnetism that are orderly in the open ocean reroute themselves into a cul-de-sac at shorelines, bunching into unreadable currents. The shore may have scrambled its navigation, especially if it was in poor health.

I cannot tell you what this is, why this shark has come. It may be that it is ill. For all of the curative properties claimed from various parts of the shark, liver for acne, cartilage for cancer, fin for nearly anything, the animal is susceptible to sickness. A captive museum shark once turned up with tapeworms, roundworms, liver disease, two possible tumors, and meningitis. If it had grown sick in the ocean, it would not have lived long. Sharks do not have the buoyancy of bony fish. They will sink if they are too ill to swim. An injured shark is quickly fare for surrounding sharks. Occasionally one caught on a fishing line will be hauled in missing everything behind its head, having been consumed by other sharks on the way. Some live-birth sharks consume one another while just past the embryonic stage, still inside the mother. Escaping the undaunted predation of its own species may have been the impetus to come here and die. But conjecture is all I have. The shark lies at my feet, grappling with the air.

By the statistics, it is easy to malign the shark. Its single-mindedness is eerie. Its penchant for what could be called violence is legendary. It consumes flesh with a regularity and industriousness nearly equal to humans. Being cold-blooded, however, it has no need to consume the daily allowance required by humans, who must fuel these hot mammalian furnaces.

People do get eaten, especially people in black wet suits who look like seals. It is not often, but sharks make a quick meal out of people. Human body parts occasionally show up in the stomach of a shark. But it is misleading to say that sharks share a taste for death with us. Four million sharks are killed for each known attack on a human. Waters around Hawaii are regularly cleaned out after attacks, first by the government, then by vigilantes with fishing boats. Certainly, the shark's evolution never prepared it for such slaughter. Even some of these ancient and impeccable species are running up against extinction as we rifle through with hatred and gaffing hooks. For all the creatures adept at meat eating, it is surprising that more humans do not end up on the menu. It is especially surprising that sharks claim only a couple thousand historically recorded attacks on humans. We are treated like prima donnas and are generally pampered and protected in a world of predation and consumption, as if we were God's own children.

There must be something in the human form that represses attack patterns. We do not look like the usual prey. But for sharks, common attack patterns sometimes involve a toolbox dropped off the back of a boat. How could we appear any less appetizing than a paisley seat cushion or a box of coal? Even if a shark does discover at the last second that a man in a black wet suit is indeed not a seal, why would it decide not to feast?

It has been observed repeatedly, a shark passing between divers, coming within inches, and never altering its course. People on the deck of a boat once watched a tiger shark weave among snorkelers, and the snorkelers never saw the animal. These are the stories I like. The more common stories, those least told; the shark making a pass without toying, nudging, or even biting. The shark continuing with its life, living outside of our bloodbath tales, confirming that there is far more here than we care to believe. The just-so stories of life itself.

The shark is a 455-million-year-old design of refined predation little changed by time. It came long before the dinosaurs; in fact, before the first amphibian ever waddled its way to land. There have been ancient sharks dwarfing the largest great whites living today. Holding a single fossilized tooth of such a shark, you will find that it occupies far more than your one hand, that its edges are serrated into even smaller teeth, that where it would have met the gum it is heavy like a block of steel. Many tons, this shark, and forty feet long. An unthinkable tool for the eating of flesh.

The shark has honed its senses since that time, like we have honed our tools, and used them to establish a firm position in the continuous motion of evolution and extinction. When it is pinned to the beach, out of its element, it is difficult to disfavor this shark. It is an animal of elegance, its form refined in outward simplicity.

Suddenly I feel intrusive standing here, watching a shark die. I am ashamed and I have to step away. My friends and I are here staring at a naked shark, deciding what it knows and what it doesn't know, how its fins work, the angle of its teeth. I take photos of it. My mother, who is on the hike with us, covers her mouth with her hand, about to cry. None of us understands. People begin to walk back, one by one. Some turn to look, wondering what has happened. The shark is moving less, gaping its mouth.

Two ravens with black, wide wings sweep to the beach. They are unusually bold for birds often hesitant to be the first to land at a carcass. The signal has been sent out. There will be a feast on the beach. I hurl a rock and they scatter with loud, exigent calls. In seconds they are back. They hop close to the shark. The shark arches to show that it is not time. The ravens swing out, lifting to the air with broad wings. The ravens will be patient for only so long, and the shark can respond to them for only so long.

I grab another rock to throw. The shark bends like a snake and the ravens patrol just out of its reach. I drop the rock and walk away slowly, turning back several times to look. Then I do not look back at all.

Prionace glauca

HUMAN

I used to walk the bombing ranges of southern Arizona. At night I would sit alone at camp and watch cherry-red flares descending on parachutes, illuminating troop maneuvers in the deep desert. I was far enough away that I could simply enjoy the show, listen to the distant thunder of bombs, sometimes watch jet fighters chase each other through the stars. During the day sonic booms split the air where sudden bursts of vapor appeared in the sky.

Other than unexploded missiles lying about and a scattering of brass shells dispensed from war games—and the infrequent crater where a fighter jet had crashed—the bombing ranges had an aura of pristine wilderness, no roads, no ATVs, no trails. Humans were a thin, strange veneer over the landscape. I walked with an enchanted sense of isolation, arroyos and broad sand washes winding toward the horizons.

On my back I carried mostly water, enough for a few days. The rest I would find in ragged, dry mountain ranges where old rainwater waited in shadowy pools. I moved from one mountain range to the next, looking for this water, crossing miles of arid basins in between.

In one of these basins, wide as the Salton Sea, I passed the carcass of a bombing target, a twisted metal sculpture chewed apart by erosion and wind. Otherwise, there was no sign of human presence. My mind dissolved into the cadence of footfalls on gravel. I breathed the hot, still air of midday. I noticed something out of the corner of my eye, almost beyond my conscious range. I paused and looked south, where a speck was floating off the ground. It glinted in the sun like glass, and I thought it was a beetle in flight before I realized it was much farther away than that, and it was getting bigger. I squinted. It had to be a plane. But I couldn't hear it at all.

Then I saw that it was a fighter jet skimming the deck of the desert. It looked eye level as it approached from a distance, heading straight for me at about the speed of sound.

There was a good chance my eardrums were about to be exploded from my head. From even half a mile away, the shock wave of a jet breaking the sound barrier can shatter windows, blow people off their feet, knock them unconscious. With the jet's 27,000 pounds of thrust, its velocity of 1,500 miles per hour, and its location approximately 30 feet off the ground, this was an encounter I could not have been mentally prepared for. Even knowing I was on a bombing range didn't help. I saw that I was going to panic when it hit; piss my pants, scream uncontrollably, who knows? I tried to add up the possibilities as fast as I could, gathering myself, bracing my muscles, tightening all orifices.

The distant fleck swelled instantly into an F-16 jet fighter, filling my entire sky. The air exploded. A deafening concussion hit me, shooting through my bones into the ground. My body tried to run, but in all directions at once. My brain stem lashed electricity straight down my spine. I became an animal. Not caveman, not *habilis*. I was something older, mammal, furred beast. The plane's shadow cut me like a whip.

I swear I could see the screws on the underside of the fuselage. With the jet traveling at some thousand miles per hour, a blink of a quarter second, I don't know how that would have been possible. Still, they swept across my eyes in all their greasy detail.

Then the plane was gone. That fast.

I seemed to be intact. My heart was still beating, very quickly. My eardrums were not ruptured, though they rang loudly.

I turned, looked north. The jet was already a dot on the horizon. I watched as it vanished miles away, arcing across the desert into nothing.

My world returned to me, clothes back on my skin, feet in hot leather boots. Stillness poured in behind the jet like water filling a hole. In this new calm I began walking again, placing one foot, then the other. I started across the desert at my own slow, subsonic pace, human again.

Homo sapiens

Animalia

ANIMAL

I finally knew what I had to do. There was so much else that needed mending, buttons and wire, holes to dig, screws to tighten, but I emptied my hands and walked into the woods. Here, old voices have always gathered—woodpeckers call one another, their codes tapped through the bullhorns of dead trees. Elk stand between naked white aspen trunks, while the aspens themselves migrate across mountains in great, thick herds, singing like water whenever the wind blows.

I arrive in one of these aspen forests, shambling on my two feet, searching for paths in underbrush and flowers. I kneel to wash my face in a cold, swift creek full of brown stones. I eat August's raspberries from thornbushes and catch cutthroat trout, cook them over a fire.

For a few days there is a stock trail. Eventually, I walk off of it. Older trails show themselves, blazes that some industrious person chopped into tree trunks with an ax, but they also fade. I pass the last hunting camp, logs rolled out for sitting, a rusted woodstove packed in by horse, a date carved on a tree, 1968. After that there are no more numbers to mark the years. Days lose their names. Spiders sew veils that I wear across my face. The map is made of bears trudging into serviceberries and lacy flowers, bending over stiff stalks of alpine lilies, giving me a place to walk.

The way grows steep. Sweat drips onto the ground, big drops like rain. The mountainside is a cascade of aspen trees where I fall to hands and knees, fingers scrabbling into dead leaves and wormy soil for purchase. A deer bolts. I stop, heart pumping, head craned to see the animal in this dense stand. At a distance the deer pauses and peers back at me through a gap in the trees. This is not the deer browsing mums in the yard, not one wearing a tidy little name tag of genus and species. It is an antlered buck living in a house of ten thousand doors. It breathes through its nostrils, ears big as oven mitts. After a moment, the deer bounds away. I watch it as long as I can and it becomes branch, leaf, shadow, light.

I am heading for a pass still a few thousand feet higher. My hands are powdered white from trunks that I grab like ladder rungs. Bracken ferns uncurl at my waist. Long after the deer I stop again, not because I hear something but because an animal is here with me. There is a smell. It is like sex and fur and sweat. Studying the perimeter, I do not see the animal. A bear maybe. Mountain lion? It is a predator, I am sure.

A chill creeps down my spine. I am being watched. I am not telepathic or supernatural. It is a knack I believe we all still share, becoming alert, seeing how shadows are aligned, that there are places where a watcher can lie in wait. I have stumbled into a predator's lair. It knows I am here. It saw how I slipped under the weight of my pack, grabbed hold of tree branches, clobbered the ground with my knees. I am no threat to it. Why not stick around to see what else I am made of?

Could be a grizzly, I think, deepening the chill I feel. There are no grizzlies documented here in the southern Rockies, but some believe, even hope, that small populations still exist in isolated mountains where there are no humans to see them. This is the West Elk Range of Colorado, one of those lesser ranges, very few visitors.

It would be a candidate for reclusive grizzlies. That is what I am thinking now. I strain my senses, but no new information arises. I straighten up and climb ahead with mustered confidence.

Something moves behind me. I turn quickly and see a path bending through the ferns. But I don't see any color of fur. More paths materialize, more ferns bend, and the sound of wind enters the grove. It was nothing. Wind. I turn and keep going.

Now I am listening to everything. I follow the chattering warnings of squirrels and birds. Are they telling of me, alone?

I come into a clearing, a place where the earth is freshly torn up, rocks clawed from the ground. I walk to the middle; it's about ten feet wide. What happened here? Branches are broken, roots ripped up, detached leaves not yet wilted. I touch the soil with my fingers. This was not intentional digging, not a hunt for grubs or ground squirrels. It was a fight. A killing. But there is no blood, no carcass.

Off to the side, I find a single strip of elk skin, curled where it is just beginning to dry. The skin still has tawny fur, and I stretch it out, about nine inches long. It is hardly the width of a fingernail, the width of a claw. I can feel raking pain, a claw swiped down the back of an elk, peeling off a ribbon of flesh. Whose claw, though? It could be lion as easily as bear. The fight was intense, tearing everything from the ground, paws and hooves scrapping hard, somewhere between six hundred and a thousand pounds of animals battling for survival. Tooth and nail, as it is said.

The strip of skin is all I can find. Everything else is gone, no evidence of a successful kill. Maybe a dead elk was dragged off. Or maybe the elk survived and this unknown animal is still hungry, now interested in something smaller, with less kick.

I can't tell whether I'm being watched or my senses are merely elevated beyond logic. I like the feeling. We guard our bodies until they are old and tasteless, when we could have fed ourselves to claw and fur, been literally reincarnated in the cells of a lion sleeping in the sun, the wall of muscle that is a bear crashing through a rotten log in search of ant eggs. Why not return again and again, glistening, gilded every time?

I pocket the skin and move out of the clearing. I'm not ready to get eaten, not just yet. I move fast and with strong shoulders.

Shadows deepen through the forest. I need to set a camp, but not here. I keep going, pushing harder, throwing sweat until I am skirting timberline, where evening storm clouds roll by, hiding and revealing bald summits. This elevation is utterly exposed, trees all gnarled and bent to the earth; rocks and flowers and the press of dry avalanche chutes. Little rabbitlike pikas peep at me, while marmots chirp and trundle away. A rock outcrop directly over my head is crowned with the rack of a buck deer who is watching me cross below.

At sunset I finally reach the pass and drop my gear in a rocky saddle drawn between two mountains. I look behind me, where aspens lead down and enter isolated valleys, forests like green seas. I wonder what animal watched me scramble through its territory earlier in the day. It knows me now, made the acquaintance of my smell, saw how I move. At this moment it is alert, as it has been since it was born, peering through the dusk of its aspen grove, perhaps bedded down in softly folded ferns, its whiskers testing the air.

To the west of the pass lies open country, and as evening deepens, the lights of small towns begin to appear, ranching outposts, orchard growers. The world has been very busy making more and more life, always looking for a place to put it all. My town is down there. My house, with its glass windows, doorknobs, and porcelain sink.

I remember the many times I have sat at my table for dinner, not thinking once of creatures roaming the earth, forests laced with territories and birdsong. I remember being absorbed in my world of letters and numbers, so many tasks that needed doing. It would be easy to stare down there, imagining all of my life. Instead, I turn the other way, watching forest and mountain become black, imagining all that is alive.

Animalia
....

ACKNOWLEDGMENTS

My gratitude goes to my editors: Gary Luke, who first urged me into this project, and Terry Adams, who saw it through to the end. Thank you to Dawn Reeder and my copyeditor, Karen Landry, both of whom shored up the last of these words. Also, thanks to Victoria Shoemaker and Kathy Anderson for clearing the way.

ABOUT THE AUTHOR

Craig Childs—naturalist, adventurer, and frequent contributor to National Public Radio's *Morning Edition*—lives with his wife and their two sons at the foot of the West Elk Mountains in Colorado. His highly acclaimed books include *The Secret Knowledge of Water, Soul of Nowhere, The Way Out,* and *House of Rain.*

Reading Group Guide

THE ANIMAL DIALOGUES

Uncommon
Encounters in the Wild

by
Craig Childs

A conversation with
Craig Childs

Many of your confrontations with animals seem fraught with danger. With distance, what is the riskiest situation you've been in with a wild animal? And did it seem more or less terrifying at the time than it did in retrospect?

There is not that much true danger in this book. Episodes may seem perilous, but mostly it is unfamiliarity or momentary shock. I am trying to convey what I immediately felt in those instances. At a rattlesnake's buzz or the sudden silence of a jaguar in the bush, my body was certainly dosed with fear, but if I had been in great danger I certainly would have died by now.

My run-in with the mountain lion in the Blue Range stands out in my mind as the most dangerous encounter. Since then, however, I have questioned how much jeopardy was perceived and how much was real. As I've played the event though my mind I have seen it more as an act of curiosity on the lion's part than as straightforward aggression. It wanted to see who I was, otherwise it would have come at me much faster, or it would have stayed clear. I look back at it more as a conversation than a conflict. I wonder what would have happened had I not pulled my knife, had I simply stood there and spoken calmly to it, asking the same question it may have been asking of me. Perhaps I would not be here to tell the story, or I would have been left unharmed, understanding so much more about the cat.

What do you make of animal-to-animal violence? Does it take mental effort to see balance in, say, an eagle viciously ripping apart a crab?

I don't see predation as necessarily vicious. An eagle eats a crab in the same way we eat domesticated stock, an act of biological violence but not one of malevolence. The balance shifts with territorial matters, such as ravens mobbing and killing an owl. Animals do what must be done: attack, avoid, kill, communicate. Violence is simply one of their (our) tools and expressions, and it seems as natural or appropriate as any other gesture.

The envy you feel for certain animals is palpable in many of the chapters. Which animals are you most envious of and which of their attributes do you covet?

Ravens are the ones that have most left me longing. You have quizzical conversations with them, and then they lift off and fly away, leaving you stranded on the ground. To move with their intelligence through a dimensional landscape that includes the sky is something one merely dreams about.

Ravens aside, I aspire to the attributes of every animal I can imagine, treading the back-walls of my house like a mouse, gliding across sand with the fluid perfection of a sidewinder, standing with the impenetrable stillness of a heron. Each of these animals lives daily in a state I am hard-pressed to fully acquire even a handful of times in my life.

And, as a human, which animals do you already feel the most affinity with?

Bears seem the most familiar to me, their mannerisms like my own, like people I know. Part social, part solitary, they are living lives similar to ours, only without all the filing cabinets and removable clothing. Recently I crawled into a dimly lit winter bear den, not knowing it was a den. When I found myself nearly nose to nose with a black bear woken from hibernation, I saw in its face and eyes an expression I could not mistake. It was not angry or aggressive. It was simply wishing I was not there, that this was not happening. It was cringing at the thought that I might be real. I muttered to it, "Oh, excuse me," and backed away, left immediately. I knew what the bear wanted. It wanted me gone. I obliged and no doubt the bear fell back asleep thinking, like you might, it was only a dream.

How do you decide when you've intruded far enough into an animal's habitat? You intercede to save the drowning raccoon, but you decide to turn around before catching up to the pack of coyotes you've been skiing behind.

I treat the domain of animals the same way I treat that of humans. I would save a person trapped in a waterhole, but I might not stalk someone through the wilderness only to leap out and surprise them at the end. It is not a matter of habitat so much as personal transgression. We share habitats all over the place, but there is a moment you know when you are intruding on something personal, something that is none of your business. That is the point where I turn back and let the animal go on without knowing I was ever there spying.

Most of your encounters occur in the wild. How can city dwellers translate your experience and outlook to their interactions with urban animalia: mice, rats, pigeons, and roaches?

I've been watching rats in Manhattan, marveling at how they appear from their underworld, and then vanish back into the maze of their secret lives. I notice the way they lay their tails on the subway rail, detecting an oncoming train before I hear the slightest rumble, and are gone that instant.

You can see these things the same way in the city as in a forest or in a desert. You cross paths with an animal, and when it disappears you follow it with your imagination. Where do squirrels sleep? How do pigeons raise their chicks? What do raccoons imagine of us, lumbering and oblivious suppliers of garbage?

You can be equally removed or engaged in the wilderness, noticing the movement of creatures around you or blithely passing them by without more than a glance. I have found pleasure watching sparrows shooting over the heads of indoor commuters at Denver International Airport, and the starlings of Seattle have made a phenomenon of themselves. The point is that animals are everywhere living their lives. They use our cities like nests. It's whether you look up or not.

What is your approach toward domesticated animals, from pet cats to show horses to barnyard pigs?

Domestic animals are strange ones, the wild trained and bred out of them. They are a link for us, something between wild and human. You watch a tabby stalking through a house, peering diligently at a chair, a potted plant, and you can see the intrinsic animal mind. But it is warped, made partly human, and I have felt an empathetic pity for them. The dog that can't stop chasing the ball, that is me, too. The most domesticated of all, I believe, is us. We are the other end of the spectrum from the wild. Without these domestic counterparts of pets and pigs we might be lost from the visceral animal world all together.

You write that we humans are naive for "believing that the world is built of words and numerals." Nevertheless, you write about beings that "have no use for pronunciations of superiority, are intent on survival, reproduction, and life." What is your process for converting raw, intuitive encounters into language that still conveys the urgency of out-of-language experience?

Of course writing is a step removed from the actual experience, and there is no way I can take you 100 percent there with me. But I try to get as close as possible, using these symbols and words to conjure every sensation that came to me at the moment. I write the way I see the world, the way encounters seem to me. I try to touch the animal with one hand and the reader with the other, send the details straight through. I've been accused of hyperbole, told just to say it like it is rather than be so descriptive, but this is everything the moment is made of. I want the reader and me to become each other, for you to inhabit every shade of the experience. When I sit to write, I fill my senses with the memory, and then convey those senses to paper.

How have you gone about amassing your knowledge of naturalism, botany, and science? What's the best way to learn to identify tracks, scat, or sounds?

What I know has come to me one curiosity at a time. I have no formal training in most of the fields I write about, so I turn to libraries, journals, and countless interviews with specialists in the field. The best way to learn is by following, pausing, and getting down on hands and knees. The questions come freely.

Do you have, or have you ever had, a pet?

I don't have a pet. I've had some cats in the past, but they are long gone. I am not home enough anymore to feed anything, and when I am in the field I don't want a dog bounding ahead scaring everything away, or whining, unable to climb into a sheer canyon with me. Pets are surrogates for what I am already seeking more directly in the wild.

You say, as the grizzly bear stalked away from your camp, that "the world became far more elaborate since I knew that this bear and many more surrounded me." Can you elaborate on how the presence of all those animals we don't encounter still enriches, complicates, and beautifies the world?

The brief encounters we have with animals imply much more going on around us. It is lonely imagining we are the only ones, but when you begin to understand the business of creatures moving in and out, living according to their own unique needs, you become part of something much larger. You are, simply, one of them. Even if you never see even a millionth of them, you know they are there. The potential for awareness and apprehension magnifies around you, extending through the kaleidoscopic eyes of a millipede, the fingering wings of a hawk. Knowing animals are living whole existences beyond you is like discovering the world is not flat, but round. It does not end at the boundaries of your perceptions. It keeps going.

Questions and
topics for discussion

1. Do you think a human can ever understand what it is like to be an animal? Are there encounters in the book in which it seems possible to inhabit an animal's mentality? By contrast, when do the minds of bears, birds, and bugs seem thoroughly off-limits?

2. What role does the wilderness play in a meaningful encounter with an animal? Is it important to have left the confines of society behind?

3. In your opinion, can a human interfere too much with wildlife? Should we let the animals have their woods and deserts, or is it possible to observe without meddling?

4. Is it a bad idea to anthropomorphize wild beings? Does it give you more or less respect for an animal to imagine that it is in some ways like us? Or to believe that it shares few similarities with man?

5. What kind of ethical accountability should a human have if he or she stumbles upon an animal that is suffering? Is it crucial to help simply because we *can?* By contrast, is it wrong to harm or kill an animal merely because we are able to?

6. In the "Mountain Lion" chapter, Craig Childs finds himself face-to-face with a lion he believes is going to attack him. Luckily, he has a knife. Of course, Childs had gone into the wilderness at his own risk. If the lion had pounced and he had wounded it, would

Childs have been overstepping his bounds? In such a situation, must the human simply resign himself to fate?

7. What is your mosquito-fighting strategy? How does it compare to what we learn in the "Mosquito" chapter—to move slowly, breathe slowly, and try not to stink?

8. In the "Smelt," "Rainbow Trout," and "Blue Shark" chapters, there are distinctions drawn between fishing with ease (with dinner as the upshot), fishing without making a catch, and having the fish (or shark) actually be the predator. How do encounters with these aquatic creatures differ from those with land-bound animals—especially when mediated by a fishing line?

9. In the final "Animalia" chapter, Childs writes that sensitivity to animal presence is "a knack I believe we all still share." Do you agree? Or does modern life squelch this knack, even if it's inherent? How can we dust it off and make it usable again?

The Secret Knowledge of Water

"Utterly memorable and fantastic.... Certainly no reader will ever see the desert in the same way again."
— Suzannah Lessard, *Washington Post*

Soul of Nowhere

"Awe-inspiring.... Childs uses the desolate places he writes about as an existential testing ground where, in facing the prospect of his extinction, he discovers an abiding will to live."
— Rand Richards Cooper, *New York Times Book Review*

The Way Out

"Craig Childs walks because he knows that everything in the backcountry has a story. He writes these stories and turns them into books, wonderful books that capture the essence of the Southwest."
— Ron Dungan, *Arizona Republic*

House of Rain
Tracking a Vanished Civilization
Across the American Southwest

"Childs's blend of anthropology, geography, and archaeology may not satisfy all critics, but his beautifully written travelogue provides a highly original answer to the Anasazi riddle."
— Tina Jordan, *Entertainment Weekly*

Back Bay Books
Available wherever paperbacks are sold